Beloved
Peace, L[illegible]
Abundance to you!
It is your divine
Birthright
Much love Peace
to you

Moving Mountains

The Journey of Transformation

Rev. Dr. Raymont L. Anderson

AuthorHouse™
1663 Liberty Drive
Bloomington, IN 47403
www.authorhouse.com
Phone: 1-800-839-8640

Published by AuthorHouse 05/15/2012

ISBN: 978-1-4685-9785-1 (sc)
ISBN: 978-1-4685-9786-8 (hc)
ISBN: 978-1-4685-9787-5 (e)

Library of Congress Control Number: 2012907762

Table of Contents

Dedication....vii

Acknowledgements....ix

Foreword by Howard Falco....xi

Preface....xiii

Introduction: Sisyphus....xv

Chapter One: The Sacred and The Profane....1

Chapter Two: What in the "Hell"....24

Chapter Three: Get the "Hell" Out
—Move that mountain!....43

Chapter Four: What In The Heaven?....99

Chapter Five: Living the Life You Are Meant to Live....120

Chapter Six: Practically Perfect?....152

Chapter Seven: Carnegie Hall?....167

Chapter Eight: What Now? Chop Wood
Carry Water. 186

Chapter Nine: Mountain or Molehill....198

Chapter Ten: The Creator is You....209

Chapter Eleven: Divine Orchestra....215

Chapter Twelve: My Story....223

About the Author:....267

Appendix: Workbook exercises....273

Bibliography:....299

Further Reading:....303

DEDICATION

This book is dedicated to the family and friends who have believed in and continue to believe in me and those who have been most supportive during my journey and during its page by page, sentence by sentence, word by word, letter by letter writing.

My parents
Lois and Charles Anderson

My friend and soul sister
Tracy A. Rhymes

My friend and soul brother
Rev. T.J. Simmons

My beloved sons
Kenneth Grimmett III, Cody Lewis, and James Park

ACKNOWLEDGEMENTS

I'd like to acknowledge and give special thanks for the support and assistance of several mentors and friends who have been instrumental in this text being brought to you. While several of these individuals were active supporters who assisted me with direct and personal communications, some were sources of inspiration and influential in other, more indirect ways through such things as their writings, workshops, etc.

Howard Falco, teacher, coach, and author of I AM

Salvatore Sapienza, author and former Catholic monk

Beverly Love, admissions coordinator of The American Institute of Holistic Theology

Rev. Paul Hasselbeck, Dean of Spiritual Education and Enrichment at Unity Village

Rev. Paulette Pipe, Unity minister and founder of Touching the Stillness

Louis Oliveri, Licensed Unity Teacher

Laura Sheppard, co-host of Absolute Living on Unity.Fm

Dr. Sheri Rosenthal, coach, author of Banishing Mind Spam

Navasha Daya-Collins, Musical artist, Reiki Master Teacher, Minister

Michael Beckwith, Founder, Senior Minister of Agape International

Rev. Ellen Debenport, Unity Minister, Host of Absolute Living on Unity.Fm

Ester and Jerry Hicks, Authors, Teachers

Colette Baron-Reid, Speaker, author, Intuitive Counselor

Ellen DeGeneres, Stand-up comedian, television host and actress

Deepak Chopra, American physician, public speaker, spiritual teacher and writer

Oprah Winfrey, American media proprietor, talk show host, actress, producer and philanthropist

Iyanla Vanzant, inspirational speaker, New Thought spiritual teacher, author, and television personality

Wayne Dyer, American self-help advocate, author, spiritual teacher and lecturer

Fr. Morton Kelsey, Author of over 30 books on spiritual life and development

FOREWORD BY HOWARD FALCO

A lighted path

At any given moment along the journey of life there is an endless stream of information at your fingertips related to any question you have about life. A collection of the amazing awareness from some of the best minds of history fills the libraries of the world and now the online libraries of the world as well. The greatest treasures of the mind are all now amazingly only a mouse click away.

There is so much of this information at our disposal that it needs to be condensed or put into a context where it can be absorbed and appreciated for its greater meaning. Often there needs to be a shepherd who has been down the journey and because of his or her struggles, questions and perseverance, can lead readers to the clearest and most powerful path to the knowledge and understanding they seek from the world. This book you now hold in your hands is exactly that kind of work. Raymont Anderson is the shepherd who by way of his own beautiful journey through life, with all its ups and downs, moments of joy and moments of sorrow, has produced a wonderful piece of work. This book combines great stories of wisdom and insight from many minds with a powerful message about life and the journey we are all endlessly traveling on.

We live in a beautifully elegant universe that is here to support each one of us along the creative road of life. **Moving Mountains** is a great guide for those who seem to have consistent stream of "obstacles" at every turn. It is for those looking to understand more about how it all works from a deeper and more profound level of creation. The book offers not only very powerful insight but valuable exercises as well that allow the reader to work to dissolve old limiting thoughts or "obstacles" and replace them with ones that free the thought feelings and actions that produce new possibilities.

There is so much that is yet to be discovered about what is possible as it relates to creating the reality of our deepest dreams, hopes and desires. It is what makes the journey of life so exciting. You never know what you are going to discover each day about who you really are. The journey to this understanding is what every moment of your life is really about. Raymont Anderson, like so many who are a light to others, presents a lifetime of study and experience as it relates to uncovering more of the majesty that is YOU. The pages are filled with the wisdom that will lead you to see less of the "can't" and more of the "can" as it relates to the opportunities that surround you every day, a wisdom that is always and only waiting on you. It is waiting on you to realize that nothing is impossible, including the great power to truly "move mountains". The next turn on your creative journey awaits!

With endless love and gratitude,

Howard Falco
Author of "I AM: The Power of Discovering Who You Really Are"

PREFACE

We have all had at one time or another, moments when everything in life seemed to be getting in the way of where we wanted to go. Seemed like everything and everyone was blocking us from obtaining our desires, goals, and preventing us from reaching our destination. When these moments have hit a point of great frustration and anger, many of us may have exploded in angry outbursts, "Get the hell out of my way!" This often heard phrase can be heard in traffic, in crowded department stores and on busy streets. Yet, many do not realize in that moment of anger and frustration, that the person we are directing this outburst towards is not the one who is in our way. It is we ourselves that need to move!

Having learned this lesson, as many would say, "The hard way," I now present this text to you in the blessed assurance that it will serve as a guide, a sort of written GPS that outlines not only how I made my descent into "hell" and eventual ascent to heaven but how you can and will ascend from your personal "hell" as well.

This book is written as much to myself as it is to you . . . Hindsight is 20/20 and "If I could have known then what I know now" was a reoccurring statement I frequently made at various times in my life. Then I realized two very important things. First, had I known then or had the lessons been presented to me then, I would not have been in a place to truly hear or learn from them. The pupil was not ready so the teacher could not appear. Secondly, on a deeper spiritual level, I did already know. It was this knowing that led me to the choices I made and the experiences that I had so that I could grow and develop as my Higher Self knew was necessary. Therefore, I did know what I know now; I simply was not ready to acknowledge that I knew it and live from that knowing. Every experience, misfortune, failed relationship, accident, injury, illness, success, book, chance meeting, etc are all "divinely" ordered. Synchronicity is all around us all the time and what we call accidents are miracles of providence.

I know from experience and from an intuitive realization that all things happen for a reason and that as I said there are no accidents therefore it is no accident that this book has crossed your path at this time in your life. You are now on a point in your journey where you and I are meeting to share in this spiritual synergy of creation, manifestation, demonstration, and allowing!

It is a clear sign that as the ancients have said, "When the pupil is ready, the teacher will appear." You are ready to learn, to grow, and to teach your story to others.

Even if you don't realize it, you are exactly where you are meant to be. Enjoy the journey!

Namaste'

Rev. Dr. Raymont L. Anderson

INTRODUCTION: SISYPHUS

While there are various versions of this myth . . . the core of it introduces to us Sisyphus who was the founder and king of the city of Corinth or Ephyra as it was called in those days. He was quite well known as a notorious individual and as the most cunning and dishonest human on earth. He is well known for having such hubris that he betrayed one of Zeus' secrets and for cheating death. The betrayal begins when the river god Asopus did not know where Zeus had hidden his daughter. Sisyphus informed the river god the whereabouts of his daughter in exchange for creating a spring on the Corinthian Acropolis.

Zeus, became quite annoyed by the betrayal and ordered Thanatos, (also called Hades) god of death, to chain and bind King Sisyphus in Tartarus. King Sisyphus slyly and with his usual cunning asked Thanatos to demonstrate how the chains worked. When Thanatos did so, King Sisyphus secured them and trapped Thanatos. This caused an uproar on Earth since humans could no longer die now that Thanatos was held prisoner by Sisyphus. A soldier having been at war and suffering grave wounds, resulting in disembowelment or decapitation would still show up at camp for dinner.

Eventually Ares (god of war) became annoyed as well because his battles had lost their fun because his opponents would not die. He decided to intervene by freeing Thanatos. Ares then captured King Sisyphus and turned him over to Thanatos. Sisyphus was ordered summarily to report to the

Underworld for his eternal assignment. But the wily king had another trick up his sleeve.

Putting his plan into action, he told his wife not to bury him and then she was to complain to Persephone, Queen of the Dead, that he had not been given the right and proper funeral honors. Some versions of the story have him complaining to Persephone himself that his wife had not done as she should in honoring her dead husband. In addition, as an unburied corpse, Sisyphus had no business on the far side of the river Styx and to make matters even more problematic, his wife hadn't placed a coin under his tongue to secure passage with Charon the ferryman. Surely her highness, Persephone, could see that Sisyphus must be given leave to journey back topside and put things right.

Kindly Persephone assented, and Sisyphus made his way back to the sunshine, where he promptly forgot all about funerals and such drab affairs and lived on in a very self-indulging manner for quite some time. But even this paramount trickster could only postpone the inevitable for so long. Eventually he was hauled back down to Hades, where his indiscretions caught up with him. For a crime against the gods—the specifics of which are variously reported—he was condemned to an eternity at hard labor and most frustrating labor at that. For his assignment was to roll a great boulder to the top of a hill.

The catch however was that every time Sisyphus, by the greatest of exertion and toil, attained the summit, the boulder rolled back down again leaving Sisyphus to repeat his task over and over again for all of eternity!

THE JOURNEY BEGINS

Everyone who achieves success in a great venture, solves each problem as they came to it. They helped themselves. And they were helped through powers known and unknown to them at the time they set out on their voyage. They keep going regardless of the obstacles they met.

W. Clement Stone

CHAPTER ONE:

THE SACRED AND THE PROFANE

"Can you get the hell out of my way?" as I mentioned in the preface is a phrase that many of us have heard if not uttered ourselves at one time or another. I remember one time, after having started studying acting, when I heard the phrase and a totally different meaning came into my mind. Let me explain something I learned about acting which will make my explanation much clearer. In acting when going over a script we are taught to be mindful of the words as written and how those words or the meaning behind those words can change based upon where we place our emphasis. For example the phrase, I said no elicits a different kind of feeling when you emphasize the "I" . . . ***I*** said no. Same if you emphasize "said" . . . I ***said*** no. And lastly, "no" . . . I said ***no***. Each of these seemingly minor changes colors the emotional expression differently. So here I was one day at the mall I think and I heard someone say, "can you get the hell out of my way?" actually I think he said "could you get the hell out of my way?" either way, my point is the same. At first, it sounded like the person was telling someone to move out of their way via this pointed question. Upon closer examination of how I heard it, it sounded like he was asking the person to help him move something almost as if he were saying, "could you move the table out of my way?" The hell then became an obstacle, a tangible something that he wanted help moving. I then had an interesting realization; we often want others to move our obstacles for us when in fact it is only we who can get "the hell," the obstacles, the mountains out of our own way.

Then it dawned on me again that there is a third possible meaning to the phrase when the emphasis is changed again. It becomes a question asking if the person can, is able to get the hell, move the hell, remove the obstacle from the person's path. In other words suppose I said, "Can you move the car?" I could be asking one of two things: I could be asking you to move the car or I could be asking if you are able to move the car. So here we return to the can you get the hell out of my way phrase and we have a phrase of anger and frustration being sent out into the world. Secondly we have a question where the person is asking you to move the obstacle, in this case the hell, out of their way. Lastly, we have the question where they are asking is it possible for you to move the obstacle for them. To which I once again say no. The only one who can move my obstacles is me! With that in mind, I want to address this idea of hell and how the concept of it shapes the lives each of us lives and creates builds the obstacles we perceive.

Hell . . . The word itself conjures a vast array of ideas and images in one's mind depending on what you have chosen to believe about hell. For some, hell is simply a difficult period in one's life, a struggle or period of tribulations. For others, it represents an actual location where a damned soul will suffer for all eternity. Still for others, it represents a state of consciousness in which one believes in separation, scarcity, duality, pain, sin, and evil . . . it is in essence a belief in an impotent God.

The idea of hell is built upon the idea of duality between that which is sacred and that which is profane; two very important words intertwined by the thread of race consciousness. The Buddha once said, "All that we are is the result of what we have thought. The mind is everything. What we think, we become." In the Bible, Proverbs chapter

23 verse 7, “as a man thinketh in his heart so he is.” These words are mirrored around the world and throughout the universe by the enlightened ones. Their words and teachings are written on walls, stone tablets, scrolls, and parchments around the world. And despite the truth encapsulated in their words, many people do not live their lives knowing these truths. Many people, still living in the illusion, prefer to complain about “what the hell is in their way;” not taking the time to realize that they are the ones in their own way and that the hell they are going through is of their own creation. The Spiritual Warrior, the man, woman, or child who puts on the full armor of God, goes forward in truth, knowing that empowerment and healing are not only possible but are inevitable. These spiritual adepts are people who make lasting empowered changes by being willing to take an honest look at the truth and once knowing the truth have the courage to live from their new awareness.

It is far easier for people to live the life or the “lie” that they have agreed to live. These agreed upon lies are based upon what Don Miguel Ruiz refers to as Domestication.

> "During our early life we began making agreements. Our parents rewarded us when we did what they wanted and they punished us when we didn’t. We also learned behaviors and habits in school, church, and from other adults, and children on the playground. The tools of reward and punishment were often emotional and sometimes physical. The impact of other people’s opinions and reactions to us became a very strong force in the habits we created. In this process we created agreements in our mind of who we should be, what we shouldn’t be, who we were, and who we were not. Over time we learned to live our life based on the agreements in our own mind. We learned to live according to the agreements that came from the opinion of others. In this process of domestication it turns out that the choices we make and the life we live is more driven by the opinions we

learned from others than one we would choose on our own (Van Warmerdam).

The human mind or consciousness is filled with the programming of the race mind or mass consciousness and because of this; the sins of the father are visited upon the sons and daughters. Mankind suffers and lives a life of bondage because his mind is centered on the profane and not the sacred; man sees the condition and not the truth and calls the illusion fact. Suppose for a moment the thoughts of racing down the road to get to an appointment on time could be heard by anyone? Or those of the average shopper in Wal-Mart or Kohl's on a relatively busy day. How often do you think utterances of profanity or insolence would be heard? "Damn it, I wish he would hurry up!" "Get the hell out of my way" "These fools should have stayed home." "Why are there so many idiots out here all at once?!" Phrases such as the preceding could be heard numerous times as people who are often in such a hurry to get from point "A" to point "B" scream, shout, or silently murmur in anger and frustration that their way is being blocked by something or someone outside of themselves. They do not see or realize that *they* are the ones creating the obstacles in *their own* lives. The person is then in fact both the offended and the offender who is getting in their own way. Not realizing this, they are quick to blurt out a phrase of profanity and point the finger at someone else rather than taking stock in the truth by looking at the source of their frustration. This would be like looking in the mirror and screaming at the reflection for looking at you. Absurd right? Yet, that is precisely what many do on a daily basis.

People watch the news daily and as a result of all the tragedies and horrific occurrences, think how bad the world is. Based upon these thoughts, they then make comments to co-workers, family members, and complete strangers at a bus stop about this being, "a rat race" or "a dog eat dog world" filled with pain, suffering, corruption, and of course the final knock down, death. Very often have people uttered the phrase, "Life is a bitch and then you die." With affirmations such as these, is it any wonder that we see and experience more and more negativity which reinforces our already negative beliefs; beliefs based on error consciousness. Because of such error thinking many people continue to "lead lives of quiet desperation," as Thoreau once said, "going to the grave with their song still in them." These people have become members of the epidemic, "the epidemic of the lie."

The epidemic of the lie is the continued belief in the condition (the fact) and not the substance back of all conditions (the truth.) Many are quick to judge and quick to hide behind the barricade of anger because of the epidemic. Many people are not only prisoners, but they are prisoners of their own choosing as well as being the architects of the prison, the prison guards, the warden, and the executioner. Their prison of choice has been fashioned brick by brick, chain by chain, from the energies of hate, prejudice, alcoholism and other addictions, selfishness, fear, self righteous indignation, compartmentalization, scarcity, and of the refusal to love and to forgive. This is what living in the realm of the profane entails and is why many suffer.

If man is to be free, the sacred must take its rightful place in the mind of man and in so doing man removes, as Jesus said, the plank from our own eye before we can see clearly to remove the speck from our brother's eye. Hypocritical, ego based living is easy however and this is precisely why Ruiz says living based upon The Four Agreements is also challenging,

> "Through our domestication we have also learned to take things personally. We assume that when someone has an opinion about us that their opinion is valid. Their opinion becomes our belief about our self. We end up having an emotional reaction to our own belief because we assumed

their opinion is true. We can also take personally our own opinions. We take personally our own self judgments. These self judgments are nothing more than an assumption. Over years the mind has developed many habits of making assumptions and taking them personally." He goes on to say, "When you decide to change your life and adopt the Four Agreements you are challenging the beliefs you learned and the habits you practiced since your childhood domestication. Adopting the Four Agreements creates a conflict in the mind between expressing your self impeccably with love and your existing fear based beliefs (Van Warmerdam).

Here in lies the path of the Spiritual Warrior; a path from bondage to one of liberation. A path, like the great Exodus from Egypt, which if traveled, will take you from slavery and death to the Promised Land and to freedom and life. This journey is not to be taken lightly. Many assume the spiritual path must be an easy path where you live the life of a hermit or monk off in some monastery where you meditate, pray, and read sacred texts all day. I don't think you could get further from the truth. Because of this often held misconception and the many questions I am asked when I teach, coach, or counsel regarding this is a topic, I address it much more in depth in my book "The Spiritual Warrior." Along the way there will be many experiences. These experiences are what some call trials and tribulations. These experiences provide us with the lessons along the way; very similarly to a student in a math class where the teacher gives you a problem to solve. The teacher is not there to torture or punish you with the problems, but instead is there to use the problem to teach you the solution through mathematical thinking. Likewise, through spiritual thinking the "problems" experienced in life are seen for what they are, lessons to be used which will serve as beacons of light to kindle the spark of awakening within.

Now it is important to keep in mind that despite my math teacher analogy, there is not a God up in heaven giving you problems to solve, giving you tests throughout your life for you to work out, allowing Satan to tempt, torture or strengthen your character and or spiritual resolve! Let me take a moment now to address this idea of God for a second. God is not some anthropomorphic deity sitting in heaven like Zeus or Odin. God is the Divine All that Is; it is the power that is the truth of all that you are. It is expressed as the Christ or Buddha consciousness that is the full expression of you and it out-pictures or manifests in your life via your thoughts and the beliefs held in mind. You, therefore, are both the teacher and the pupil in my analogy. Your Higher Self which is the Christ that IS you is using everything in the entire universe to provide for you. It is the Father's good pleasure to give you the kingdom. So back to the initial idea of life's experiences being manifested to assist you in becoming more of what you are. As the student, you get what you give. The math student who gives her all to studying, working the problems and exercises, taking the risk to be innovative and creative with the mathematical premises and equations is the math student who yields amazing results where as the student who does not study, does not read, does not risk is the one who will have to take algebra 101 again!

"Whatsoever you sow, so you shall also reap."

Getting "the hell" or the mountains out of the way is the journey of self discovery. This journey guides the traveler to a place where they identify with the capital "S" Self and not the lower case self which is linked inexorably with the ego. Knowing who and what you truly are is quite a liberating realization. Then you will know the truth and the truth will set you free. Rev. Dr. Michael Bernard Beckwith says in his book, Spiritual Liberation,

> " . . . spiritual liberation, which I define as becoming free from the narrow confines of fear, doubt, worry, and lack, and living instead from a conscious awareness of one's Authentic Self, one's true nature of wholeness. Spiritual liberation

> results from discovering and expressing the intrinsic qualities of enlightened consciousness that have been ours since the moment we came into existence. Simply put, all that is required to live up to our highest potential is already inside us awaiting our conscious activation. Living up to our potential is about becoming more ourselves, more of who and what we are as awakened beings . . ."

There are many stories told of the days after slavery had ended in America when many former slaves continued to behave as slaves. These people though free had held on to the belief that they were slaves. The slave mentality kept them bound. Many people live their lives like these "freed" men and women; free yet because they still hold a limiting belief, they remain bound to the limitations within their own minds.

What master do you continue to bow down to rather than standing as a free man or woman?

Having gotten "the hell out of the way", the individual becomes liberated; becomes awakened to what he already is, was, and will forever be, which is free. This person becomes free to express the divine potential that is ever present. The person becomes free to live a life based upon what God has dreamed for them not what the little self or ego would dream. Within the acorn, patiently waiting, is the potential to become the mighty oak; so too is the divine potential of God awaiting the conditions of growth and development to be awakened and realized within each man, woman, and child throughout the universe. For the individual who has yet to look squarely at his mountain and do what is needed to remove it, life remains one of constant cursing, dreading, blaming and complaining.

It is said that necessity is the mother of invention; if that is true, what was the necessity that invented both complaining and finger pointing? Complaining and finger pointing are two things that humans have grown quite skilled at doing. While neither of them is necessary, the reason for them is simple to see—protection. The ego desperately needs and wants to protect itself. This is why gossip, for some has been exalted to status of an Olympic sport. The ego holds a definition of what it is and what it wants and it is from this definition of itself that the beliefs and actions of the individual are born and grow. The ego wants to defend its concept and its image of itself; an image which is based on an illusion. It is based on the epidemic of lies and as it would so happen the egos' self is not the "true self." People may wonder how complaining is protecting the ego and that too is easy to answer if it is understood why complaining occurs.

> "To "Complain" is defined as "to express pain, grief, or discontent." Surely, it makes sense to express pain, grief or discontent occasionally but most people do so constantly. In so doing, they are talking and thinking about what they do not want in their life and, thereby, attracting more pain, grief and discontent. Instead, think and talk about what you are grateful for. Talk about what you DO want and not what you DON'T want (A Complaint Free World Website).

The website goes on to say that people tend to complain fifteen to thirty times per day. Complaining becomes a maze into which mankind spirals farther and farther into the abyss. The research also says that venting, blowing off steam, and getting stuff off your chest is not healthy and that "studies have shown that complaining about one's health actually tends to make a person's health worse. (A Complaint Free World website)" Complaining offers the ego a scapegoat. The ego doesn't have to assume ownership of the actions of the individual. This protects and allows the egoic self to "save face." Should the ego relinquish this control, release the mask, and allow the light to enter, then the ego would fade into the background and it would become a tool used by the mind; no longer would the ego be the captain of the ship. Despite what many profess about how bad and evil and wrong the ego is, the ego can be useful when it is used by the conscious mind and not the one using the mind for its own gain and self preservation. The ego serves a purpose. It exists to protect us; sort of a throwback to the reptilian brain that helps us with Fight, Freeze, or Flight.

The problem comes when the ego has so much control of protecting us that it will create the very situations to prove that we need protecting. It would be like a parent who wants their children to be safe yet takes the children to the worst and most dangerous places in town where they are exposed to dangerous situations and in the end the parent says, "See that's why you should listen to me. I keep telling you how dangerous it is out there." The child now afraid lives a life of codependency and fear. The ego left unbridled is that parent run amok. For those people who continue to allow the ego to reign supreme and continue to complain, they will continue to have more and more to complain about. Complaining does not create positive energy, rather it multiples the negative energy and in fact does the opposite of what people think it does.

Complaining alienates people; it builds more mountains of separation. No one wants to be around a constant complainer except maybe another complainer since misery loves company as like energy will attract like energy. Complaining protects the egoic self by creating what the ego perceives as a barrier between what it desires and this experience that it does not want. By talking about the thing that is not wanted, a perceived distance is created. It creates an argument, like a defense lawyer at trial, to support why or how much this experience is truly unwanted. Yet, as has been said, no one can get the thing they want by focusing on the thing they don't want. James Arthur Ray in his audio series "The Science of Success" gives an example of this by telling the listener to, "not think of an ice cream cone," which he then says, "you have to think of the ice cream cone in order to think about what not to think about. And that parents tell their children not to spill the milk, the child must think about spilling the milk in order to think about not spilling the milk" (Ray). No driver can maneuver the vehicle forward to the destination by looking into his rear view mirror at the cars behind him. Common sense says that to drive forward while looking backwards is not only impractical but it is not safe but and yet that is how many people live their lives.

If you listen to someone complaining it often boils down to a lack of awareness. For example, the person who complains about the rainy day is speaking from a lack of awareness that the rain is falling not as some personal attack to mess up their plans. Rather the falling rain is a part of the natural cycles of nature and in reality is neutral in its happening. Once this is realized, the person complaining has nothing to complain about. While a comment could be made about changing plans since a picnic in the rain is undesirable, this is a comment and not a complaint. It is often stated that "knowledge is power," however I would add that power comes from the wise use of knowledge. This is an age where more wisdom could be utilized in the processing of information. This is an age where people have information at their fingertips through traditional books on paper, books on the World Wide Web, and handheld electronic books by way of the Kindle and Nook as well as via IPADS and PDAs. Anyone who seeks information, seeking answers to questions has no real reason not to have access to an answer. There are many people who, unable to buy the books, will go to Barnes and Noble and read the book in the store. It is almost as if the store somehow serves as a surrogate library. These people may even sit in the coffee shop and take notes if necessary. Confession? I have done that to get a homework assignment or two completed. Most of those books ended up being bought and added to my library though. I love to highlight as I read!

In the book, "I AM," Howard Falco tells the reader, "When you are ready, the answers will flood your experience from every direction, providing you with the choice to accept or to reject the wisdom for which you have so earnestly asked (Falco)." This seems to be his way of saying, "When the pupil is ready, the teacher will appear." When you are ready to shift in awareness, to wake up and evolve, the Universe conspires to assist you. You no longer need to blame anyone or anything. There is no one to point a finger at or anything to complain about. This is one reason I loved Howard's book. His technique for assisting the reader in discovering self is beautiful artistically and empowering spiritually. Reading his book was one of the divine sparks that guided me even deeper into my Self where God and I are One.

In similar fashion, The great New Thought visionaries, sought answers and understanding and when they were ready, they were given the insight to grow beyond the limiting confines of old paradigms. The answers flooded their experience giving them the means to make the necessary shifts. Myrtle Fillmore, Charles Fillmore, Ernest Holmes, Malinda Cramer, Nona Brooks, and many others began an intensive study into the Oneness of Spirit and in their search they found the means to unshackle their minds from old limiting paradigms based on the illusions that have been handed down and are still being handed down to many. What they sought, freedom, love, truth, they found. "Ask and it will be given to you; seek and you will find; knock and the door will be opened to you." Matthew 7:7 Were it not for the Fillmores there would be no Unity movement. Were it not for Holmes there would be no Religious Science centers and were it not for Cramer and Brooks there would be no Divine Science. The three major denominations of the New Thought movement were born of the hunger to know the truth. Had they simply complained about the church and the beliefs of the time, New Thought would not have been born. "Many of the world's great religions assert, 'Ask and you shall receive' (Falco). If you pause for a moment and assume this to be true, what are you asking for? Do you really want to receive what you are asking for? What I mean by that is, every complaint is a request for more to complain about, is that what you want? Every thought and every word has creative power and if you look at the mountain that stands before you, it will reveal what you have been asking for of some level of consciousness.

Through an analysis of the knowledge available in such texts as The Science of Mind, I AM, Practical Spirituality, Sacred Contracts, The Peaceful Warrior, Spiritual Liberation, Beyond Fear, The Four Agreements, The Power of Belief, and The Millionaire from Nazareth, as well as many others, a clear path through each person's version of Dante's Inferno can be laid out. There is a plethora of information available for the avid truth seeker. Anyone desiring a map need only go inward to find the compass that will direct the way. By outlining the problem, the path, and the perfection in this thing called life, a clear "True North" will be identified and once the direction is in sight and the individual takes the journey, the peace of empowerment is assured; this is what true healing is about.

Despite the bickering, complaining, finger pointing, and needing of scapegoats, man has within him the power to undo all the ills of the world; however, this must begin with healing the ills of Self and this is a most frightening journey for most. Despite the fear, it is not only possible it is inevitable that each person will learn to get the hell out of their own way by moving any and all mountains.

As a part of this critical analysis it is important to begin by looking at a few key words that will assist in defining and clarifying what it means to become empowered and not only healed as a spiritual warrior but someone who is able to move the obstacles, mountains from their path. I'd like to define and clarify the following: sacred, profane, damnation, hell, religious, spiritual, warrior, empowerment and liberation. You may be wondering what these words have to do with moving mountains so let me explain the connection. In order to move any mountain, it takes s shift in belief, shift of paradigms, and a shift in faith. As it says in Matthew 17:20, "I tell you the truth, if you have faith as small as a mustard seed, you can say to this mountain, 'Move from here to there' and it will move. Nothing will be impossible for you." In order to know why the mountain is there, it helps to know what it represents and that begins with knowing what you believe and have faith in. I have found that many people's mountains are connected in some way or another to the list of words I've chosen to define. So let's get to it!

Around the globe, man has identified certain artifacts, locations, buildings, words, and people as being "sacred." To go on the supposition that this is correct is to imply that there are likewise artifacts, locations, buildings, words, and people which are less sacred or as will be defined later, profane. Before one can determine what is sacred or not sacred, it is important to know how sacred is defined.

According to Miriam-Webster Dictionary online sacred is:

1 a : dedicated or set apart for the service or worship of a deity <a tree *sacred* to the gods>
b : devoted exclusively to one service or use (as of a person or purpose) <a fund *sacred* to charity>
2 a : worthy of religious veneration **: holy**
b : entitled to reverence and respect
3 : of or relating to religion **:** not secular or profane <*sacred* music>
4 *archaic* **: accursed**
5 a : unassailable, **inviolable**
b : highly valued and important <a *sacred* responsibility>
— **sa·cred·ly** *adverb*
— **sa·cred·ness** *noun*

If this definition is accepted then to a certain degree there must also be the belief that some are not sacred and that some are the antithesis of sacred—profane.

According to Miriam-Webster Dictionary online profane is:

transitive verb

1: to treat (something sacred) with abuse, irreverence, or contempt **:** desecrate
2: to debase by a wrong, unworthy, or vulgar use
— **pro·fan·er** *noun*
See profane defined for English-language learners »
Examples of PROFANE
<the once-lovely landscape had been *profaned* by ugly factories>
<*profaned* his considerable acting talents by appearing in some wretched movies>
Origin of PROFANE
Middle English *prophanen,* from
Anglo-French *prophaner,* from
Latin *profanare,* from *profanes* First Known Use:
14th century

Were it not for the concept of the profane, horror movies such as "The Exorcist," "Paranormal Activity," and the film "Devil" would not only be far less successful in the box office but far less threatening to the human psyche as well. There is deep seated fear because lurking within the recesses of the ego are the shadows of what mankind calls evil. People fear this imaginary evils that writers such as Stephen King have captured on paper, and those that movie directors such as M. Night Shamalan and George Romero, have captured in celluloid. People also fear the "real-life" evil of man against man as demonstrated in the actions of Hitler and the Nazis, Islamic fundamentalist terrorists, the Jeffrey Dahmers, Ted Bundys, Charles Mansons, and Jared Lee Loughners in our neighborhoods. Were it also not for the archetype of evil, stories such as Harry Potter would have far less appeal since the hero's journey would lack the evil antagonist of Lord Voldemort to oppose the good. What would Star Wars be without Darth Vader and Batman without the Joker? Man believes in evil and because of this belief we see evil demonstrated, manifested, and proven to exist in the physical world. The interesting thing to ask is, does evil exist and so we believe in it or does evil exist because we believe in it? Those are two very different paradigms and are worthy of more in-depth analysis. Suppose for an instant, just for a moment, that it is our belief in evil that creates evil. What would that mean to you personally if it is true?

The Christian belief that man is inherently evil has been a belief held and practiced and handed down for centuries. According to the general Christian doctrine, man was born in sin and as a sinner is prone to act on his sinful nature. Such evil, sinful actions, beliefs, and happenings are said to be made worse or more likely because of the influence of a power for evil; a devil, an enemy of God or an opposite god, a demon or god of evil, who influences the minds and hearts of mankind. Many have heard and maybe even uttered the phrase, "The devil made me do it." Likewise, many have heard the biblical story of Job. The Old Testament tale of how Satan was given permission by God to test Job's faith. This concept of an incarnated evil is deeply entrenched in the culture and the minds of people the world over. For many, the belief in evil is easier to profess than the belief in good!

Evil has been given many names. Satan is Hebrew for "Adversary" and is the name given to Lucifer after his fall from grace. Lucifer is the Latin term for "Light-bearer" and the name most often used to signify the name of the most beautiful angel in heaven whose pride caused him to attempt to overthrow God thus causing God to cast him out of heaven. *Set* is the name given to the Egyptian god of darkness or chaos. There are countless other names given such as the Romanian word *Dracul* which is said to mean "the devil" and was eventually changed and used in the Bram Stoker classic "Dracula." There is also the Russian word *Chernobog* which means "black god." Demons and devils haunt the world over in the minds and hearts of those struck with the epidemic of the lie. Once healed of the epidemic, the cloud of illusion is lifted and it is realized that evil as an entity, regardless of the name given to it is erroneous; there is no force or power that can or ever will oppose God. The concept of evil serves a guidepost. It merely points the way from error to right thinking, from the darkness to the light.

Believing that evil lives as a separate existing entity that affects mankind and opposes the good of God is thinking in error, living blindly, and seeing the illusion and believing it is truth. Regarding this, Ernest Holmes, founder of Religious Science said,

> "One of the most illuminating things that mysticism has revealed, is that evil is not an ultimate reality. Evil is simply an experience of the soul on its journey toward Reality; it is not an entity, but an experience necessary to self-unfoldment; it is not a thing of itself, but simply a misuse of power. It will disappear when we stop looking at or believing in it. We cannot stop believing in it as long as we indulge in it; so the mystic has always taught the race to turn from evil and do good (Holmes)."

Throughout Holmes' text "The Science of Mind", he reminds the student that fear based thoughts must be erased and replaced with faith and love based thoughts where consciousness is focused on and centered on the Oneness of God; There is only God.

> "A central, ruling thought in the Babylon state (state of confusion) of consciousness in man. This thought is foolish in that it looks upon worldly pride, pomp, and power as worthy of one's effort to attain; it also believes in outer, limited, error conditions as real. Persons who behold the outer constantly, and believe in error seemings, bring about strife and confusion in mind, and body, and affairs (Fillmore)."

Here we see that Charles Fillmore, co-founder of the Unity movement, was pointing out that the suffering of man is due to man's incessant focusing on the error and in building his faith on such a faulty foundation, man is forced to experience and to demonstrate strife and suffering in his life. "It is as if there were a Universal Ear, listening to and hearing everything that we say, feel, or think and reacting to it (Holmes)." Again the words, "As a man thinketh, so shall he be" are echoed as a constant reminder that whatever man sows in mind and heart so shall he also reap in life. "We are ceaselessly setting our words afloat on the great sea of life. And our every word works in a positive or negative way in our bodies and in our lives" (Mauss).

Many researchers estimate that people has anywhere from 12,000 to 66,000 thoughts per day. Regardless of which number is more accurate, the point is that the average person spends a lot of time thinking. The more important question is not the number of thoughts per day but the quality of those thoughts. "Thinking is the way in which we manifest that which we desire to have added to our lives and change that which we need to alter in some form or even eliminate completely" (Jones). A frequent phrase used in New Thought circles states, "Thoughts held in mind produces after their own kind." Just as apple seeds produce apple trees which in turn produce more apples so too do thoughts produce after their own kind. Thoughts have a kind of cosmic or spiritual DNA and like any DNA they have the capabilities to reproduce offspring that share their DNA traits. An orange will never be produced from the planting of a watermelon seed nor will the DNA of a bear produce a human child. The DNA of a thought which is ruminating on and thus reproducing offspring of lack, scarcity, illness, and fear, will not produce a life of prosperity and health. The DNA of a thought that is centered on lack, fear, and evil is easily remembered by the acronym Downright Negative Affirmations and that D.N.A. is the hell, the obstacle, the mountain that must be removed if empowerment, healing, and liberation are what the truth seeker seeks.

Charles Fillmore says that both heaven and hell are states of mind and that one need not die in order to experience either. He goes on to say that, "If one's mental processes are out of harmony with the law of man's being, they result in trouble and sorrow; mental as well as bodily anguish overtakes one, and this is hell (Fillmore)." This is one reason that man prefers to remain in a state of ignorance. For him ignorance is bliss and from this state of mind he can continue to fool himself into believing that all is well and all is right according to what he believes. Despite those that prefer to remain in the illusory land of blissful ignorance, the road of the spiritual warrior is actively and consciously walked by more and more people. This era is finding more people increasingly feeling the itch of divine discontentment and they are awakening and consciously choosing this path of awakening and awareness.

The traditional systems of religious dogma typically point the finger to an outside source as the cause of man's misfortune and yet the divine truths say otherwise. Joe Vitale said on one of the several DVDs where he is being interviewed, "If you ever want to know what you are thinking, look at the life you are living." The thoughts that people are thinking shape their lives in every way, shape, and form. The thoughts man thinks form the beliefs which are the foundation upon which his life is built.

> Watch your thoughts, for they become words.
> Watch your words, for they become actions.
> Watch your actions, for they become habits.
> Watch your habits, for they become character.
> Watch your character, for it becomes your destiny.
> **Author unknown

It is unfortunate that many have slowed their awakening by having built their foundation upon sinking sand.

> "We make up stories about how everything is, and become so invested in our story that we will defend it at any cost. We collect evidence so we can easily justify our stories. Why this is possible and that is impossible . . . We describe ourselves with stories. I have a temper. I'm not a morning person. And I've always been this way (Dodd)."

These stories are what people believe in at their core. These core beliefs are the subconscious programs which determine everything. They determine their choices, likes, dislikes, interests, motivations, fears, and obstacles. These core beliefs are the keys to the gateway of either heaven or hell.

Imagine for a moment what life could mean for a person if classes on awakening were offered during a person's formal education from kindergarten through high school and college. Suppose these classes were taught alongside the traditional academic courses; however, these select courses were in place to orient the student to the workings of his or her mind. The educational system seems to believe that math, science, and history are important. As a former public school teacher and former college professor, I agree that they are important and serve a purpose and yet there are no lessons on how your thoughts have power; these equally if not more important classes are missed. Even in the school systems that have high school psychology courses they do not teach, to borrow Emily Cady's book title, "Lessons on Truth."

A primary tenet in the book "The 7 Day Mental Diet" states that, "If you change your mind your conditions must change too. We are transformed by the renewing of our minds (Fox)." Emmett Fox goes on to say that, "You must train yourself to choose the subject of your thinking at any given time, and also to choose the emotional tone, or what we call the mood that colors it. Yes, you can choose your moods." For many this is a radical concept in a society dominated by the illusion of a lack of control where people are quick to say how someone made them mad while never stopping to think about how this is impossible. How can anyone *make* anyone else feel anything that the person does not *consent* to feeling?

"No one can make you feel inferior without your consent."
**First Lady Eleanor Roosevelt

While it is certainly true that there are certain feelings that may be felt in a given moment. Feelings ranging from anger, sadness, or fear to joy and love are all possible. However, no one makes anyone else feel any of these. The individual feels what they feel as a result of the core beliefs they hold sacred. The empowering realization is that no one has to stay in that vibration as Esther Hicks would say. "Never mind what is. Imagine it the way you want it to be so that your vibration is a match to your desire. When your vibration is a match to your desire, all things in your experience will gravitate to meet that match every time." Esther Hicks continuously points out in her writings and workshops that, "What you think and what you feel and what you manifest is always a match, every single time. No exception." For many that is a scary rather than liberating thought. There is great power in that realization for the one who releases the fear. Similarly, Viktor Frankl realized during the holocaust that he did not have to live in fear of the Nazis or the kapos and that when man has meaning to living his life has power, purpose and direction. It was this power as found in his meaning for living that gave him the strength to survive the holocaust and see that even the suffering had meaning.

"If you want to make your life happy and worthwhile, which is what God wishes you to make it, [sic.] you must begin immediately to train yourself in the habit of thought selection and thought control (Fox)." So here it all boils down to a simple or not so simple choice; a metaphysical crossroad where each person will one day arrive and being unable to go backwards must choose which road to take. One road leads to more of the same, the same addictions, the same pain, the same rat race, the same slavery. This is the road where the traveler gets more of the race conscious rigmarole. The other road, offers authentic living, peace, joy, love, and freedom. Frost reminds the reader in his poem, "I took the one less traveled by, and that has made all the difference." The road less traveled made all the difference. It was not the road that was popular. It was not the road that is the easiest or most comfortable. It is not the road that has been chartered and discovered by others. The road that offers the greatest benefit, the one that makes all the difference is the road that each person charts for himself. It is the road of self discovery where following someone else is not an option. This course is for one and one alone. Many still fear this road despite its benefits. Stepping out of the comfort zone, away from the majority, out of the pack of sheep can be a frightening step towards liberation. That step often results in isolation and ridicule from those remaining in the safety of their comfort zone. They are the ones quick to call someone a sinner, crazy, or a cultist. They are quick to say how the person is turning their back on their family and friends or the church. This isolation, ridicule, perceived abuse gives many reason to pause and reconsider being different. This gives many the motivation to stay comfortable, to avoid the road less travelled for they fear being damned by friends, family, and church.

According to Miriam-Webster Dictionary online damnation is:

1: the act of damning **:** the state of being damned
Examples of *DAMNATION*
The minister spoke about death and *damnation*.
First Known Use of *DAMNATION*
14th century

Damnation isolates and keeps the fear of death alive as it condemns them to a fate they desire to avoid. People feel the pangs of loneliness and it frightens them. The threat is also preached from pulpits across the globe of man's eternal damnation. This threat continues to enslave the hearts and minds of the children of God. Damnation scares man because of what man believes hell to be. As has already been mentioned by Fillmore, hell is a state of consciousness, yet many still hold fast to the traditional concept of hell as preached and shown in the dictionary. If liberation is to occur, man must unlearn the old paradigm and learn a new theology of liberation. They must learn to release the fear of being condemned to hell, release the fear of being judged and isolated, and release the fear of change by stepping out on faith and embracing the truth rather than the illusion.

CHAPTER TWO:
WHAT IN THE "HELL"

As we prepare to venture into "hell" where we will see the foundation upon which the mountain stands, I would like to continue with the study of the words and the definitions as used in our society. This is something I tend to do when teaching or coaching; this gives us an opportunity to gain a deeper understanding of what ideas we allow to occupy our minds and thus to create in our lives. I would like to continue from where we left off. In chapter one, we looked at sacred, profane, and damnation. Having a general definition gives a sturdy foundation or introduction upon which our discussion can then be built. That being said thank you for indulging me. Let's continue by look at a few words which are interwoven into our collective psyches and will prove to be quite relevant to this text and our journey out of and away from hell.

Hell, it would seem has many uses in the English language. If we look at how Miriam Webster defines hell, we shall see that our language is proliferated with the idea of hell.

According to Miriam-Webster Dictionary online hell is:

1a (1) **:** a nether world in which the dead continue to exist **:hades** (2) **:** the nether realm of the devil and the demons in which the damned suffer everlasting punishment—often used in curses <go to *hell*> or as a generalized term of abuse<the *hell* with it>
b *Christian Science* **: error** 2b, **sin**

2a : a place or state of misery, torment, or wickedness <war is *hell* —W. T. Sherman>
b : a place or state of turmoil or destruction <all *hell* broke loose>
c : a severe scolding; *also* **: flak**, **grief** <gave me *hell* for coming in late> **d :** unrestrained fun or sportiveness <the kids were full of *hell*> —often used in the phrase *for the hell of it* especially to suggest action on impulse or without a serious motive<decided to go for the *hell* of it>
e : an extremely unpleasant and often inescapable situation<rush-hour *hell*>
3 *archaic* **:** a tailor's receptacle
4—used as an interjection <*hell*, I don't know!> or as an intensive <hurts like *hell*> <funny as *hell*>; often used in the phrase *hell of a* <it was one *hell* of a good fight> or *hell out of* <scared the *hell* out of him> or with *the* or *in* <moved way the *hell* up north> <what in *hell* is wrong, now?>
— from hell
: being the worst or most dreadful of its kind
— hell on
: very hard on or destructive to <the constant traveling is *hell on* your digestive system>
— hell or high water
: difficulties of whatever kind or size <will stand by her convictions come *hell or high water*>
— hell to pay
: dire consequences <if he's late there'll be *hell to pay*>
— what the hell
—used interjectionally to express a lack of concern about consequences or risks <it might cost him half his estate . . . but *what the hell* —N. W. Aldrich *b*1935>

Examples of HELL

1. Getting the loan approved was pure *hell*.
2. He *went through hell* during his divorce.

3. She had to *go through hell* to get where she is today.
4. Living with the disease can be a *hell on earth*.
5. The pain has made her life a *living hell*.

Origin of HELL
Middle English, from Old English; akin to
Old English *helan* to conceal, Old High
German *helan,* Latin *celare,* Greek *kalyptein*
First Known Use: before 12th century

As this definition shows, our language is inundated with "hellish" and "hell-full" uses. It is no wonder that man is full of hell and can't seem to "get the hell out of his own way" as mountain after mountain seems to block people from happiness, joy, and more. Hell seems to be on many people's tongues and that is a dangerous place for it to be since scripture tells us that, "We have the power of life and death in our tongue" which metaphysically indicates that our words literally have creative power. "We must continually remind ourselves of the power of the Word, and our ability to use it (Holmes)."

Many people flippantly use words never taking into account what enlightened mystics, teachers, and masters throughout time have told us—"words have power." Words are thoughts given verbal energy and therefore are powerful as well. Charles Fillmore, said, "Words are also seeds, and when dropped into the invisible spiritual substance, they grow and bring forth after their kind." This is precisely why scripture says, "You have the power of life and death in your tongue." It is also why the Bible begins with, "In the beginning was the Word, and the Word was with God and the Word was God." This is added demonstration that we are to be mindful, conscious creators who control both thought and word.

If we are people who superficially or jokingly speak of hell, is it any wonder that hellish conditions are demonstrated in our lives? Do you talk about solar flares if you are not thinking about them? Do you talk about Jane Goodall if you are not thinking about her? We tend to talk about what we are thinking, what we believe and we talk about what we are focusing our energy onto at the time; this is precisely why we must be vigilant. The master teachers of all cultures have reminded us that it is done unto us according to our beliefs. If you notice two people sitting in a crowded coffee shop talking about something in a very passionate manner, we often refer to that as a heated discussion. Heat is energy, so if they are in a heated discussion we can assess that on one level or another there is energy being expressed. It is important to realize that the discussion need not be "passionate" or "heated" per se to be one where energy is brought forth. Every time you speak a word, energy is expressed and sent out into the world—metaphysically and literally! This reminds me of one of the lessons from the Kybalion that I will discuss in the "Spiritual Warrior" as that text is sort of the next step to follow what I am teaching in this book.

Metaphysically your words have spiritual power to create or as many say, to co-create with the Divine. Your words have the ability to inspire hope and lift a nation or depress and incite destruction. Adolf Hitler used the power of words to provoke and ignite the flames of hatred and death where as the Rev. Dr. Martin Luther King Jr. and Mahatma Gandhi used words to enliven and create a climate for change and freedom! Their words, born of the spirit touched within their listeners a chord that was made to resonate to the tune of love or in Hitler's case, that of hate. Then there is the literal energy created as your vocal chords vibrate the air which then travels through space until reaching the ear drum of the listener causing it to vibrate, as well as, send signals to the auditory center of the brain which then translates those vibratory signals, also known as sound, into something we assign meaning. All about us are sound vibrations. Have you ever taken a moment to sit in a crowded place and center yourself in order to notice how much you truly hear at any given moment? The eardrum picks up far more sounds than we are aware of or paying attention to at any given minute. And to my deaf friends, who may assert that they do not hear the sounds, the vibrations are still present and their affect on you while different are still worth noting. A blind person does not need to see the sun to feel the warmth of the sun on their skin; likewise, you do not need to hear to be affected by the vibrations of sound. The body by way of the atmospheric space receives the vibrations that have traveled through the air much like the opera singer whose voice travels across a space and shatters a crystal glass.

Now, there are many who would argue that words are not that significant. They argue that words are merely words. Many in the rap industry and other musical genres would argue that using profanity, sexist and homophobic references, as well as rampant use of the "N" word are all simply poetic and artistic musings. Yet, they fail to take into account that music has an amazing ability to amplify the power of the voice, the power of the word! Music is an amazingly powerfully creative medium that has been used all over the word as part of spiritual practices. Many mantras are sung. Many monks chant scriptures. Even in consumer driven societies advertisers have realized the power of the musical jingle to make their product memorable and the movie industry spends billions of dollars on the development of the film's soundtrack to not only enhance the movie going experience but as a product to be sold via ITunes or CD. Teacher, musician, and authority on sound healing, Jonathan Goldman says that "Sound Healing, as the name implies, is the use of sound to create balance and alignment in: the physical body, the energy centers called "chakras", and/or the etheric fields. The sound may be applied by an instrument or by the human voice. Sound Healing is a vibrational therapy and can be understood as being energy medicine." All of this attests to the fact that music and sound does in fact have a profound effect on us. Therefore, it stands to reason that the words set to music will affect us. At the end of the book in my "Further Reading

Section", you will notice a book by Yvonne Oswald, "Every Word Has Power." This is an excellent book that can assist you further in understanding your responsibility to be mindful of your speech and of your thoughts as well.

Speaking of being mindful of our thoughts . . .

What is hell? Does hell exist symbolically, metaphysically or literally? Does hell exist because people believe in it and because they talk about it? That is a question many of us may want to take the time to ask and consider. Each of us would benefit at some time or another in our lives from questioning each and every one of our beliefs. So much of what we act upon was part of our childhood programming and we never take the time to assess that programming's validity in our lives. I love the analogy that Sherri Rosenthal uses in her book "Banishing Mind Spam." She offers the idea that the mind is filled with spam that messes up the workings of the mind and that we have the ability to banish and quarantine the spam or mental viruses that run through the system. Picture that for a moment, how do you feel when working on your computer and suddenly some bit of unwanted spam or virus affects what you are doing? Many people opt to do nothing and simply continue to fuss and fight with the computer as if the computer is at fault. Others do what they can by taking the computer to an expert to have them fix it so it can run more effectively. Our mental systems are no different. Some of our beliefs serve us and some do not. All of our actions are backed by and are the effects of a belief in something. Everything you eat is because of something you believe about the food. Everything you buy is because of something you believe about the product. Everything you wear is because of something you believe about the clothing. Think of it like a GPS, you tell it where you want to go and it calculates the route. Your beliefs do the same thing; the difference however, would be, suppose I place the destination in the GPS and don't tell you. You would have no idea where you are going since you did not select the destination. Similarly, someone may have chosen to become a vegetarian not by conscious choice but because somewhere in their childhood they were told they were a fat and ugly child and made fun of when they ate pork chops or beef and they were told that they were going to end up as fat as the cow or pig. This person may well have internalized those words and as they grew up may have dismissed or suppressed them and yet they eventually changed their diet becoming a vegetarian not because of any conscious health reasons or ethical choices but because of that early childhood programming that labeled them as fat and ugly. All of our actions are influenced by our beliefs and this is why it is in our best interest and serves us best to lay them all out on the table and assess which beliefs truly serve us now and which beliefs are out dated and no longer do. Making a conscious choice is far more empowering than continuing to run on the default settings of the subconscious and ego.

While there are in fact many who do believe in hell as a literal place in the bowels of the Earth, hell as a place of fire and gnashing of teeth is not what is being referred to here. What I am referring to is the consciousness of hell. There are also those who would use the Bible as their support to say that hell is in fact a literal location and I do not disagree or dispute that fact. What I am pointing to is that many believe in something without knowing why they believe it or what it is they truly believe. Why do so many staunchly advocate that we are to follow the Bible word for word as the inerrant word of God and yet as a culture of Christian believers, pick and choose which passages to actually follow and which ones to dismiss as out dated? There are those who believe the Bible as a literal document and yet most of those who do so do not take *the entire* document literally. To do so would drastically change the manner in which we as a society function. For example: If we were to do as Leviticus 15:19-30 says and put the menstruating female apart which some have translated to mean out of the house for seven days because she is unclean, how would this affect our modern world? If we treated women as property which can be sold into slavery as is mentioned in Exodus 12:7, how would that impact a woman's right to live as the Declaration of Independence states or would that not apply to her? How would marriage be affected if we followed Deuteronomy 22:13-21 and only allow virgin women to marry? And stoned those who mislead the man by lying about it? Speaking of stoning, what if we still stoned people as the mob that Jesus stopped were preparing to do in John 8:3-10?

Were we to remove the "sting of hell" by removing the literal concept of hell, of damnation, of Satan, and of sin, many argue that it would drastically alter the significance of the sacrifice, the resurrection, and the gift of salvation given through Jesus. If we are to put in faith in the teachings of Jesus, the master teacher, then we must keep in mind that Jesus said he came that we might have life and have it more abundantly. How do we really believe that he came to save while at the same time offering a fate worse than death (eternal gathering) to those who did not follow or accept Him and His teaching? Why do many hold and continue to believe in such a contradictory teaching? If Jesus, being the Way Shower, came to educate, illuminate, and enlighten mankind by raising the consciousness to unconditional love, then how could this same teacher profess to the existence of eternal separation from God? Jesus broke from Jewish law on several occasions; one such occasion, the stoning I mentioned earlier when he stopped the crowd from stoning Mary. The law gave them the right to kill her due to her "sins" and yet Jesus, demonstrating compassion, love, and true Godly justice intervened and taught them a valuable lesson which resulted in the accused being left to live. If Jesus was a believer in sin, punishment, death, damnation, etc. then would he not have followed the law and allowed them to judge, condemn, and sentence this sinner who was going to hell? Jesus believed in forgiveness, love, justice, and life for all!

> "The mystics have taught the ultimate salvation of all people and the immortality of every soul. Indeed, they have taught that immortality IS HERE AND NOW, IF WE WOULD BUT WAKE TO THE FACT. "Beloved, now are we the Sons of God." Since each soul is some part of the Whole, it is impossible that any soul can be lost. "God is not the God of the dead, but of the living." Damnation has been as foreign to the thought of the mystic as any belief in evil must be to the Mind of God (Holmes)."

Waking to the fact, as Holmes puts it, is what the spiritual warrior's path is about. It is about awakening and remaining awake because it is easy to be lulled to sleep by dogma and religiosity which Rev. Beckwith speaks of in his book "Spiritual Liberation." There is also the dogma of consumerism which seduces many men, women, and children into believing that for them to be healthier, happier, more attractive, and more alive, they must buy, own, and use some particular brand of products. These people now sick with the epidemic of lies become addicted to the plague of acquisition where they are possessed by the demon of acquiring. Note: I use the term "possessed by the demon of acquiring" for poetic affect, I do not believe in and am not referring to or advocating a belief in a literal demon though the feeling of being possessed by the need to buy and acquire is quite real. This acquisitive nature which is based on a core belief in scarcity takes over. The person constantly affirms, "I am not complete and not good enough unless I have the new IPAD, IPOD, HD television, Blue-ray machine, etc . . .____________" You can fill in the blank with any number of "things" that people can be heard saying, "I have to get this or get that!"

Ironically, one day people reading this will laugh at the items I listed realizing how out of date they are. Like people today thinking about records, radios, and cassette players as being out dated. Each day new gadgets and gizmos are created, new fashions given someone's stamp of approval as being the hip thing to wear. As each new day comes, the fads and fashions find themselves old and outdated and those people who are bound to them find themselves feeling lost. This belief in acquisition is not limited to electronics, clothing, jewelry and the like, it can also manifest as acquiring the right job, the right spouse, the perfect body, needing to belong, needing to be thought of highly, needing to fit in by having and getting some "thing" they feel they are missing. These people continually find themselves always running to keep up in a race they have already lost. These people, like the cocaine addict whose high has left, begin to feel the pain of not having the false power coursing through their veins as a new high must be sought after. And like the addict who overdoses, so to do those addicted to material substance. They give up living to become zombies and junkies of the illusion. Saks Fifth Avenue, Wal-Mart, and Target become the corner where they get their next fix. These places have become their place of worship as they practice the religion of "Acquisition" and worship at the altar of "I Must Have It."

Interestingly, this version of religion practiced by the "gotta get, gotta have" addicts is not far from the drug of limiting dogma that is peddled in many synagogues, churches, mosques, and temples around the world. Many people believe and strictly follow the doctrines espoused within these hallowed locations. Yet, much of the doctrine is based on control, on fear, and on lack. People lack salvation and therefore need someone or something outside of them to be responsible for giving it to them but only if they are deemed worthy of it. This worthiness is determined by someone other than the seeker and by them practicing a series of actions that must be honored daily and failure to honor the religious code runs you the risk of being excommunicated, ostracized by community and family, mocked and condemned, and in some instances killed.

Some form of daily prostrations must be made. This could be in the form of literal prostrations or prayers, tithing, reading the scriptures, reciting mantras, knocking on doors, handing out pamphlets, selling incense, conforming to the clothing standards, and on and on the list can go. So few of them truly realize that their "salvation" is not won or obtained by doing these things; that does not get them to heaven. This kind of thinking impedes growth. Like hell, heaven is a state of consciousness and not a literal place in the clouds with streets of gold and pearly gates. Heaven is within as Jesus stated. Heaven is experienced in the here and now when one's consciousness is raised. Anytime someone lives thinking that by giving some financial indulgence, by saying a prayer a certain number of times, by believing in *this* religion, going to *this* church or following *this* pastor, they are fooling themselves into believing that they have assured their place in heaven by gaining God's grace and favor. Far too many people actively believe in that anthropomorphic God I mentioned earlier. They believe God to be a Zeus or Odin like being sitting in some far off place above the clouds sitting on a throne; a "man" who can be placated and appeased in order to garner the favor of Heaven. And even worst, when he is not appeased or placated, he grows angry and wrathful and damns us to the Hades, the underworld, hell! This belief is the result of the dogmatic doctrines in religion that are still being taught and followed today. For that reason many people not wanting to be compared to or placed in the same category, have begun to say that they are spiritual not religious. This is their attempt to escape from and separate themselves from the dogma and doctrine of separation, damnation, and hell.

This kind of statement gives the impression that religion is a bad thing and spirituality is a good thing. It is wise to remember what Shakespeare said, "Nothing is good or bad but thinking makes it so." There are many so called "spiritual" people who have fallen asleep while proclaiming to be awake. Religion in and of itself is neither good nor bad. What a person thinks, feels, believes and does within the walls of their chosen religion is what is important. There are many interfaith ministers who honor and embrace the practices of other religions while still engaging in their own.

According to Miriam-Webster Dictionary online religious is:

1: relating to or manifesting faithful devotion to an acknowledged ultimate reality or deity <a *religious* person><*religious* attitudes>
2: of, relating to, or devoted to religious beliefs or observances <joined a *religious* order>
3a : scrupulously and conscientiously faithful
b : fervent, **zealous**
— **re·li·gious·ly** *adverb*
— **re·li·gious·ness** *noun*

Examples of RELIGIOUS

1. My *religious* beliefs forbid the drinking of alcohol.
2. *Religious* leaders called for an end to the violence.
3. His wife is very active in the church, but he's not *religious* himself.

Origin of RELIGIOUS

Middle English, from Anglo-French *religius,* from Latin *religiosus,* from *religio*
First Known Use: 13th century

According to Miriam-Webster Dictionary online spiritual is:

1: of, relating to, consisting of, or affecting the spirit **:incorporeal** <*spiritual* needs>
2 a : of or relating to sacred matters <*spiritual* songs>
b : ecclesiastical rather than lay or temporal <*spiritual*authority> <lords *spiritual*>
3: concerned with religious values
4: related or joined in spirit <our *spiritual* home> <his *spiritual*heir>
5a : of or relating to supernatural beings or phenomena
b : of, relating to, or involving spiritualism **: spiritualistic**

— **spir·i·tu·al·ly** *adverb*
— **spir·i·tu·al·ness** *noun*
Examples of SPIRITUAL

1. Doctors must consider the emotional and *spiritual* needs of their patients.
2. I regularly consult our pastor about *spiritual* matters.
3. The Romantic composers saw Beethoven as a *spiritual* ancestor.
4. France will always be the *spiritual home* of wine lovers.

Origin of SPIRITUAL
Middle English, from Anglo-French & Late Latin; Anglo-French *espirital, spiritual,* from Late Latin *spiritualis,* from Latin, of breathing, of wind, from *spiritus*
First Known Use: 14th century

Dr. Alberto Villoldo of *the Four Winds Society* said in an online interview with *kripalu.org* that, "religion is based on belief and spirituality is based on experience." The individual has an experience and feels a profound sense of the sacred and upon that experience is formed the belief, the story, the dogma, and as I believe Don Miguel Ruiz would say, "the agreements." These beliefs that the individual has formulated based upon the experience have become the foundation of that individual's religion, they have become the agreements by which they move within the religion. This is the process by which all of our beliefs and practices are formulated. 1. You have an experience. 2. You evaluate the experience and how you feel about it and this becomes your belief. 3. You begin to live according to the belief you have which was based on the experience. Seen another way: 1. You have a terrifying experience where a neighbor's dog attacks a friend of yours. 2. You evaluate the experience and your feelings of fear and create the belief that dogs are dangerous! 3. You do not like dogs and you live your life disliking and avoiding dogs. You talk to people about how much you do not like dogs and you may even mention that they scare you although you may not even recall that childhood experience that planted the seeds and started the fear. So you go from the initial experience, to building of the belief, to living life based on the belief, and then your life is shaped accordingly.

Both Yeshua ben Yosef (Jesus) and Siddhartha Gautama (Buddha) had spiritual experiences and as a result of these experiences taught others. Their disciples under their direct instruction had similar experiences and from those the disciples began to develop certain ideas and they believed certain things based on those experiences and from those experiences the religions of Hinduism, Buddhism, and Christianity were formed. There is nothing inherently wrong about this process or formation. The error or disconnect occurs when the person no longer seeks the personal experience. They are content with the form and not the essence. This is like the thirsty man being satisfied with a photo of a glass of water rather than being permitted to drink an actual glass of water or the young bride given a painting of a bouquet which she sniffs hoping to take in the fragrance rather than being given a fresh bouquet full of the aroma and feel of the flowers. Many people do this on a daily basis; they are satisfied with empty prayers, crosses, statues, and choir songs rather than having the full experience of their oneness in God. This is the sign of a spiritually immature person.

The spiritually mature individual realizes that first that there is a choice and then they realize that they must make a conscious choice between the form and the essence. They know as The Science of Mind states, "We cannot live a choiceless life. Every day, every moment, every second, there is a choice (Holmes)." This is where the development of the spiritual warrior begins, with the initial awakening. This is also why the term warrior is being used. The warrior archetype must first awaken to the quest before being trained and skilled to do what he or she is meant to do.

The warrior is also someone who is willing to do the work to learn, develop, evolve, and then go and serve others.

According to Miriam-Webster Dictionary online warrior is:

1: a man engaged or experienced in
warfare; *broadly* **:** a person engaged in some
struggle or conflict <poverty *warriors*>
Examples of *WARRIOR*

1. a proud and brave *warrior*
2. <a program of tough training and discipline that turns untried civilians into *warriors*>

Origin of *WARRIOR*
Middle English *werreour,* from
Anglo-French **werreier, guerreier,* from *warreier, guerreier* to wage war, from *werre* war—more at war
First Known Use of *WARRIOR*
14th Century

The warrior of the spiritual is a person who understands not only his or her responsibility for creating their world, but their responsibility for affecting change in the world for others and they understand how to actively participate in this creation. This person takes on the task of identifying and eliminating by way of transmutation each of their addictions, their fears, and their erroneous core beliefs. They take on this responsibility one hundred and ten percent. They do not blame others, point fingers, criticize or complain. They assume the fullness of the responsibility despite the challenges they may face in the world. They maintain a constant vigilance to remain in the light and to be the light. They do not fight against anything because they know that whatever is resisted will be persistent. Fighting *against* the race consciousness and *against* the ego gives more power to what they do not want. They understand that they cannot move the mountain that is in their way by pushing against it. This is why the spiritual warrior must understand what it means to be in the world but not of the world and this, as well as, the many other lessons occurs after the spiritual warrior's initiation.

> "*Initiation* is the shaman's art for transforming emotions such as anger, fear, and despair, into love, purity, and compassion. Initiation is the way the spiritual warrior heals her emotions, lets go of the need for growing through adversity, and becomes a creative force in her own life (Villoldo)."

The warrior's initiation can occur in many ways; simply making the intention to move in that direction can serve as a strong enough catalyst for the warrior's initiation to begin. Once the initiation begins, the training also begins. It is through the training that the spiritual warrior becomes empowered and the mountain's foundation begins to crumble.

IT'S NOT AS BIG AS YOU THINK

A hero is an ordinary individual who finds the strength to persevere and endure in spite of overwhelming obstacles.

Christopher Reeve

CHAPTER THREE:

GET THE "HELL" OUT—MOVE THAT MOUNTAIN!

What does being empowered mean to you? We use the word quite often and yet I venture to say many do not truly embody the word as a quality they possess. According to Miriam-Webster Dictionary online empowered is:

transitive verb

1: to give official authority or legal power
to <*empowered* her attorney to act on her behalf>
2: enable 1a
3: to promote the self-actualization or influence
of <women's movement has been inspiring
and *empowering* women—Ron Hansen>
— **em·pow·er·ment** *noun*
Examples of *EMPOWER*

1. seeking changes in the workplace that will *empower* women
2. <the federal agency *empowered* to collect taxes>

First Known Use of *EMPOWER*
1648

To be empowered is to be self actualized; it is the evolution of a man to be all that he is capable of becoming. Abraham Maslow describes "Self Actualization," as,

"the desire to become more and more what one is, to become everything that one is capable of becoming . . . in order to reach a clear understanding of this level of need one must first not only achieve the previous needs, physiological, safety, love, and esteem, *but master* (emphasis added) these needs (Wikipedia)."

This call to become self actualized/empowered is in many respects not optional. Maslow said, "What a man *can* be, he *must* be (Cherry, Kendra)."

That is a powerful declaration and it speaks directly of the divine discontentment that each person feels when they are settling for less than what they can be. Divine evolution will always call the spiritual warrior forward to be the best he or she can be. Settling for complacency is not an option. The self actualized/empowered are quite different from the un-actualized/dis-empowered or un-empowered individuals. They have a unique set of characteristics as identified by Maslow.

- Self-Acceptance and Democratic World View
- Realistic
- Problem-Centered
- Peak Experiences
- Autonomy
- Solitude and Privacy
- Philosophical Sense of Humor
- Spontaneity

It is only through self actualization, through becoming an empowered person that true mastery can occur. Once mastery of one's life via mastery of one's mind is achieved, liberation is inevitable.

According to Miriam-Webster Dictionary online liberation is:

1: the act of liberating **:** the state of being liberated

2: a movement seeking equal rights and status for a group<women's *liberation*>

— **lib·er·a·tion·ist** *noun*

Examples of *LIBERATION*

1. The *liberation* of the city took weeks.
2. <the *liberation* of the slaves was one of the key results of the Civil War>

First Known Use of *LIBERATION*

15th Century

Gandhi often said that upon his death he would like to have the name of god (Ram) on his lips and as the story is told, when Gandhi was assassinated, he uttered the name of god at the moment he was shot. I mention this because for many people there very well may be panic, fear, worry and dread at this moment and yet for Gandhi there was peace. From what I have learned, studied, and experienced personally, this occurred because Gandhi was already liberated. He was already free from the confines of fear and death. Liberation is the state that Rev. Dr. Martin Luther King Jr. was in when he delivered his "I've Been to The Mountain Top" speech which gave a sense that he knew he too would be assassinated if he continued on the path he was on. Undaunted, he continued, liberated from the paralyzing fear that could have caused him to stop his involvement in the civil rights movement. It was this same kind of liberation that allowed Father Mychal Judge to go serve the men and women in NYC on Sept. 11. When others were fleeing the World Trade Center site, Father Mychal went to the site to do whatever he could to serve. Father Mychal died there doing what he had done every day prior to that—serving, helping, and loving. Liberation is what gave Jesus the Christ the ability to say "not my will but thine" when he was in the garden of Gethsemane meditating on what was to come.

"Spiritual Liberation is . . . living instead from a conscious awareness of one's Authentic Self, one's true nature of wholeness (Beckwith)."

Once the spiritual warrior reaches the state of liberation, the next step, “healing,” occurs automatically.

According to Miriam-Webster Dictionary online heal is:

transitive verb

1 a : to make sound or whole <*heal* a wound>

b : to restore to health

2 a : to cause (an undesirable condition) to be overcome **:mend** <the troubles . . . had not been forgotten, but they had been *healed* —William Power>

b : to patch up (a breach or division) <*heal* a breach between friends>

3: to restore to original purity or integrity <*healed* of sin>

intransitive verb

: to return to a sound state

Examples of HEAL

1. You’ve got to give the **injury** time to *heal.*
2. After the divorce, he needed some time to *heal.*
3. The ointment will help *heal* the wound.

Origin of HEAL

Middle English *helen,* from Old English *hǣlan;* akin to Old High German *heilen* to heal, Old English *hāl* whole—more at **whole**

First Known Use: before 12th century

This is the journey of empowerment, liberation and healing for the spiritual warrior who seeks to “move mountains.” Getting the hell out of one’s consciousness is the process of exorcising the demons (note this is poetic use meaning demon consciousness). So picture for a moment that you are at a friend’s house and she tells her ex-husband to get the hell out! Is she making a request or is she making a demand? Without presupposing the pathology behind their relationship and simply looking at the statement itself, we see that getting the hell out comes from a place of strength. It is this same place that the warrior must come from in order to move mountains and get the hell out of his own way. More and more people are waking to the fact that they are not moving forward and that their inability to develop, grow, and live a life of true joy is because they have allowed the consciousness of hell to hold them captive in the underworld in a cell constructed by each and every thought of scarcity, fear, doubt, worry, hatred, prejudice, and separation from God.

Whether it is grade school or post high school, people are "hungry" for positive, empowering education. They want the knowledge that will allow them to change and grow. They want the knowledge that will not only open the cell door allowing them to be free but dissolve the cell itself. The current systems of mainstream education and religion are not supplying them with the "spiritual" nutrients they desire. Many are "spiritually" famished. While there are more and more New Thought churches and centers popping up around the world and more and more people being trained and educated as ministers and practitioners to meet the needs of the community, there is still a vast amount of people who feel the weight of despair, fear, pain, and struggle. This is why I offer you this book, to share with you the lessons I have learned, the changes I have made and to give you the necessary tools so you can let your light so shine. As your light shines, others will be affected and given the means to become illuminated and through your fruit they are nourished and are given the tools to be free.

"By their fruit you will recognize them." Mathew 7:20

In a 2011 radio broadcast on KPFK.ORG, Rev. Michael Beckwith spoke with Bishop Carlton Pearson and in that interview the two very distinguished and articulate ministers agreed that there is a change coming in the spiritual community, that many so called Fundamentalist Christians are leaving their old paradigms for the New Thought Ancient or Ageless Wisdom teachings that are becoming more and more available. People are not only hungry for the truth, they are ready for the truth; the truth that will set them free. This message of being ready to be set free is masterfully taught by singer, songwriter, and Agape licensed practitioner Ester Nicholson. Ester, a woman who at one point in her life was an alcoholic, learned about true freedom. Through her journey she learned and evolved and as a result has developed what she calls "The 12 Keys To Freedom: *for those experiencing addiction of any kind.* (Emphasis added)" This list of 12 keys gives the spiritual warrior an excellent training. On her website she says,

> "The 12 Steps of the Alcoholics Anonymous program (including AA, CA, NA, OA and all of the A's) are extremely powerful. They were the steps that healed me from drug / alcohol and food addiction—and all of the other deep seated illusions that I suffered from. However, there came a time in my 25 years of sobriety, when the steps were no longer enough for me. I referred to what Bill Wilson, founder of Alcoholics Anonymous wrote in the Big Book, "We know only a little" and "we must enlarge our spiritual lives." There is a scripture that speaks to this part of my evolution. It says, 'When I was a child, I spoke as a child, I understood as a child, I thought as a child, but when I became a man, I put away childish things (Nicholson).

This is what it means to become spiritually mature. The immature individual focuses on the acquisition of toys and having fun at the cost of their physical, emotional, and or intellectual health and wholeness. This is seen in the actions of many young people today who go off to college and party in ways that place them in undesirable situations; in jail, in the hospital, or in the morgue. They treat college as if it were an amusement park or an extended house party. Their focus is more on having fun than on education. Due to their immaturity they end up learning their lessons in the school of hard knocks. The mature individual on the other hand knows how to balance healthy fun with the work that must also be done. This person, if they were in college, would see not only each class as an opportunity for growth, but each experience in the registrar's office, financial aid, or academic advisor's office as an opportunity for growth as well. Though they may not particularly enjoy the course or the professor, the mature student would understand that there is more to learn than just the course work from the syllabus. The mature individual understands the value and purpose of each experience as part of the process of awakening. Ester goes on to explain,

> "When I needed to believe that I was powerless and that my life was unmanageable, in order to become humble enough to really listen, heal, grow, and follow someone else's directions, Step 1 worked in my life. When I needed to believe that I was insane so that I could be open-minded enough to know that my thinking and behavior was irrational and out of perspective, and that something more powerful than me could restore my sanity, Step 2 was crucial to my healing. When I needed to turn my will and life over to a Power greater than myself because without it I was going to kill myself with drugs and alcohol, Step 3 saved my life.
>
> But once I turned my will and life over to a Power greater than myself and practiced the rest of the steps which allowed me to have a direct connection to that Power, the strangest thing happened; I realized that the Power wasn't greater than me, It WAS me. It was nearer than my hands and feet, closer than my breathing. Oh, what a revelation. What a break-through. Once I had that realization, I could no longer affirm that I was powerless and that my life was unmanageable. I'm only powerless and out of harmony with life when I ***believe*** I am separate and apart from the One Power.
>
> There are times even now, after 25 years of sobriety that I somehow find myself hypnotized into believing I am separate

> from the Universal Presence. I can tell when I've stepped out of Reality into illusion, because my thinking gets out of whack and I start eating like it's my last meal. When I catch myself in the midst of the illusion, I say "oh, you've forgotten who you are again, you've forgotten what's real". This has led me to create 12 Keys To Freedom, which are not steps of powerlessness, but keys to the inner Power which we all possess. When I am consciously connected to the one Power, I am restored to balance, harmony and order. Cravings and out of balance behaviors dissolve because I am no longer operating at the vibrational frequency of powerlessness when I'm connected (Nicholson).

That connection she speaks of is what the spiritual warrior learns via the journey. One of my favorite movies of all time, the archetypal story of The Matrix is an excellent example of the journey of a man from sleeping to awakening. The path of the spiritual warrior, as shown in this modern day myth is made clear and serves as a compass of sorts which can be followed as it points the way for the viewer willing to see the film as metaphysical road map rather than simple Hollywood entertainment. For the student who is ready the movie, a clear map is laid out on the table and can be followed. This map indicates how one can move from a life based on scarcity, limitation, bondage, and fear to a life full of prosperity, limitlessness, peace, freedom, and love. The journey, as told in The Matrix, reveals the life of Thomas Anderson, a man living in a world of illusion believing the illusion to be the truth. He believes the illusion until he is, by way of his newly adopted mentor Morpheus aptly named after the god of sleep, shown the illusion for what it is. Upon knowing the truth, Thomas, later to simply go by the name Neo (the Greek prefix for "new"), is given a choice to either return to the dream, the illusion, the lie or awaken to the truth and to do what he is being called to do. Neo chooses the truth. This is where many choose the opposite, preferring to dwell in the land of ignorance believing that ignorance is bliss. As is shown later in the story, one of the rebel warriors, Cypher, desires to return to sleep; which he never achieves. No one, once awake can return to a state of being asleep. As Oliver Wendell Holmes said, "Man's mind, once stretched by a new idea, never regains its original dimensions." You cannot un-know what you know. While you may have moments where you forget and you may doze off, you cannot unlearn. So, in an attempt to be put back to sleep and to un-know, Cypher makes a deal with the Agents to be "plugged back into" the matrix where, once back in the system his mind would be cleared of his betrayal and where he would no longer have any awareness of what he has done in giving the Agents what they wanted—Morpheus. He adds in his negotiations, that he also wants to be someone rich with influence in the world of illusion. How fitting that many people, like Cypher, prefer the epidemic of the lie; they prefer to live a life that is a lie, hiding behind several façades simply to avoid awakening to the truth and living free.

What is it that makes man prefer to live a lie rather than to embrace and live the truth? It is a simple yet complex four letter word, fear. Man fears many things, fear of success, fear of failure, fear of loss, fear of the unknown and despite all of the degrees or things man fears many great master teachers have said that all fears when boiled down to their root reveal the fear of death, the ultimate loss. Man fears his death, the end of his existence and all that he believes himself to be, and then there is death as the greatest of the unknowns. The life that is the lie is a life that is known; it is a life that is safe, predictable, and built on a foundation of complacency. The alcoholic knows the pain and degradation that comes from being an alcoholic. He does not know what a life without alcohol, his addiction of choice, is like. Fearing the unknown, he continues to drink. The abused wife knows what will irritate her husband to the point of violence. That is a predictable existence where she, despite the pain of abuse, has a roof over her head and the financial "support" of her husband. She does not know what a life of independence would entail or if she could even live on her own. Fearing the unknown she continues to remain in the abusive relationship. The fear of the lie keeps her blinded to the possibility that her death could one day result from the beatings. The church going, God fearing man continues to go to the same church he has gone to for as long as he can remember. He hears the rhetoric of hate being preached from the pulpit on a regular basis. He sits there week after week listening to a message of hate towards anyone unlike and unacceptable by the pastor, most notably gays. He hears the condemnation and feels the hatred burning around him. He does not know what church would be without such preaching. He does not know what a life of self acceptance would mean. Fearing the unknown, he remains in the closet until he can take it no longer and chooses to take his life instead because he needs the pain to end and suicide seems the only option.

Fear is a powerful motivator keeping man firmly entrenched in the concretized morass of the illusion. Fear keeps the mountain firmly in place and unmovable. However, as the great mystics have said, one day all will awaken. I remember the first time I heard the story of how Siddhartha became the Buddha and how when he touched the earth as his witness, he not only became enlightened but that his awakening awakened everyone all at once and that we need not awaken but are charged with realizing that we are already awake, that Buddhahood is not something to obtain but something to realize is already ours. We can only delay the inevitability of our enlightenment for so long.

> "Neo believes he's living a normal, but slightly troubled life in 1999. By day, a computer programmer for a large, generic software company; by night, a hacker, providing the fruits of his labors to other troubled souls. He lives alone, he doesn't sleep, and there's a profound emptiness in his life, but it's something he can't put his finger on—until he is contacted by Trinity. "It's the question that drives us", she whispers in his

> ear, to which he correctly responds "What is the Matrix?" It is this question that has gnawed at Neo seemingly his entire life, yet he's never put it into words before now. It is the voicing of this question that begins his transformation into The One (The Matrix Meanings).

It is that gnawing, that divine discontent, which propels humans to evolve their thinking, their consciousness. This growth occurs only if the person listens, as Rev. Beckwith has said, "with the ear behind the ear," meaning that we are to listen to the still small voice of God which is not coming from some outside source but is rather from the very essence of who and what we are. There is no where that God is not. So listening to the still small voice is done with the spiritual faculties. Neo listened to his divine discontent and as a result was open to the contact made by Trinity. He sought the truth without even knowing what the truth, capital "T" Truth, was.

> "Neo's journey in the movie bears many hallmarks of classic myths. He is the Chosen One, the reluctant hero, the savior, and the one who will lead his people to freedom. In order to do that, he must sacrifice himself, and rise from the dead. He faces progressively greater challenges through the course of the movie, and as he begins to believe in himself, he is able to overcome these challenges, including beating his ultimate adversary, Agent Smith (The Matrix Meanings).

Instinctively all who hear the call also know that sacrifice is necessary; it is impossible to fly while still holding onto the earth below. Few are willing to sacrifice what they know and to leave that which they have grown accustomed. "There is a distinct purpose for each person and each situation that gets presented in your life. A true gift from the experience waits to be realized (Falco)." The path of the spiritual warrior can mean relocating to a new city where you will assume your right livelihood and serve the community. It could mean leaving behind family and friends who are not ready to change and who chose to label you as the evil one or the black sheep because you changed from what they were accustomed to. The sacrifice could be leaving your old paradigm of religion and transforming into a new expanded inclusive faith which is built on unconditional love. Regardless of what benefits the sacrifice offers, many people hold tight to the old and comfortable, due to their fear of change. Gandhi said, "Be the change that you would see in the world." A simple yet very profound statement for it takes an awake, aware, and dare I say enlightened individual to live this creed daily. Living this creed means that if you desire to see more love in your life and in the world then you are to be love in the flesh. By being love in the flesh you are being more loving, expressing love, and welcoming love; this energetically sows seeds of love which will be reaped by others in the world. If you desire to see peace in the world, then you must be peace. Note that Gandhi did not say that you must "DO" anything . . . he said to "BE" that which you desire to see. By being peace you will do things that reflect, express, and demonstrate peace, however, you must innately be it.

I liken this to a person going through the motions, but not feeling it within. And since I know I would wonder, some of you may also be wondering if "Faking it until you make it" or "Acting As If" is valid based upon what I am saying about going through the motions. Yes, they are valid IF you are committed! If you have set the intention to live an abundant life then you have in effect turned on the inner light switch of awareness. In order to act as if you are abundant, you must have a concept of what that means and it is from that intention and concept that you think abundantly and live from an abundance consciousness. You refrain from believing what the outer world might show you to the contrary and instead you choose to see only what someone who is already abundantly living life would see. Your intention sets the tone of being that which you desire to see in the world; so that when you begin to do various things you are doing them from a place of beingness and not a place of emptiness where you merely go through the motions. This would mean that you say I am abundant and you may profess to others that you are abundant yet when you pray you pray *for* abundance, when you watch TV or go shopping you still have scarcity thoughts running rampant you just are not consciously aware of them. Simply going through the motions is pointless and is what Jesus advised against when he spoke of the hypocrites who do what they do to be seen and praised by men rather than doing so from a place of true worship. “And when you pray, do not be like the hypocrites, for they love to pray standing in the synagogues and on the street corners to be seen by men. I tell you the truth, they have received their reward in full.” (Matthew 6:5 NIV)

Taking the road most travelled is far easier to do than it is to stand up and let your light shine amongst men. Guiding each man, woman, and child is an inner oracle of sorts, much like The Oracle that Neo encounters in the story. The Oracle serves as his guide; using her words to guide him into becoming the fullness of who and what he is meant to be. She initiates him. In a key part of the story, Neo and The Oracle discuss why Morpheus brought Neo to see her. In the exchange of words we find that she, The Oracle, is one who tells each person exactly what they *need* to hear which is quite different from telling someone what they *want* to hear. We can only receive from the Divine what we are ready to receive. This is why Iyanla Vanzant said to Oprah that she could not hear what Oprah was telling her so many years ago. She was working from the pathology of welfare consciousness and in that consciousness she could not see the gifts, the blessings, or the possibility that was within her. The Oracle could have told Neo that he was in fact The One. However, Neo’s state of mind would not and could not have heard, nor could it have accepted her words. In his state of disbelief, resisting her proclamation that he was in fact The One, Neo would not have moved forward as he did. Therefore, The Oracle does not tell him, she lets him find the answer to the question within himself.

> "**The Oracle**: You know why Morpheus brought you to see me?
> **Neo**: I think so.
> **The Oracle**: So, what do you think? Do you think you're The One?
> **Neo**: I don't know.
> **The Oracle**: You know what that means? It's Latin. Means `Know thyself'. I'm going to let you in on a little secret. Being The One is just like being in love. No one can tell you you're in love, you just know it. Through and through. Balls to bones.
> **The Oracle**: Well, I better have a look at you. Open your mouth, say Ahhh.
> **Neo**: Ahhh.
> **The Oracle**: Okay. Now I'm supposed to say, `Umm, that's interesting, but . . .,' then you say . . .
> **Neo**: But what?
> **The Oracle**: But you already know what I'm going to tell you.
> **Neo**: I'm not The One.
> **The Oracle**: Sorry, kid. You got the gift, but it looks like you're waiting for something.
> **Neo**: What?
> **The Oracle**: Your next life maybe, who knows? That's the way these things go.
> **The Oracle**: What's funny?
> **Neo**: Morpheus. He . . . he almost had me convinced.
> **The Oracle**: I know. Poor Morpheus. Without him we're lost.
> **Neo**: What do you mean, without him?
> **The Oracle**: Are you sure you want to hear this? Morpheus believes in you, Neo. And no one, not

> you, not even me can convince him otherwise. He believes it so blindly that he's going to sacrifice his life to save yours.
> **Neo**: What?
> **The Oracle**: You're going to have to make a choice. In the one hand you'll have Morpheus' life and in the other hand you'll have your own. One of you is going to die. Which one will be up to you. I'm sorry, kiddo, I really am. You have a good soul, and I hate giving good people bad news (The Matrix Meanings)."

Using choice, The Oracle provides Neo with a powerful nudge to his already present feelings of divine discontent. Her words spur Neo forward. Based upon what she told Neo, his goal shifted from thoughts of being The One to his need to save Morpheus which meant he would have to sacrifice his own life. "Greater love has no man than this, that a man lay down his life for his friends (John 15:13 American KJV)." Once Neo was willing to make the ultimate sacrifice, he unwittingly stepped directly onto the path of the being a spiritual warrior, The One. "For whoever may will to save his life, shall lose it, and whoever may lose his life for my sake, he shall save it (Luke 9:24 Young's Literal Translation)." It is his respect and love for Morpheus that sparks the divine fire within him. A fire within his very soul which tempers him; as the master sword makers of Japan tempered the Samurai swords, Neo was tempered into being The One. This is the sacrifice that each person must also make. We must lose our life. Before you panic, the life I am referring to is the life you have been tricked into believing is real. Like Neo, we are tricked into believing the matrix is truth when in fact the matrix is a lie fashioned to keep us in check as good little automatons. This lie is what has convinced you to believe that you were anything less than happy and joyful, anything less than abundantly prosperous, anything less than surrounded in and by love, anything less than whole, complete, and healthy, and anything less than perfect and divine. What do you suppose Jesus meant when he said, "I and the Father are One." Have you ever stopped to consider that this also applies to you? You and the Father (Mother, Divine Source) are One! This must in fact be the truth otherwise Jesus was less than truthful when he said, "Timeless truth, I tell you: 'whoever believes in me, those works which I have done he will also do, and he will do greater works than these, because I am going to the presence of my Father.' "(John 14:12 Aramaic Bible in Plain English)

Assuming that Jesus was in fact speaking a timeless truth losing one's life means relinquishing the lies and seeing beyond the veil of illusion to the eternal truth of all that is. To lose one's life is in truth only the losing or the loosing of the egoic mind's control over your life. Once again, I am not advocating the death of the ego for it serves its purpose when seen from the right perspective. Like fire, the ego does harm when out of control yet warms a home or cooks a meal when used properly. The ego is meant to be servant not master. Its job is to protect you and once taught what and how to do its job it no longer acts as an obstacle to your growth and development. The ego believes that keeping you safe means staying in your comfort zone and living a life of quiet desperation. However, it can be retrained to understand that unconditional love, adventure, and living by the creed "Carpe Diem" (Seize the day) is a life well lived.

"The purpose of life's journey is not to arrive at the grave with a well-preserved body, but rather to slide in sideways, completely used up, yelling and screaming, what a ride!"

A full and thoroughly lived life is what this journey is all about. Because man fears losing something that truly cannot be lost he allows his ego to protect that life at all costs. Somewhere I once read that "The true test of a man's character is what he does when no one is watching." So much of what we do is based upon not only who we think is watching but what they might think about us as well. We allow our ego to entertain itself with the endless tirade of negative 'what if' questions. What if they don't like me? What if she divorces me? What if they find out I'm gay? What if I lose my job? What if I don't finish school? What if I don't pass the entrance exam? What if this and what if that . . . on and on and on! What does any of that serve? Let's put a spin on that quote, "What would you do if there was no death?" Some people might say they would take more physical risks like driving as fast as they want, go sky diving, or swim with sharks. Others might eat and drink whatever they want. Still others would do any number of other immature things. However, what we are really speaking about here beckons a more mature point of view, a more metaphysical look at the question. If what we tend to refrain from stems from a root fear of death, what would we do if that thing we fear was non-existent? For example—What if failure was not possible? If you could not fail, what would you do differently with your life? Life cannot truly be lost and it is the fear of losing one's life that forces man to cower in the corner to afraid to grow. In truth, the you that refers to having a body is not the body. You are something beyond what words can even describe or explain. And it is precisely because you are a spiritual being experiencing life in a human form that you cannot die nor can you fail. To do so would imply that God can die and that God can fail and this is not the case.

God is eternal, without beginning and without end and God is life; therefore Life is eternal. This has been demonstrated and taught by masters the world over. No matter if the concept is expressed in reincarnation, in a soul that goes on after the body, or in a more scientific manner which focuses on "energy" which cannot be created or destroyed. The central idea is that our consciousness, the essence of what we are is energetic in nature and is immortal. Therefore no matter what point of view you take, death is merely a metamorphosis a transition from one form to another; life is eternal! Once that idea can be embraced and accepted as truth, it is possible to live a life from a much more liberated plateau where you can look out on your experiences and see them from a place of victory and not victim.

In order to move from victim to victor a degree of courage must be employed. Courage must well up within and the thing that is feared must be faced and the sacrifice that must be made must be given. Sacrifice what you ask? Sacrifice the worry, doubt, low self esteem, victimhood, blame, and finger pointing for starters. Sacrifice the waiting. Waiting for the fear to leave before you relocate, waiting for the fear to leave before you change careers, waiting for the fear to leave before you follow your inner calling, or waiting for the fear to leave before you decide to be the change you know you are meant to be in the world. Sacrifice anything and everything that will result in you staying in your comfort zone. Feel the fear and do it anyway!

Courage is not the absence of fear, but rather the judgment that something else is more important than fear. ~Ambrose Redmoon

Courage is resistance to fear, mastery of fear, not absence of fear. ~ Mark Twain

Had Neo waited until he was fear free to go save Morpheus, Morpheus would have died. You cannot grow while being "comfortable," growth is change and change takes work and is at times uncomfortable. It takes the butterfly work to stretch and push its way out of the cocoon, were it to not have this challenge, its wings would not develop and grow strong and it would not be able to fly! The decision to "do it afraid" is the only thing that will give you the ability to fly when you thought you would fall.

Courage isn't an absence of fear. It's doing what you are afraid to do. It's having the power to let go of the familiar and forge ahead into new territory. ~John Maxwell

Within each person is an oracle, an intermediary of sorts between man and God or flesh and spirit. Some call this intermediary the Higher Self, others the Atman, others the conscience, and to others the subconscious. As Shakespeare said, "A rose by any other name would smell as sweet." Do not get fixated on the name; the concept is far more important. This is why men fight over God and religion; they fixate upon a name rather than the essence or concept that is behind that name. What sense does it make to fight over any of these labels or names: Mizu (Japanese) Agua (Spanish) Eau (French) Shuǐ (Chinese) Acqua (Italian), or Pānī (Hindi)? Though the names are different they speak of the same essence which is water, H_20. The name is merely a linguistic tool we use to convey an idea, to express a concept. The name is not the thing itself. The word water cannot quench thirst, wash a dish, or fill a tub. The experience is what is most important not what you call the experience. Each person has within at this present moment now the ability to know and be known. "Ask and it will be given to you; seek and you will find; knock and the door will be opened to you (Luke 11:9 NIV)." This is the assurance given in scripture reminding mankind that when the pupil is ready, the teacher will appear; when the question is asked, the answer will be revealed. Nothing is hidden when you are ready and willing to know the truth. When Neo was ready to know the truth, nothing, not even the bullets that Agent Smith pumped into his chest prevented his resurrection, his rebirth into the conscious realization that he was in fact—The One. Likewise, when each of us is ready to awaken, nothing will stand in our way. The mountains, worries, problems will all be seen for what they are, foggy mists of illusion which were believed to be truth.

From sleep and curious stirrings, to disbelief, doubt, and disappointment, to determination and sacrifice, to death, resurrection, and awakening is the journey of the spiritual warrior. Each person is called and in some form or fashion each and everyone is chosen to do their part in the grand tapestry of life. How does anyone know that they have been called and chosen? The answer is simple. Every man, woman and child that is alive is an individualized demonstration of God. God has individualized itself to more fully express itself and as such, every man, woman, and child has a divine mission, purpose, and reason for being—everyone is called to be a spiritual warrior—time to wake up!

THE PROBLEM: WAKING UP BECOMING AWARE

Spiritual awakenings can be much like physical ones in that when the person first wakes up he may have to take a moment to become cognizant and fully conscious after having been dancing in the realm of the subconscious all night. Hitting the snooze button once or twice or even five times may even be part of the process; however, sooner or later waking up occurs. At which time he reorients himself to the physical once again, he may rub his eyes, stretch, and even yawn, all of which are very important steps in the awakening process. He rubs his eyes so that they adjust to the light in the room; allowing him to see. He stretches so that his body is limber and ready to serve as the vehicle of action which allows him to move and do that which must be done. He yawns so that his lungs are filled with fresh air. Each breath then becomes a reminder of the breath that God used to make Adam a living soul—*Ruach*. Like Adam, that breath which inspired him and gave him life is the same breath that each person breathes causing them to be inspired, to be filled with the *Ruach* of the Divine—the breath of God. Once the person has re-acclimated himself to the physical world he is ready to go through the next steps of preparing himself for the day ahead. No one goes to work before having woken up. People may opt to go to work without having brushed their teeth, bathed, or combed their hair, but waking up is not an option. Before anyone can begin the activities of the day ahead they must first wake up. The spiritual journey is no different.

The problem, for lack of a better word at present, is that many prefer to hold onto the state of sleep for as long as they can. They then jump up from bed, racing to get the day started in an awkward and hurried frenzy of confusion, sloppiness, and mayhem. That is no way to start one's day if peace calm and order are what you desire. For those people who prefer to remain asleep, the alarm buzzes, the snooze bar is hit, and they roll over and assume the next warm comfy position. This does not just occur in the physical world of sleeping and waking, it also occurs in the mental/spiritual as well. There are many instances when the call to awaken comes and many prefer to remain asleep. They do their best to ignore the call and fight against the light. Their resistance resembles the young child who pulls the blanket over their face when mom opens the curtains and lets the sun shine in. Look at the life of Gandhi. His life served as an example and his teachings lead to independence of his nation and the end of war. Despite this great growth there were those so determined to remain asleep who made the decision to silence the alarm that would have them awaken. Rather than embrace freedom and empowerment, and peace, there were those who felt it better to silence this teacher of a better way to live.

There are many who focus not on the positive lessons and examples of the teacher, but focus more on the positive reasons he should die as they plan his assassination so they can remain in their comfort zones. They argue that the teachers are evil, misguided, and wrong and must therefore be stopped. Jesus, Rev. Dr. Martin Luther King, Malcolm X, Gandhi, Harvey Milk, and many others are examples of wayshowers, teachers, leaders who were assassinated by the fearful. The fearful see the assassination as a viable option to free them from change. They are mislead into thinking that someone can kill another or take another person's life and it is this belief that gives them even more evidence and reason to be fearful because they reason that if I can kill him, he can also kill me, so I must get him first!

This presents us with two important things to realize: Death is an illusion and therefore murder is illusory as well and no one can take your life for your life is the life of God and no one can take God's life. Life is eternal as I said before; there is neither beginning nor an end to it. This is quite a challenging concept to grasp considering we are so bound by the confines of what we physically experience as we experience such things as time as we look at the ticking hands of the clock. However, I challenge you to sit with the idea that there is no death and that life is eternal. Does the caterpillar die to become a butterfly? Does the seed die in the soil to become the plant? Does childhood die to become adolescence? These are transformations, changes, transitions; they are not cessations of life. Death is a change of form not an end of life. Life cannot end. People fear death because,

> "Our instinctive desire is to live and to go on living, and death is a savage end to everything we hold familiar. We feel that when it comes we will be plunged into something quite unknown or become someone totally different. We imagine we will find ourselves lost and bewildered, in surroundings that are terrifyingly unfamiliar (Rinpoche)."

Despite this fear of the unknown, there is much reassurance that man is an immortal being and that death is a change not an end. "Jesus revealed himself to his followers after his resurrection, to show them that death is but a passing to a higher sphere of life and action. TO KNOW THAT WE MAINTAIN AN IDENTITY INDEPENDENT OF THE PHYSICAL BODY IS PROOF ENOUGH OF IMMORTALITY (Holmes)."

Despite man's apparent immortal, powerful, spiritual nature, many people prefer to avoid embracing this nature.

Like the depressed person who closes all the curtains to keep the apartment dark and prefers to remain in bed, under the covers, asleep, these people behave as if they are fearful of the sunrise of a new day and the hope it represents. For them, the dream world is far more appealing than the waking world. These people fail to understand that sooner or later they *will* awaken and that they must engage and participate in their life; no one can remain asleep forever. The desire to remain asleep is rooted in the desire to avoid something. People avoiding getting up and going to work, people avoiding getting up and walking the dog, avoiding the gym, avoiding the realization that they are not going to bed early enough to get adequate rest, avoiding the realization that those who frustrate them the most are merely mirroring back to them some aspect of themselves that is calling to be healed and avoiding the responsibility and changes that comes with being awake. Many prefer the world of dreams where they can have the cars, the sexual adventures, the money and mansions. For them remaining plugged into the matrix is a preferred false reality. For them the epidemic of the lie has seduced them into believing that the hallucinations are in fact the real thing.

Then there are also those people who so desperately *try* to wake up. However, their version of waking is merely waking to a dream within a dream. It becomes reminiscent of a scene from the movie "Inception" starring Leonardo DiCaprio where there were dreams within dreams within dreams and knowing the dream from real life could be quite difficult. That is why DiCaprio's character said that there was a tool used to help them know when they were in fact still dreaming. For him it was the spinning top. Many people think that once awakening occurs, once they become "awakened" that things change and they may somehow now be "magical." This is merely the ego, wanting to be special, trading one dream or one lie for another. This is a huge illusion for many in the spiritual community. When this illusion is examined more closely and looked at much deeper than many of us are willing to dig, we come to find a continued belief in separation and suffering based on fear. Expecting to become or desperately desiring to become someone or something great the individual may wonder or worry if they are truly up to the task. They may question their sense of worthiness. Hidden beneath their monks garb, prayer beads, choir robes, and prayers exists a form of escape. They desire to escape the dull humdrum world, they desire super powers. Powers that enable the newly awakened "superwoman" to leap tall buildings in a single bound. Powers that enable her to become the something *special* rather than simply being the mother or teacher or waitress she is being called to be in that moment.

Each person is great as they are. Nothing outside makes anyone great. The person who feels a need to awaken so that they can become something better, to become something that they perceive to be greater than they are, is based in fear. It is still selling one lie for another; it is trading one sleeping dream for another. Do you believe that you are great just as you are right now? Do you believe that you are perfect just as you are right now? Do you believe that something outside of you can give you peace, joy, happiness or love? So much time, effort and energy is expended as we worry about changing, getting, and becoming something we feel is lacking and yet we are reminded in Luke 12:25 "Can any of you add an hour to the length of your life by worrying?" What this is telling us, plain and simply is that worrying is pointless, fruitless, and useless! We are being asked to shift our consciousness from a lower vibration (worry, doubt, lack of worth, fear) to a higher vibration (assurance, faith, worth and love). As we raise our vibration, as we be the change, as we live life consciously in alignment with Source, others will see the light and be influenced by it.

Raise yourself to a higher level of thought and you will raise others with you. ~ Howard Falco

We awaken in order to more fully express who and what we are. We do not seek to awaken in order to escape what we perceive as a boring life. If you are called to be a mother, then that is a holy calling when you are willing to see it through the eyes of God. And truth be told, there is no such thing as a job that is not holy. Radical concept right? Colin Tipping proposes in his book Radical Incarnation that each of us has a soul contract of sorts which we play out on the stage of life and that each of us is doing precisely what we need to do in order to bring about the necessary shifts in the universe. What this implies is that not only was Dr. Martin Luther King Jr. on a holy mission, so was his assassin. It's like the biblical references seen in the interaction between Judas and Jesus. Had Judas not betrayed Jesus, there would have been no crucifixion. Had Pharaoh not pursued Moses and the Israelites, God would not have used Moses to demonstrate His power. Had Satan not tempted Job, Job's faith would not have been proven. Without dark there is no light and vice versa. What I glean from the concept of a soul contract and from the book Radical Incarnation is that each person as a piece of God is holy and can be nothing less than holy and that each person is moving through life as they are "meant to" for lack of a better word. As each of us lives, part of the process of this incarnation is to awaken to the realization that we are holy, divine, and perfect and that as we awaken to that and change within ourselves, the ripples of energy are sent out and affect change in those around us and in the universal whole as well; that awakening is enlightenment.

It is often said when referring to enlightenment, "before enlightenment, chop wood and carry water; after enlightenment, chop wood and carry water." This simple yet profound quote serves as a reminder that enlightenment does not make anyone into some kind of "superhero" or "super" human. Enlightenment is found in everyday living, it is walking, bathing, doing dishes, feeding the doing, mowing the lawn, bagging groceries, changing a diaper, and laughing with friends. There is as story that Rev. Dr. Beckwith relays on the DVD "Transforming Awareness" where he speaks of an enlightened laundry man. Here is a slight variation of the story he told; the moral of the story is the same.

This old rural monk is walking down the road to the stream, a big bundle of clothes slung over his back because it's his turn to do the laundry. A guy from the nearby village stops him to chat just a bit. He's mystified by the great spiritual work they do at the monastery, and asks him, "What is enlightenment like?" The old monk slips the big bundle off his back and straightens up with a bit of a stretch and a deep, contented breath at the release of the burden. The guy also sighs at the thought of it. He then excitedly asks, "Then how about after you are enlightened? What's life like then?" The old monk just picks the laundry up, hoists it onto his back, and starts walking again toward the stream. Hence the saying, "After enlightenment, the laundry."

"When an ordinary man attains knowledge, he is a sage; when a sage attains understanding, he is an ordinary man." **Zen saying

As Gordon Deitrich from the film V for Vendetta says, "You wear a mask for so long, you forget who you were beneath it." It is easy to forget, to become seduced by the lie, to believe in the personas we have built. As our consciousness shifts, as we awaken we no longer see through a glass darkly, we realize and know as we have been known. As we are enlightened we see the truth beyond all outer appearances and here we know that that we have always been and will always be God's divine offspring. All that you desire to be, you already are! There is nothing missing, what you are called to do is to remember, re-member, connect once again to the One for this is your birthright. One should not desire becoming enlightened or awakened out of a misplaced belief in becoming something "better" than they are nor should they flee the idea of becoming enlightened or awakened out of a misplaced belief or fear of losing themselves and their routine of daily living by assuming that they have to become the next Gandhi, Mother Theresa, or Dalai Lama. Just as Gandhi, Mother Theresa, and the Dalai Lama have their *Raison d'être;* their reason for being so too does everyone and everything else. A great thing about the reason for being is that each person creates it. It is not predetermined in the way that many people tend to think of predetermination or predestination. God's will is the same for all—for greater expression and expansion of itself in you, through you, as you.

For many people they hold onto the belief that God predetermines what everyone will be and what they will do and that there is nothing anyone can do to alter their destiny. For them, if God wanted Oprah to be a truck driver then nothing she could have done would have altered or changed her destiny and she would have been a truck driver. This belief in predestination goes beyond just the idea of what you are here to become and to do, this idea is for many carried further into who gets to go to heaven. This idea is fueled by a belief in scarcity.

> "The Western monotheistic traditions that arose in the Middle East assigned much power to the role of God in determining our destinies, while still placing a large burden on the individuals to follow God's laws or reap the consequences. The Protestant doctrine of predestination preached by John Calvin and others in the sixteenth century, however, tipped the balance entirely on God's favor. According to their beliefs, our purpose in life is to fulfill the duties and responsibilities that God has assigned us, but because human nature is essentially corrupt, we cannot achieve salvation (the reward of Heaven) except by the grace of God. Moreover, to the Calvinists, God has predestined certain people to receive that grace and not the others, leaving us dependent on a kind of luck controlled by the Divine, which has already decided our fate. Acting morally is all but

reduced to a form of hoping that one is already among the elect (Myss)."

This position is held firmly in place by many Christians today because of the belief in scarcity. There are a select number of slots to heaven and those slots are *already* filled; doesn't get much more limiting than that. This position or belief is acted out with judgment as those who believe themselves to be on the VIP list serve as judge and jury for the rest of mankind who may or may not by God's grace already be on the list and thus guaranteed salvation. This belief is permeated with fear and confusion and anger as each person lives their life unsure if all their right living, deeds, and prayers have been for naught since God has already selected his chosen few. How does anyone truly live a life of peace and joy? Somewhere in the back of the mind would be the constant nagging questions and potential anger associated to never knowing if this is all one big waste of time and energy since they could be damned to hell no matter what they do. In my mind I find that this creates quite a confusing religious practice as the believer does all that he thinks God wants him to do and does all that his religious dogma dictates and still no matter what he believes, confesses, and does, his fate to damnation is already sealed. Think about that for a second and see if that resonates with you on any level. Here is a young woman who "religiously" goes to church and based upon what the powers that be in the pulpit tell her she does her best to live according to the Good Book and yet she will not find out until she dies if she receives salvation, if what she has done all her life has any lasting merit or if there has been any point since she very well may not be one of the preselected. Belief in this kind of theology makes you wonder and question why a loving God would create so many people and then only chose a select few to save.

Suppose the maker of the Titanic had created the ship with the conscious plan of sinking it and not only that but he knew that of the two thousand two hundred and seven people on board only the seven hundred and twelve he selected would be saved. Would that make him a criminal who could be charged with murder? Based on this fictional analogy, yes I would argue that he would be liable of a criminal act and yet this is precisely what many believe and teach? This kind of theology is but one of the paradigms that prevent true empowerment and healing from occurring. Until this limiting paradigm and all other similar core beliefs are removed, man will continue to run around the hamster wheel of a self induced purgatory.

You have heard me mention this shift of paradigms and the importance of waking up and so by now you may be asking how then does one wake up in order to move mountain so that they can proceed unencumbered by the illusions. First and foremost is the realization of what you believe. It is assessing your core beliefs. As I have explained earlier, there are many things that we do that have their genesis in some long forgotten childhood experience and it is there that we delve in order to know what paradigms we hold as truth. For example suppose I ask you what is your favorite color? Your answer is based upon your belief and feelings about that color. You may say that red represents vitality or sexiness and you feel energized or sexy when you wear or see red. What is your favorite film? Who is your favorite actor or singer? What does being a democrat or republican mean to you? What does it mean to be a Christian, Muslim, Jew or Buddhist? What is evil? What is good? Do you believe in the death penalty as a viable deterrent to crime? Do you think spanking kids is appropriate? Each of these questions on some level asks you to access what you believe and how you feel. Beliefs and feelings are closely intertwined. For example, you might feel disgust at the thought of eating broccoli however if you were told that it would help you reduce your weight you might change how you feel about it as a trade off for losing the weight. So in order to begin the awakening process and make the shift you have to know what you are shifting from and shifting to. Your beliefs serve a purpose, even those that are not as healthy as they could be. Some people believe they are stupid, fat, ugly or untalented. I have had coaching clients argue that they did not chose to believe that about themselves. They argue that their mother or father or older brother made them believe it. I ask, really? And once I see the head nod, I proceed to ask, so if they told you that you were a bunny rabbit would you believe them? They say no. What about Santa Claus? Again, they say no. What about a Leprechaun or the Tooth Fairy? By now they get my point and they see that somewhere they made the choice to agree with the person and believe what was being said. Now we can begin to find the hidden benefit of holding onto their beliefs. For some it may be a sense comfort and acceptance because when they agreed and accepted the belief, the teasing or the abuse may have temporarily stopped. For others, it protects them from rejection. The possible reasons are too numerous to go into but know that there is a reason behind each and every one of them.

Yet we have chosen to believe them for a reason and in order to change them we must look at them and consciously decide to make the shift. Many people feel a deep sense of loss and isolation which stems to their belief that God is separate from them. For those feeling lost, their lives are ever tugging at the ever persistent nudge to find their way back to God. It is the belief that, each person has been cast out of Eden, like Adam and Eve, due to our disobedience to God that shows up as obstacle after obstacle. That lie and the others like it are the paradigms that must be sought out and replaced with more empowering beliefs.

When I was an adolescent practicing martial arts and studying the philosophy of the East, to help me understand the concepts which I was reading, my father use to quote a phrase that at the time made no sense to me. He would say, "All roads lead to Mecca." I remember many times wanting to say, "Dad, I am reading about Lao Tzu, what the hell does Mecca and Islam have to do with Taoism?" It wasn't until many years later that I truly understood his point. All are on the same "spiritual" journey. While the routes may vary, the destinations are the same. No matter their position, the avatars, bodhisattvas, teachers, ministers, parents, atheists, and government officials are all on the same spiritual journey—A journey to remember who and what we are. It is a journey of atonement which is the realization of At-One-Ment, where we awaken to the truth that no one is now separate from the One Divine Source, no one has ever been separate from It, and no one can ever be separate from this Universal Mind which many call God. This realization must be more than an intellectual exercise in understanding, it must be a full on embodied experience because it is from our realization of Unity and Oneness with the Divine that man evolves and becomes enlightened. From this enlightened state, man becomes self actualized, empowered, liberated, healed, and at one with the Divine.

Despite this grand metamorphosis that awaits each person, many still fear the change. Many fear the light, thinking that the life of the enlightened master means meditating for hours each day, eating rice and vegetables, wearing saffron colored robes, and chanting in some sacred temple. They fail to realize that the awakened master lives the life of the poet, actor, writer, artist, mother, father, business man, janitor, senator, teacher, and waitress. Each person has within, already in this present moment, the master; the Christ; the Buddha and Brahman, and once awakened, their lives will change but not in some drastic fearful way that they may imagine. Many of their daily routines and actions taken will not change. Remember the story I told about the monk and the laundry?

> "On one level, you brush your teeth and have a cup of tea in the morning like everybody else. On a deeper level, more internal level, you are in communion with all of nature at all

> times, and your practice is one of finding how you can be of service, as a steward of nature and to the world that you want your children's children to inherit. So the core task of the Shamanist is to dream her world into being. Otherwise, she has to settle for the Collective nightmare that is being dreamt by others (Villoldo)."

On one level, the person continues to go about their daily life, yet beneath the surface they are intimately aware now of the connection, the divine thread that interconnects everything and everyone. Having that awareness alters how they express the divine and what they demonstrate. That awareness creates a different mental equivalent for the spiritual warrior or what Dr. Villoldo referred to as the Shaman. It is from that awareness that the shaman can manifest, or as Dr. Villoldo says, " . . . dream her world into being." He goes on to say,

> "We now know that whatever you vibrate, you create and attract to yourself. So you work on healing yourself in order to create peace around you. The world mirrors back to you perfectly the condition of your love and of your intent. And if the world you're living in is not a world that is at peace and at joy and at grace, then you have to find peace, joy, and grace within you. The shaman no longer looks for meaning in life, but brings meaning to every situation. The shaman stops looking for truth and instead brings truth to every encounter. You don't look for the right partner, you become the right partner. And then the right partner finds you. It's a very active practice focused on healing (Villoldo)."

It becomes the job or the responsibility of each person to wake up and take full control of his thoughts and in turn of his life. It has been said throughout the ages that whatever man thinks, man shall create and yet so few people truly pay attention to that admonishment. Many continue to be unconscious creators, creating by default and suffering as a result. The realm of the sleeper is a realm of *unconscious* creation, for creation will and does occur whether we are consciously doing it or not. If a person is continuously complaining about the racist teacher their child has in school, their mind is unconsciously creating a life filled with racism whether real or imagined. If a person is constantly focusing on losing weight, their mind subconsciously will continue to create a weight issue for them to focus on. If a person focuses on all the ills of the world that seem to only worsen as time goes on, then their unconscious creation is that same self-fulfilling prophecy—a world that is damned! All the more reason for people to look around them and determine if what they see in their lives is something they desire and if it is not, take the steps to wake up and re-create their lives as they consciously desire. It begins with waking and being aware.

THE PATH: INITIATION AND TRAINING

Once awake the day begins and the individual actively moves about the day creating their world. For many, this idea of conscious creation is something of which they are unaware. Many go about their day believing they are merely victims of the weather, the traffic, and the crowds at the store, their jobs, the economy, and their relationships. For them life is something that happens to them. They do not realize that they can affect each and every area of their lives by shifting their perspectives and training their mind. Life then becomes something that happens through them instead of to them. In the Star Wars saga, episode five, The Empire Strikes Back, the character Yoda tells the young Jedi initiate, Luke Skywalker "to do or do not, there is no try." Luke did not grasp his wise teacher's words at first. It took Yoda's demonstration of his mastery of the Force to prove to Luke that it was his own mind and not the size of the jet fighter, which caused him to fail! Luke was being initiated into the ways of the Force and like him the spiritual warrior is initiated into the ways of Universal Mind which in many ways is similar to George Lucas' Force concept. Initiation begins when the initiate sees behind the veil so to speak. When there is a realization that this current way is not working and that something better something more whole exists and that something needs to be done to change, the initiation begins with the *intent* to step into something greater.

Waking up is when the individual officially begins the quest; as I said before you cannot go to work and do your job if you are still asleep. The initiation is the process of getting out of the bed, getting washed, dressed, nourished, and stepping out the front door into the world. This is in essence the activity of getting out of the comfort zone and taking the necessary steps to move forward in spite of fears that may appear. It can be quite intimidating to look in the mirror and not recognize the face looking back. It is the process of cracking the mask, the façade that has been carried for so long and now seeing the face spoken of in the ancient *koans* (a challenging question or statement used to bring the student to a higher level of awareness)—In Zen (Japanese) and Chan (Chinese) Buddhism.

> "The term (Original Face/Original Self) appears most famously in Case 23 of the koan collection *Mumonkan*, or "Gateless Gate," in which the monk Myō, jealous that the Sixth Patriarch Enō has received the robe and bowl of their master, chases him through the mountains and tries to take them by force. Enō places the robe and bowl on the ground and invites Myō to take them. However, Myō finds that they are too heavy to lift. Overwhelmed with shame, he asks to be given the teaching instead, and Enō responds, "Without thinking good or evil, in this very moment, what is your Original Face?"
>
> What face did you have before your parents were born? The question isn't hard. It's like asking a sunflower what it was before it was a sunflower, or the wind before it was wind? A true Zen master never asks to see something that isn't already there (Strand)."

Once the individual is given a glimpse of his or her original face, the individual begins to understand his quest more fully. He now realizes that there was something to the discontent that nagged at or tugged at his mind and soul. He now realizes that there is in truth something more to life than the "Rat race" that he was conditioned to run in as a hypnotized participant. There is more to life than growing old, making a living, and then dying. The individual now realizes that there is a way to get back home; there is a path to wholeness which paradoxically is also a quest to find and obtain something he thought he lacked which in reality is simply something he must become reacquainted with because it is, has and will forever be a part of him! This is something he must rediscover for and within himself.

The initiation in "The Matrix" begins when Neo takes the red pill and awakens to what Morpheus called "Wonderland", referencing the Alice in Wonderland mythos. This Wonderland would be where Neo would see just how deep the rabbit hole goes. Once awake to the Wonderland his mind was in a place where his training could begin. Luke Skywalker woke up and embarked upon the path of training when he made the decision to tell Ben Obi-Wan Kenobi that he wanted to become a Jedi and for Dorothy, her path and training (quite artfully illustrated) begins after exiting the comfort of her house into the land of the Munchkins and walking the yellow brick road. Waking up is when the warrior has decided that they have slept long enough and they set the intent to change and begin this new journey rather than go about life as they have done thus far or as they are expected to do. The warrior is consciously ready to embark upon the divinely appointed journey. A journey that will take them to a destination that is new and unchartered, a journey that will have challenges and moments of uncertainty; yet a journey they know they must take, for their Higher Self has called and appointed them to take this quest that they may become all that they can be, the full expression of God in physical human form.

This journey or quest involves the acquiring of certain skills and abilities that the spiritual warrior has not actively or consciously utilized before, however, they are skills that are now needed to assist them in their growth and evolution. Luke had to learn to use the Force and wield a Lightsaber, Neo had to learn that his only limitations were those within his own mind. It is through their training that the initiation obtains the ability to move mountains. Unlike *Sisyphus* from Greek mythology, the obstacles that have been in their way for so long, can and will be moved. The hell in their way is the hell they created and have allowed to be in their way. For those seeking a "quick fix" or some new trend in personal health and healing, the training of the spiritual warrior will prove to be disappointing for some and painful to others. The training, while simple in concept is complex in practice and does offer several challenges. And though the challenges may not be as grand as those of *Perseus* or of *Hercules,* they should not be underestimated or undervalued. The training is life changing as major shifting occurs and the very foundations of belief are shaken to the core as the initiate embarks on a major transitioning from sleep (death) to being awakened (life). The training can be stated quite simply as—Change your thoughts, change your life. If that one thing is truly understood and practiced with faith and earnestness, then the life, the outward manifestations or demonstrations will also change. "Through the medium of Mind, man unifies with the Universe and contacts a power that can do anything for him that he is able to conceive of Its doing (Holmes)." This is one of the major ideas of New Thought. It is how the mental equivalents are formed in mind and from those mental equivalents come the manifestations or demonstrations in life.

Hold an idea of poverty and poverty will manifest. Hold an idea of illness or dis-ease and disease and illness will be demonstrated. Hold an idea of fear and a reason to be fearful will manifest to keep your fears alive. This is why the primary thing to change is the conscious use of mind.

Becoming a skilled and conscious creator is at the root of all the warrior's training. Without being mindful and conscious of the thoughts held in mind, the subconscious thoughts, which often are laced with the poison of fear, lack, and limitation, will create by default without the individual's consent. Conscious, unconscious, or subconscious creations will attract to the individual whatever things they are a match to vibrationally. Emmet Fox says in his text, The Mental Equivalent, "Jesus Christ taught us saying, 'Do not judge by appearances, but judge with right judgment' (John. 7:24). So when we see the appearance of evil, we look through it to the truth that lies beyond it, as soon as we see this truth, and see it spiritually, the appearance changes (Fox)." This is what changing the thoughts will do. It will remove the old habitual actions and patterns of judging what is seen. It enables the person to see beyond the circumstances of war, illness, famine, poverty and gives them sight beyond sight to the truth behind the appearances and they then can see peace, health, and abundance. Having thus rid the mind of thoughts of negativity, "the mental equivalent of them must go (Fox)."

It is vital to understand that, "Everything you see or feel on the material plane, whether it is your body, your home, your business, or your city, is but the concrete expression of a mental equivalent that you hold (Fox)." Once this statement by Fox is understood and put into practice through the warrior's training, it will result in shifts in the physical plane. Things will begin to occur but only to the degree of the mental equivalent. Each person will receive only what they expect to receive. "We should EXPECT THE BEST, and so live that the best may become a part of our experience (Holmes)." Build first the mental equivalent in mind, build in consciousness first and it will be demonstrated to the same degree. This is why the four minute mile story is so incredible. Prior to Roger Banister achieving the record for running a mile in under four minutes, it was believed to be impossible. However, once he demonstrated that it was possible, many other athletes have since gone on to do it as well. The only thing that ever prevented anyone from achieving this prior to Mr. Banister was their belief that it was impossible. They believed it was impossible and so received the demonstration of its impossibility in their own lives. The individual that builds what they do not want will be forced to live in the prison they themselves have built. The building of a prison or a mansion is up to the architect. Whatever the individual architect chooses to build in mind by conscious choice or by default is what he will demonstrate and create.

Once the individual becomes skilled at creating consciously and purposefully that which he desires, all areas of his life will begin to change as well. I have taken the ideas that James Arthur Ray refers to as the five areas of "Harmonic Wealth"—physical, mental, relational, spiritual and financial and I have added a sixth—emotional. Law of Attraction proponents will agree that your emotions serve as an excellent indicator of what you are attracting, therefore how you feel is an area of abundance or wealth that we should be more aware of based upon my experiences. Besides, how often have we heard of the billionaire who has all the money he can spend but is miserably depressed?

So, getting back to our thoughts . . . If the thoughts held in mind are shifted and centered on right-thinking, the six areas of wealth will likewise demonstrate the changes as well. Balancing abundance in one area will set into motion a shift in the other areas as well, when done consciously. A positive shift physically will result in a boost relationally and financially as well. The web of life like an actual spider's web connects each and every area. You cannot vibrate one strand without that vibration moving throughout the web. All of these areas are interconnected and one area cannot be developed "harmonically" and not benefit the others. Likewise, disharmonic influences will adversely affect each area as well. Harmonic wealth or True Abundant

Prosperity as I like to think of it comes from knowing where to find it. "But seek ye first the kingdom of God, and his righteousness; and all these things shall be added unto you (Matthew 6:33 KJV)." The first priority to harmonic thinking is seeking the "kingdom of God" which Jesus the Christ said in Luke 17:21, "for, behold, the kingdom of God is *within you* [emphasis mine]."

James Kirk use to say on the introduction to Star Trek that space was the final frontier. Unbeknownst to him, the true space that is the final frontier is not outer space but is actually inner space; the space within that is mind. Once mankind truly understands this power, reality for each person will change profoundly and as it changes for one, it will change for all.

> "The nature of Reality is such that Universal Mind has unlimited power but so far as man is concerned It has only the power which he gives to It. He gives It power when he says 'I am weak, sick, or unhappy' It says for him what he first says for himself (Holmes)."

The great Law of Mind gives unto each person exactly what that person asks for through the words he speaks, the thoughts he thinks, and the emotions he feels.

> "Habits die hard. So many years of living in a false personality imposed by people whom you loved, whom you respected . . . and they were not intentionally doing anything bad to you. Their intentions were good, just their awareness was nil. They were not conscious people—your parents, your teachers, your priests, your politicians—they were not conscious people, they were unconscious (Osho)."

This is why the warrior training is of the utmost importance; to break this cycle of unconsciousness. Like the child of an abusive parent realizes their grandparents abused their parents and their parents abused them, and they now have the choice to follow in the footsteps of their family lineage or they break the cycle. Far too many abusers, alcoholics, welfare recipients, and victims are merely doing what has been done for generation after generation. At some point the generational curse, the chains of bondage and victimhood must be broken lest the sins of the parent continue to be visited to the children and the cycle continues.

Anyone entering a *dojo*, school of martial art study, in order to be trained as a martial artist, must realize that physical conditioning and skill training will be a part of their experience. Pushups, sit-ups, stretching, striking, kicking drills, as well as, blocks and technique drills and more will be a part of training. Sweat and sore muscles will be a daily routine until such time as the body grows stronger and more accustomed to the workouts. Likewise, the spiritual warrior must train his mental muscles through the use of meditation, affirmations, spiritual mind treatments and affirmative prayers, mindfulness, and visualizations. These tools do not give anyone anything that they do not already have. What they do is assist the individual in removing the blinders that have kept them focused on the illusion so that only the truth is what remains. This can be likened to a sculptor who chips away at the marble block. The statue exists already within the stone and the sculptor merely removes the unnecessary excess so that the work of art is all that remains. This is the training of the spiritual warrior.

Bring a candle into a darkened room and the light does nothing to force or push the darkness away; the darkness simply does what it must do in response to the light—it must withdraw. If a person moved into a new home and the windows were either boarded up or covered with paper or encrusted with dirt from age, would the new home owner sit in the dark feeling angry that they must come home and find a way to "force" the light into the house or would they simply remove the obstructions and allow the sunlight to naturally flood the dwelling? When we properly and consciously engage and utilize the tools and techniques of training, that which is false will withdraw from the presence of the spiritual warrior and only the light will remain. One cannot stand in Christ consciousness and hell consciousness at the same time.

"No one can serve two masters. For you will hate one and love the other; you will be devoted to one and despise the other."

(Matthew 6:24 NLT)

It is through the use of such tools that the perfection of all life that is already in existence comes into full view.

THE PERFECTION: LIONS AND TIGERS AND BEARS OH MY

In the Wizard of Oz, Dorothy and her buddies, the Tinman and the Scarecrow, chant the famous, "lions and tigers and bears oh my," repeatedly until the very thing they feared appeared. It was immediately after this repeated affirmation that the Lion appeared and while the Lion symbolically can be seen to represent the manifestation of their affirmation, he also represents something much more profound. The Lion, a coward, believing he needed courage, went on a quest to the Wizard in order to be given courage. Interestingly enough the Wizard, in his wisdom, tells the Lion that he is already filled with courage. Prior to the Wizard's eye opening statement, the Lion, believing the lie, went in search of obtaining what in truth he already possessed as did the Scarecrow, the Tinman and Dorothy. Each of them already had that which they believed was missing. This is the perfection in the life of the spiritual warrior. The very courage that is needed to live life is the very courage that is already coursing through the very metaphysical DNA of being. The love, the power, the peace, the prosperity, the presence of God is already within every man, woman, child, rock, tree, river and mountain. It is in everything! It is in every particle of air, molecule, atom, speck of sand. God is in, around, above, below, and through everything. There is no where that God is not. This is yet another lesson that I will explore in greater depth in the next book when we discuss the Law of Mentalism in the Kybalion.

> "Humans believe so many lies because we aren't aware. We ignore the truth or we just don't see the truth. When we are educated, we accumulate a lot of knowledge, and all that knowledge is just like a wall of fog that doesn't allow us to perceive the truth, what really is. We only see what we want to see; we only hear what we want to hear. Our belief system is just like a mirror that only shows us what we believe (Ruiz)."

It is because of the ease with which people believe the lies, which Don Miguel Ruiz spoke of, that it takes a degree of honesty and courage to shatter the mirror of falsehood. Without the honesty and courage to see rightly, people will continue to do as Ruiz says, "You don't believe people who tell you how great you are; and you don't believe them because you believe the opposite. Your faith is already invested in a belief that is not the truth; it's a lie, but your faith guides your actions."

If every man and woman courageously, honestly, boldly, and with full naked awareness, took the time to evaluate their lives, they would see quite clearly what master they are serving—God or mammon, God or lack, God or fear. Willis Kinnear says in the introduction to Ernest Holmes' book "Living without fear," "The challenge in life and living is to what degree we can learn to think constructively." Remove the fear and the individual sees the perfection. Remove the lies and you are free to live a life based on the truth. "How you interpret who you are in this moment is what is determining your present experience of life and what lays the seeds for your future (Falco)."

All of the things that man believes to be worthy of fear are in fact like the Lion. They are cowards, hiding behind a mask, who became our allies once we embraced them rather than refusing to trust them or believe in them. The training of the spiritual warrior is a training that will squarely place the warrior face to face with whatever he fears. This is why the Sedona method tools as taught on the DVD "Letting Go" can be useful. You do not repress, deny, subjugate, or destroy your feelings. You embrace them. You give yourself the space to simply feel them and sit with them. By simply being willing to look at them as they are and give yourself permission to feel them fully, you allow them to run their course. As stated in the DVD, by asking yourself three key questions you begin the process of release and you let these feelings and thoughts run their course:

1. Could you let it go?
2. Would you let it go?
3. When?

In order to be a conscious creator or co-creator with the Divine, a creator that demonstrates and manifests from an awareness of the perfection, each person must release the hold of fear and use the power of love. "There is no fear in love. But perfect love drives out fear, because fear has to do with punishment. The one who fears is not made perfect in love." (1 John 4:18 NIV) Again to reiterate, the lies that a person chooses to believe will serve as the broken compass which they are using to get to a destination; however, because the tool they are using is faulty, the journey will take far longer than it could if the compass worked effectively. What tool(s) are each of us using now to guide us along this journey? What beliefs guide and shape our actions? What affirmations are we unwittingly declaring on a daily basis?

> "Powerful and effective affirmations require a belief in your spiritual connection. God is the source of our true and divine

nature; affirming that spiritual source and nature is essential to the process of creation. **Iyanla Vanzant

"If you believe the lie that you cannot speak in public, *thy will be done*: When you try to speak in public, you are afraid. The only way to break your faith in this agreement is by taking the action and doing it. Then you prove that it's a lie, and you are no longer afraid (Ruiz)."

Suppose you want to go North and you believe the compass is pointing north and so begin your journey; however, the fact is that the compass is pointing east—What direction will you in fact be traveling? You will believe the lie that you are going north and with each action you take you will continue to move in the direction of the lie. If anyone believes that they are fat, they will live according to those beliefs and those beliefs will affect how the person eats, how they diet, and how they exercise. If the person believes they are stupid or have difficulty comprehending what they read, they will live according to those beliefs and they will find their prophecy to be true in that they will confirm daily their difficulty with reading and with comprehending what they read. If you believe your spouse will inevitably cheat on you because that is what all of your previous relationships led to, then you will act as the suspicious, untrusting, waiting for the other shoe to fall person who can never truly be in love with the person you married. If you believe, for whatever reason, that you are not worthy of a loving relationship, every possible relationship will fail under the weight of your negative dis-harmonic belief. How could you live your best with this person when you expect the worst? What would happen if this person were to reverse their beliefs?

Nick Vujicic, star of the DVD "No Legs No Arms No Worries" and author of "Life Without Limits: Inspiration for a Ridiculously Good Life" is a man who was born with no arms and no legs and yet he swims, plays golf, surfs, and travels the world speaking, preaching, and teaching about the love of God and the ability to do what you desire. Clearly he has taken the Latin motto *Carpe Diem*, to heart because he lives his life fully by doing what he *can* do, not by dwelling on what he cannot do. Nick is an inspirational speaker and says, "Motivation gets you through the day, but inspiration lasts a lifetime (Vujicic)."

There are countless people who have proven that by shifting their focus from what they don't want, from what they can't do, and from the lies they bought into, to what they do want, what they can do, and the truth, the miracles inherent in the everyday living of life appear everywhere! This may be the hardest thing for many people to do. To realize that, as Falco says, "The only way your world changes is one person at a time—that one person is always You." This is why Gandhi said for each person to "be the change that you want to see in the world." You do not focus on changing anyone else. You can't change anyone else. You can and are only responsible for changing yourself. Take the drug addict or alcoholic for example no amount of begging from family or friends can force or make this person change. You cannot convince them to change. They must of their own free will come to a point where they are ready to change. Have you ever seen an episode of Hoarders where they talk to the person about their addiction to the hoard? Sometimes it take a good minute before you can see the light bulb of realization come on and the person is willing to move the mountain. I look at it metaphysically that the expert holds the consciousness that the person is already free of the hoard and the more they hold that consciousness the more in alignment the person then shifts until they manifest a house free of the clutter—the mountain is moved. This is also what Rev. Beckwith means when he says, "it is not our job to set things right; it is our job to see things rightly." It is through the full understanding of Self, that each person steps into the position where they can shift their mental positioning and see things rightly. Seeing things rightly means seeing beyond the physical. What one person calls fat, you see as fit. What one calls poverty, you see prosperity. And from what one calls disease, you see health, well being, and wholeness. It is only from seeing things rightly that healing can occur and a cure cannot truly occur if a healing is absent. It took me a long time to understand and accept that everyone can be healed but not everyone is cured. There are many who are healed of their experience of cancer and yet they still die as a result of it. I am using the word die as a linguistic convenience not as a truth. We have already addressed that life is eternal and death is an illusion. What I am saying here is that the cancer is used as the impetus for their transition from the physical back to the non-physical, from life to life everlasting!

There are many concepts or paradoxes that are challenging to fully grasp while we are still using our physical bodies. For example, the concept that we are all one is challenging when you can see, touch, feel the physical separation between you and another. Another is the concept of death being an illusion when we have morgues and cemeteries filled with the bodies of the deceased. And grasping that we are spiritual beings despite the human experience we are intimately invested in can also be a challenging pill to swallow. Bear in mind however that there are many things we ourselves do not know that we take for granted, things that we take for face value and simply trust. How many of us who use cell phones know how they work? Very few of us I would venture to say and yet we use them, trust that they will do what we need them to do. We trust electricity, microwaves, computers, and more, even though we ourselves do not understand their inner workings. Clearly we do not need to understand them to make use of them. Likewise, we do not need to understand the paradoxes that exist in order to make use of them. There are various spiritual laws or spiritual technologies that like any scientific law and technologies when used will produce results. I do not need to understand how meditation or affirmative prayer works, all I know is that it does!

Despite what I see for example, when there is the transition from physical to spiritual that is commonly referred to as death, I choose to trust, believe, and have faith that the being that was using that body temple continues to live merely in a different form. I choose to believe this because of the experiences I have had related to the other spiritual laws and practices. I can trust that any seed when planted in the right conditions will grow. I trust this each and every time because of the experiences I have had with gardening. I do not know what it is in the soil, the water, the sun light or the seed itself that all conspire for growth and I do not need to know; it all works according to my use of the principles of gardening, doesn't matter if I intend to grow flowers or vegetables. It all works the same. What you believe about life, death, spirit, God etc. is entirely up to you to decide based upon where you are on the path and what your personal experiences are and have been. Once we have wisely made our choices and we consciously believe whatever we believe, we are able to see things rightly; we are in a state of mind, a consciousness where we assume the job title of executive producer of the show called "Life" and we produce our lives according to our intention and vision.

As the executive producer of your life, there are moments of fear where you may not feel qualified for the job. Imagine two people apply for a job as Oprah's new executive producer at Oprah's Harpo studios. One applicant has years of experience as an executive producer and the other has absolutely none. Which would most likely get the job? Now, slight twist, what if the one with the experience feels incapable of working at Harpo? Maybe they feel intimidated by the Oprah effect and reputation. The other applicant is eager and ready to learn and believes that though they lack experience they can and are willing to learn. Now who might get hired? While the unqualified person may not get the job for which they are applying, they could very well get their foot in the door due to their confidence and willingness to work. While the other person blows the interview due to their constant fear, feelings of incompetence and lack of worth to work for Oprah. This is precisely why it is imperative that each of us look at our lives and determine what is in fact not working. The fearful applicant could have taken the time to honestly look in the mirror and say, "You need to get a grip. You are qualified for this job. Go in there confident and ready!" Rather they played the CD of negative affirmations, "This is Oprah we're talking about. You know she has much higher expectations of her executive producers. How could you ever measure up?!" This is where the warrior rolls up his or her sleeves and gets down to business.

Martial warriors the world over have had to face their fears in order to go into battle. The Samurai, one of my favorite martial disciplines, could possibly be one of the most famous for facing their fears, most notably their fear of death. The Samurai of Japan are surrounded by a fog of mystery and glorified violence in many instances and yet there is a mysterious beauty and truth that can be found in the life and martial studies of the Samurai. Samurai, the name itself means, to serve or to be of service or as Wikipedia says, "those who serve in close attendance to the nobility (Samurai)." The Samurai was a warrior that was surrounded with death on a daily basis. In order for them to serve and to be the military soldiers that that were, they needed to be able to live and fight without a fear of death. This is one reason statements such as, "The way of the Samurai is found in death," are often quoted from the *Hagakure* which is a book that records Tsunetomo's views on bushido, the warrior code of the Samurai. "*Hagakure* is sometimes said to assert that bushido is really the 'Way of Dying' or living as though one was already dead, and that a Samurai retainer must be willing to die at any moment in order to be true to his lord (Hagakure)."

The Samurai faced death and in a similar way so to must the spiritual warrior. Death is, as I have repeatedly said, the greatest fear of mankind. No matter the fear, all of the smaller or lesser fears can directly trace back to the one ultimate fear—fear of death. That is the fear that keeps mankind in a state of perpetual stagnation and stuck in the morass of complacency. It is said that public speaking is the number one fear and that it surpasses the fear of death; however, under closer scrutiny it can be seen that the fear of public speaking is directly connected to the fear of death. It clearly is not a physical death and as such, can be called a small death but is a death none the less. When a person fears delivering a speech, he fears failing at the task, he fears looking foolish, and how the audience will perceive him. Thus the ego fearing ridicule and embarrassment, which to the ego is a death; a death to the façade it has spent so much time constructing and defending. The ego's façade is shattered and it suffers a death. While not the ultimate physical death, the ego sees the threat of losing a sense of self which to the ego is death and so it does what it can to protect and defend by keeping you fearful and safe. All of the things that are feared which are not "life threatening" events, like public speaking, can be traced back in some way to a fear of death perpetuated by the ego's dominance and control of the person's core beliefs. Once the ego is retrained to see that activities like public speaking are okay and are actually beneficial to the overall development, the ego will then support and assist us in doing the things we once feared.

Suppose for a moment that there is a realization that there is no death and that life was eternal and that we were actually immortal souls, what would that do to the ego? If there is no façade to protect, what would the ego do? What if there is nothing that can be lost, taken away, or stolen from us, what would the ego do? What if there are no secrets that could be used against us and there is nothing to personal to share for fear of being shamed or not accepted, what would the ego do? It is that aspect of the Samurai training that is worthy of adopting, releasing the fear of the archetypal symbol, and even the actual physical death. Each person must die to the lowercase "s" self in order to resurrect to the realization of their True existence as the uppercase "S" Self; the True Self, the Higher Self. Even the physical death that occurs is only in form and not in truth. The shedding of the physical body is no more an end of life than the caterpillar that sheds the old form in the metamorphosis to a butterfly. "There is a natural body and there is a spiritual body (Holmes)." Holmes continues by saying that, "all of the evidence should prove to us that *we are not going to attain immortality*, but that WE ARE NOW IMMORTAL! Our contention is not that dead men live again, *but that a living man never dies* (Holmes)."

This fear of death has also been one of the chief tools used by the church to scare man with the threat of hell and damnation. Once the person dies, they will suffer if they have not lived as the church officials, the experts, and God's spokesmen here on Earth have deemed appropriate. For many of these spokesmen, it is far easier to lead and control the sheep than to set them free. Keeping the sheep corralled and controlled is far more comforting and appealing. The sheep now look to you as their protector and teacher, the bringer of truth, and they trust you explicitly, they have accepted the trappings of churchianity as Rev. Beckwith might say rather than seeking a personal experience with God. For the ego driven clergy, such as these, the truth is better hidden behind the veil of shadows, kept in place through terrorist fear tactics. It is easier to control the masses with the threat of an angry old man in the sky that can and will strike you dead as your punishment for disobedience as can be seen throughout the Old Testament. Yet for those individuals that get that glimpse beyond the veil; the veil that was torn from top to bottom when Jesus breathed his last (Mark 15:38) they see that there is a loving divine presence that is in all, around all, binding all, and uniting all. This is the ether that Holmes spoke of in The Science of Mind when he said, "We know that the ether penetrates everything; it is in our bodies, at the center of the earth, and throughout all space (Holmes)." It is also the inexhaustible Source or Substance that Rev. Beckwith speaks of when he affirms, "Dr. Ernest Homes tells us that, 'Prosperity is the outpicturing of Substance in our affairs. We just receive, utilize and extend the gift.' This is another way of saying that Undifferentiated Substance takes the form of whatever is needed: health, relationship, livelihood—you get the idea. Let us joyously extend the gift by sharing our resources today! And we do so from an inexhaustible supply. And so it is."

This concept is very similar to George Lucas' definition of "The Force" which I mentioned earlier from his Star Wars saga. Obi-Wan Kenobi says to Luke Skywalker, "It [The Force] surrounds us and penetrates us. It binds the galaxy together." That is precisely what the ether or Substance, Source, or God is and does. This is the meaning of God's Omnipresence—There truly is nowhere that God is not. Having not simply an understanding of this, but a knowing from experiential awareness, it is realized that everything, being indivisible from God already has perfection about it. The person cannot help but to realize that there are no "accidents," there are no "by chance" synchronistic occurrences; there is only the realization that everything is created and co-created of, by, and with God and that it is *all* good.

There are those who would argue with the idea that everything is good. Who would dare say that cancer is good, that the events of September 11, 2001 were good, that the shootings by the DC snipers were good, or any disease, murder, natural disaster are good? Yet if there is truly an understanding and a knowing to the core that God is all there is, that Source is everywhere present, Love is Omniscient and Omnipotent, then on some level there must be an agreement that though one does not know the reason for such experiences, there is a Divine perfect inner working that is back of all things. Trusting in this realization we also can affirm that though we do not see it or understand it, there is and can only be good! Radical concept I know; however, have you ever heard someone say that getting sick or losing their job was the best thing that could have happened to them? Neuroanatomist brain scientist Dr. Jill Bolte Taylor experienced a stroke that resulted in an awakening for her and catapulted her field of studies and her life into a fascinating new direction and so for her the stroke was a "good" thing. With that in mind, is it possible to even consider the possibility that everything is good? If we are truly saying we believe in an Absolute Power called Love, the Divine, God, then we discredit that belief when we return to our "imbedded theology" as my friend Rev. Hasselbeck is known to point out from time to time. Our imbedded theology is one where we anthropomorphize God again making God out to be that big male judge in the sky. It is when we see ourselves as anything other than the God. Rev. Hasselbeck has taught about the different ways our theology connects us to God. For example, there is the hotdog perspective where God is in us like a hotdog in a bun. Both are distinct and though one is in the other they are separate. There is the plumbing perspective, were we are likened to a conduit, where God travels through us like water through a pipe. Our imbedded theology maintains a position of God being out there and separate from us, where as this New Thought Ancient wisdom the belief is that we are God!

"Jesus answered them, "Is it not written in your law 'I have said ye are gods?'" (John 10:34 NIV)

To believe in good and bad is to suppose two distinct powers—the good and the bad or a God and a Devil perhaps. I encourage you to question your belief in duality. You may choose to keep it and that is fine if it is what works for you. I personally could no longer wrap my head around the idea that there is God and the anti-god called Satan or the Devil. And this anti-god being the enemy of God was created by

God and was given the ability to make men suffer, die, and tempt them away from this loving Omnipotent, Omniscient, and Omnipresent God. As members of the Unity movement state as the first of their five principles, "There is only one Presence and one Power active as the universe and as my life, God the Good." Accepting, believing, and knowing that, is to know that goodness exists within all seemingly bad occurrences. It is to know that even though it may not be seen, there is perfection interwoven into the fabric of life.

Unity principle number two and three continue to demonstrate our perfection and power as manifestations of the Divine. Principle two states, "Our essence is of God; therefore, we are inherently good. This God essence, called the Christ, was fully expressed in Jesus." Principle three, "We are co-creating with God, creating reality through thoughts held in mind." As perfect creators, that which is being created is perfect as well. Therefore there is no sin, not as we would label it and have understood it from our imbedded theology. On one level there are the mistakes, the sins we make where we miss the mark per se; however, on a deeper spiritual level at our core, there are no mistakes, nor are there reasons for anyone to judge themselves as wrong, bad, evil, tainted, or imperfect. All that anyone does at any given moment is truly the best they are able to do at the time. If the person could have done better they would have done so. Upon learning and awakening, the consciousness shifts and with that shift new and more effective choices are capable of being made. The error thinking is eliminated or reduced and gives way to more light, more thinking rightly, and more life affirming thoughts rather than the previous death and darkness affirming thoughts that filled the mind like cobwebs and dust in an unused attic.

> "In less than one second, many of the limiting beliefs I had held about myself since childhood dissolved. All of the woulda's, coulda's, and shoulda's that I had carried in my thoughts four years simply vanished . . . As I let go

of the ideas I had about who I should be, I let go of all my resistance to who I currently was—and suddenly I was free . . . I could see nothing but the perfection of everything in my world. I felt an abundance of love as I became aware of my role and connection to the oneness of all that exists (Falco)."

Through this realization of oneness, all sense of lack and fear are washed away. There is no way to lack when it is realized that everyone is One with the Isness and Allness of God and as One with God, everyone has access to the infinite All. It truly is your Father's good pleasure to give you the Kingdom. There is nothing to fear when the realization that everyone is at one with the divine presence and that every breath is a reminder that everyone lives, moves, and has their being in that Oneness. If God be for his child, there is nothing that could ever exist in opposition; for there is only God! This gives not necessarily new meaning but a new perspective to the hymn "How Great Thou Art." The person who knows they are At One with God, knowing they are one with the divine the I Am, they can boldly exclaim this hymn as well knowing that if it be true for God, it is true for them as well, as one made in the image and likeness of the Divine—How great *Thou* art, how great *Thou* art!

To reach such a profound realization each person must be diligent to remain awake and avoid being lulled back into the illusion of fear and worry. Part of remaining awake involves what scripture refers to as proving all things. "Prove all things; hold fast that which is good (1 Thessalonians 5:21)." Scripture goes on to remind each person that many "spirits" or thoughts that come our way are based on lies. Because they are based on lies and are not of God and each person must be aware of such "false prophets" who will do their best to convince the willing victim of the failing economy, the evidence showing up on the MRI, the behavior of the child in school and their need for medication to control their ADHD. "Dear friends, do not believe every spirit, but test the spirits to see whether they are from God, because many false prophets have gone out into the world (1 John 4:1)."

> "I suggested that he have quiet sessions with himself three or four times a day and declare solemnly that the Almighty has given him inspiration and hope and all he need do is tune in to the Infinite and let the harmony, peace, and love of the Infinite move through him . . . I told him to affirm to himself: God, or the Supreme Wisdom, gave me this desire. The Almighty Power is within me, enabling me to be, do, and to have. This wisdom and Power of the Almighty backs me up and enables me to fulfill all my goals. I think about the Wisdom and Power of the Almighty regularly and systematically. And I no longer think about obstacles, delays, impediments, and failure. I know that thinking constantly along this line builds up my faith and confidence and increases my strength and poise, for God hath not given us the spirit of fear but of power, and of love, and of a sound mind . . . . These truths went into his subconscious mind and, like spiritual penicillin, they destroyed the bacteria of worry, fear, anxiety, and all there negative thoughts (Murphy)."

Once the individual has arrived at this point, they have arrived at the point of understanding the perfection and with that understanding they realize what it means to be empowered. As an empowered spiritual warrior, they know the power of their word. They begin to expect the best and as Ernest Holmes spoke of when he said, "so live that the best may become a part of your experience." The power of their word has creative power. "You shall also decree a thing, and it shall be established to you: and the light shall shine on your ways (Job 22:28 KJV)." This is a workable principle because of what John 1:1 proclaims, "In the beginning was the Word, and the Word was with God and the Word was God." Each living person exists as the individualized manifestations of God, the I AM. As the I AM, each person has the power of the Word. This is why those who decree, "I am sick and tired, I am so lazy, I am accident prone, I am never going to find a husband" walk a dangerous route for their tongue has the power of life and the power of death and they are the author who make that choice. If anyone ever wanted to know if what they are thinking or decreeing is of God, they should look at two things—Look at what they have in their lives and look at how their thoughts makes them feel. "In order to know if a thought is, 'of God,' we can check to see if it creates fear. A fearful thought is not from God . . . (Ruiz)."

CHAPTER FOUR:

WHAT IN THE HEAVEN?

If I were to ask, have you ever heard someone use the phrase, "What in the hell . . . ?" You would most likely say yes you have heard it before and might even admit that you have used it on occasion. However, how many times have you heard someone say, "What in the heaven . . . ?" I may be going out on a proverbial limb here; however, I would venture to say that you have heard it far less than the previous phrase. Why is that? Why do we speak more about hell than we do heaven? I offer that to you as something worth consideration; especially now that we know how powerful our words are.

A common New Thought Ancient Wisdom precept is that energy flows where attention goes. Based upon this I would say that Einstein's definition of insanity is applicable to many people who continue to do the same things, talk about the same things, and focus on the same things and yet they expect different results! What is that, if not insane? It is high time that people lose their mind in order to find their mind. Lose the mind that created the problem and find the mind that is higher in consciousness that can resolve the problem.

"Problems cannot be solved
by the same level of thinking that create them"
**Albert Einstein

It is also time for us take to heart and mind the words of Myrtle Fillmore co-founder of the Unity movement who said, "You should never speak about anything that you do not want to have show up in your life." Deep! If we were to actually taking that into account, what would that leave people to talk about? Would there be any more talk of depression? Not unless you wanted to see it show up in your life. What about talk about that neighbor who was caught cheating on his wife? Oh, so you want infidelity to show up in your life? No? Then why are you talking about it? Why are you talking about the unfair supervisor, the disobedient child, the adult ADHD or diagnosis of XYZ? Actually, why are you complaining at all since to talk about it is actually bringing more of it into your life? Now before you get upset at what I am suggesting, understand that I am not suggesting that you stop talking about these things all together. Realistically, how would you have a conversation with your doctor or car mechanic if you did not mention certain things? What I am saying is that the more you dwell on those things, the more attention you give to your complaints, the more those thoughts and words build emotional energy, and the more emotional energy that is sent out, the more you increase the likelihood of it manifesting in your own life. And for the sake of conversation, suppose there is no emotional energy to be concerned about and no chance of manifesting negative effects in your life experience. If nothing else, it seems plain and simple, why talk about something that is not bringing you health, prosperity, joy, peace, love and well being? "How in the hell does that do you any good?" Read in a slightly different way, how does having your mind in hell do you any good? How does complaining about the obstacle move it from your path?

I love that Oprah tells a story about how when she was eight years old, a gentleman at church asked her father if he thought Oprah could do the welcome for "the afternoon Sunday Tea" as she said they were called. Oprah went on to say that her stepmother said that they could do better than the welcome; she then taught Oprah the poem *Invictus* by William Ernest Henley. She says that at the time she didn't know or understand what she was saying but she liked the part about being the master of my fate and captain of my soul and she took that to heart and it became her mantra. Like any mantra, one's mind is being reshaped through the focused concentration and repetition of a phrase. If the mantra is uplifting, the mind and life are shaped accordingly and if the mantra is negative, the mind and life again are shaped accordingly. As the mind is conditioned, one's life has no choice but to out picture according to the dominant thoughts and feelings our mantras invoke. Clearly looking at her now one could see how that poem planted a seed within her and shaped her life. The people who live empowered lives are well aware that they are the ones in control; they also have assumed the mantle of master of their fate and captain of their soul. They consciously align themselves with the harmony of the Divine and from that state of mind, the Christ Consciousness, nothing is impossible for them to be, do, and have.

"Your intention rules your life and determines the outcome." **Oprah Winfrey

As a result of the Rhonda Britten phenomena of "The Secret" there are many people who have scoffed at such claims that people can be, do, or have whatever they desire. The critics give examples like, suppose five people all desire to be President of the United States in the next election clearly only one can hold the position. The four who did not get elected therefore cannot "be" what they have desired. Some Law of Attraction (LOA) teachers would say that is because only one of them was a vibrational match for the position and the other four were not. Other LOA teachers might say that there is plenty of what the presidency represents to go around and that those four who wanted the position of President may have, if one looks deeper, wanted what the presidency represented and not the actual position. Regardless of why one gets it and another may not is not the point at this present moment. Why not you ask? Well for starters, because if the person looks deep enough to find the essence of what it is they desire, we find that it is possible to be, do and have what is being manifested using the law of attraction; it is the essence of goal and not the goal itself that we all seek to manifest. Let me explain further . . .

Someone may say I want to "have" a new car. Why do you want a car? Do you want it so that you can get to and from work? Do you want it go you can travel? Do you want it because you won't have to do public transportation anymore? Regardless of the basic answer, there is a deeper, metaphysical reason. The new car serves as a physical representation, a physical manifestation of something he/she wants to have on a metaphysical level. So the question becomes what does the car represent? Does it represent transportation and thus the freedom? Does it represent a sense of independence or maybe adventure? Does it represent a sort of status that reminds him of his freedom to use his money and again a sense of independence and comfort? The car could represent many different things and the point is that it is not the car itself that is desired; it is the essence of what the car represents that is desired! It is on that metaphysical level that we realize it is possible for every one of us to be, do, and have what we desire. Note that these desires must be based in love and be for the good and highest of all involved. Things sought for selfish or destructive reasons will result in more and more hellish experiences cause more and more mountains to obstruct, and affect all of your manifestations negatively. Search your heart to find why you want what you say you want. It does not matter if it is a relationship, home, dog, promotion, weight loss, etc. What is the root feeling that having it would give to you? By focusing on that feeling, the deeper reason or answer to what you desire will be revealed. And after receiving the answer you further align with it by means of your spiritual practice, i.e., things like spiritual mind treatments, affirmative prayer, visioning, meditation, and visualizing. At this point you then do what many licensed practitioners say, "treat and move your feet." Meaning, once you have your destination, set your intention, begun your spiritual practice, the next thing you do is to go about your life with the mindset and heartset that it is already manifested; *past tense*, because it is already done! On the level of heart and mind, your desire already exists, done, complete and manifested. What you are now doing is giving it time to manifest or out-picture in the physical. You are using the spiritual tools and technologies which are setting into motion the vibratory match to manifesting it.

"That is why I tell you, whatever you ask for in prayer, believe that you have received it and it will be yours (Mark 11:24 International Standard version)."

The key thing to remember is that each person is solely responsible for the direction of his/her life and that by clearly asking for what they want and believing it is already present in the here and now and accepting it or being open to the receiving of it, it will manifest in one form or another to match their desires. They may not get the million dollars because it really is not the money they desire, it is what the money represents for them. That could be security or a form of freedom to travel. These elements can be enjoyed in the now and should be enjoyed in the now if anyone ever wants to manifest anything. It is not possible to demonstrate the freedom to travel if the mind is fixated on needing the million dollars to travel. Begin to find ways to enjoy travel now, today! There is no reason to put it off to some distant, I can travel when I have ___. The focus must be on the present and enjoying the desire in the present. This is why many teachers say, "act as if" or "fake it til you make it." Such axioms help the student to shift their focus to the present. The ability to focus and visualize with crystal clarity is a skill that must be developed. Having a mind that is cluttered with debris will yield cluttered debris filled results.

> "There is a close relation between riotous living and want. The word 'riotous' means 'lacking in order,' 'lacking peace.' When you just rush into your day unprepared for it spiritually, mentally, or emotionally—when you begin your day without first having a quiet time of prayer, meditation, affirmation, or study of some inspirational book or the Bible—your day can become riotous, or lacking order and peace (Ponder)."

Having a mind that is at peace is having an empowered mind, a mind that is filled with wholeness and healing. This is realization of the Christ within and from this place heaven is realized right here, right now. It was from that awareness, the Christ consciousness, that Jesus manifested what many have called miracles. In truth they are no more miracles than eating, walking, talking, picking up a pen, or breathing. I say that not to belittle what he did but to emphasize what he taught when he said, "I tell you the truth, anyone who has faith in me will do what I have been doing. He will do even greater things than these, because I am going to the Father (John 14:12 NIV)." Jesus made use of the fullness and allness of the divine. He was using the full capabilities of the God Presence within him and urged others to also make full use of all they are. From this consciousness the multitudes can be fed, the dead can be raised, the blind made to see, and the crippled to walk, seeming obstacles like water can be walked across and pure 100% unfettered communication with the One Love occurs. When we do as Jesus did and fully tap into the Power of God, the things we call miracles become daily occurrences for those who are spiritually adept. This is why the journey of the spiritual warrior is important!

Gandhi is a great example of a spiritual warrior. His life was a great example of someone who made a conscious decision to shift his focus to a holistic, empowered, and authentic life. And from that place of authenticity he was able to perform miracles which changed the world. At some point in his life Rev. Dr. Martin Luther King Jr. was asked who he thought was a great Christian. To the shock of many Fundamental Christians who anxiously awaited his answer, King named Gandhi! He named a Hindu as a great Christian? Rev. Dr. King went on to say that it was Gandhi he selected because in Gandhi were the very ideals and love that Jesus the Christ demonstrated. Gandhi exemplifies living an authentic life and from that place he was able to teach and to lead and to transform the world. If one man can in fact do as Gandhi said, "Gently shake the world," then does it not benefit each person to not only do his/her best but to "be" his/her best? "So be perfect, as your heavenly Father is perfect (Matthew 5:48 International Standard)." It is the life lived authentically that causes the most positive empowered ripples to spread out into the whole of the universe. The ideal that Rev. Dr. King saw in Gandhi is the same ideal that King did his best to also demonstrate. It was the same ideal that Mother Theresa did her best to embody as she served in Calcutta. The same ideal that Father Mychal Judge did his best to demonstrate daily to all he met around the world. It is the same ideal that each person is here to demonstrate. The same ideal that YOU are here to demonstrate!

"Nothing is impossible to the willing mind."
**Books of the Han Dynasty

So many people are unwilling to change because they believe that living from the place of heaven within to be challenging if not impossible. They believe that being perfect is impossible. They believe that they are meant to struggle simply because their vision is blocked by an enormous mountain formed by three simple letters that carry such spiritual baggage—sin. Their connection to sin prevents them from living free. You cannot be free to experience heaven if you allow the chains of sin to keep you bound to hell. Can you be a free slave? No. Either you are a slave or you are free. You cannot be a free slave any more than you can be a holistic murderer. Many people, who believe in and are bound by the concept of sin, do not know the origin of the word itself. The original Greek meaning of the term sin was to miss the mark; a military (archery) term, meaning to miss your desired target. How apropos that sin, a once used military term became a misused term to mean some dishonor to God, can now be used once again for the spiritual warrior to mean what it meant in the first place—to miss the mark. Anyone living from a place of fear is missing the mark. Anyone allowing the ego to dictate and rule is missing the mark. Anyone living a disempowered and unauthentic life is missing the mark. Anyone reliving the past or dreaming of the future without being in the eternal now is missing the mark. There can be no harmony, peace, ease, or love as long as the mark is being missed. There can only be strife, struggle, pain, and anger when anyone resists or fights against awakening to their full potential. Preferring to remain asleep only retards the individual's growth in the same way that remaining in your bed day in day out would cause your muscles to atrophy. Each person's mark is to become all that they are meant to become, anything short of that is a "sin." What are you meant to become you ask? We will get to that soon enough; however, remember this, "You were made in the image and likeness of God." In war, the missing of the mark, the target, the opponent could cost the soldier his life.

Quick added note: If we keep the idea of sin as a debt or a trespass that it is somehow an affront to the very nature of God we are limiting or in a way creating an impotent God. I say that because of the concept that God cannot know sin. This is, in the more traditional understanding of why Jesus bore the sins of the world and felt God's separation. "Then at three o'clock Jesus called out with a loud voice, "Eloi, Eloi, lema sabachthani?" which means "My God, my God, why have you abandoned me?" Again we are faced with an interesting philosophical question that asks if God is all powerful and can do all things, can God lie? Can God create a boulder that even God cannot move? I have heard many Christian argue these two questions because of what the questions are implying. First of all can God lie? Many say yes God can but chooses not to. Ok that's fine but implies that God can sin, but chooses not to. I believe that to be in error because God cannot sin. And the reason God cannot sin is because it is not in God's nature. God cannot be something God is not. I'm certain my old philosophy teacher would then ask if that means God therefore is NOT all powerful. After all this is what the whole boulder question is also pointing to. If God cannot create a boulder that He cannot move, then God is limited, and if God can create it but then cannot move it, God is still once again limited! While I love such metaphysical musings for the sheer pleasure of exercising my mind, I must also admit that this boulder question is to bait the ego not the soul. This question of God's power is something that we cannot grasp in full because as I said before we are to a degree bound by the confines of our humanness and cannot fully grasp even such tangible things as the vastness of the galaxy let alone the vastness of God. So I will leave that up to each of you to investigate and to answer for yourselves. I can only answer for myself what I believe is meant by all powerful or omnipotent.

I seem to have digressed a bit, so permit me to return to my original discussion of sin by saying that I believe God is bigger that any proposed sin and that it is not possible to offend, trespass against, or owe God. If God were the sun, what could a dark room or dark cave possibly do to affect the pure light of God? Nothing! If God were the sun, with a warm surface, or photosphere, of about 10000° Fahrenheit (5500° Celsius), what could an ice cube or iceberg possibly do to affect the pure heat of God? Nothing! God is love, light, wholeness, health, peace, joy, intelligence and beauty! Sin isn't even a concept that God can entertain because it is an illusion. The Course in Miracles sums it up quite succinctly by saying—"Nothing real can be threatened. Nothing unreal exists. Herein lies the peace of God." I will leave you with that to contemplate and return to my first proposition of sin as a military idea.

A Samurai warrior who did not draw his sword as quickly or wield the blade as skillfully as his opponent increased the likelihood that the opponent would now kill him. Therefore, missing one's mark was "unhealthy" to say the least and potentially fatal. That is why I believe it was said that the wages of sin or the penalty of sin is death. Not because God was going to punish the sinner with damnation and hell but because in war the missing of the mark could mean death to the warrior. In order to live the healthy and empowered life, "sin" must be forgiven and as Mark 2:9 reveals Jesus' teaching, "Which is easier: to say to the paralytic, 'Your sins are forgiven,' or to say, 'Get up, take your mat and walk'?" Upon receiving forgiveness, the paralytic man arose and walked away. Each person has the same choice to allow sin, mistakes, or error thinking to keep them paralyzed or to be free of it and walk. Jesus asked, which is easier? Yet we make it so much more difficult.

Any person desiring to make a change in the world must first make a change in themselves. As Michael Jackson said, "I'm starting with the man in the mirror. I'm asking him to change *his* ways (emphasis added)." He is not asking anyone else to change. He is asking himself to make the change. The information as outlined here identifies the beginning aspects of that change. In identifying the perceived problem, you are able to identify the belief system that supports it. After identifying the beliefs, you can more actively move on to the subsequent steps along the path. By realizing the perfection within everything, each individual will awaken the sleeper as did the character in the Frank Herbert classic Dune. In case you are not familiar, let me summarize so you get the gist of why I made that comparison; I mean besides the fact that I love the story and symbolism. Paul Atreides is prophesized to be the Kwisatz Haderach or Messiah. In order for Paul, who later is given the name of Muad'Dib, to become all that he might be, he must awaken. In the film adaptation of the book there is a climactic awakening scene. Paul Muad'Dib, having imbibed a substance (the bile of the worms) that has killed all previous males who have taken it, cries out in the dessert, "the sleeper has awakened!" This awakening in line with the prophecy spoken about by the Reverend Mother Ramallo who says, "He will come . . . the voice from the outer world, bringing the holy war, the Jihad, which will cleanse the Universe and bring us out of darkness. He will have been born of a Bene Gesserit mother."

The jihad or holy war, which she speaks of in the story and the journey of the spiritual warrior are, one and the same, in essence. Each person who is alive will come to a point in his life where the call from that still small voice beckons the person to a more authentic life; the divine discontent becomes a gnawing that can no longer be ignored. Hearing the call is easy. It can and does come in many ways; often through what many call an "Oh No" moment which Oprah has called an "Aha" moment! That moment when the person knows that they know that they know that they cannot ignore, deny, or run from what they just realized! Once hearing the call, the individual's next step is to respond. Responding to the call is a tad more challenging. This is when the individual decides what he will do as a result of the call. Does he shrink back in fear and cower hoping the voice will go away and the Aha moment will fade back into the shadows of forgetfulness, or does he stand up and decide to live authentically? Many people unfortunately because of the disempowered ways in which they currently live reduce their likelihood of responding with any significant power. The reason many respond in disempowering ways is because many people live from a place of ego, from unconsciousness. From that state of mind people cannot see where their point of power truly rests. Anytime someone exclaims what someone else has done to them, i.e., "she made me mad" the person is giving their power away. Anytime they blame their husband, the girlfriend, the parents, the school system, and the weather, the Devil or God as having done something to them of somehow causing them to be where they are, they are dismissing their inherent power and responsibility for creating their own lives. From that place of unconscious disempowered living, making a conscious choice to awaken can be challenging; however, it is still possible and in the grand scheme of things one day will happen to everyone.

Awakening to the authentic life is the point; it is *the* mark. Once awakened, the ability to consciously create is realized. Once awakened, the ability to serve is magnified. Jesus the Christ could feed the multitudes because he stood in the center of God and knew where the power originated. "So Jesus explained, I tell you the truth, the Son can do nothing by himself. He does only what he sees the Father doing. Whatever the Father does, the Son also does. (John 5:19 NLT)." Jesus understood that when he aligned himself with the power of the omnipotent, omnipresent, omniscient Divine Presence many call God, that he was able to do things that seemed to defy logic, defy nature, and defy human understanding, yet in truth, with God all things are possible and Jesus knew this at an *experiential* level. It was this kind of knowing that was held in the consciousness of those participating in the DC crime study of 1993 where the crime rate was significantly lowered due to the effects of meditation.

Authentic living is a life of service where you unite with the divine to be of service to the world. By transforming the only person that can be transformed, the self, the whole of humanity reaps the transformative benefits as well. In Matthew 25:37 scripture tells of a time when the Lord will separate into two groups those who served and those who did not serve. "Then the righteous will answer him, Lord, when did we see you hungry and feed you, or thirsty and give you something to drink?" Those who serve receive heaven and those who do not serve receive hell. As has been revealed, heaven and hell are states of consciousness. Therefore it is understood that service is in alignment with heaven consciousness and hell with lack of service, ego, or self centeredness. In Luke 13:6-9 we find Jesus doing his parable thing again telling a story about a fig tree that was not producing fruit. When we are not producing what we are here to produce, like the barren tree, we are once again missing the mark! Our purpose is to produce fruit, to be all that we are as divine manifestations of our Mother/Father God! "By their fruit you will recognize them . . . (Matthew 7:16)." That is being in heaven. When all that you do is sacred, when all that you see in the world around you is sacred, and when all that you are is sacred, you are living from a consciousness of heaven. So it comes to a choice; do you want to live in a state of hell on Earth or a state of Heaven on Earth? Making that choice sets the intention which in turn sets the ripples in motion. There is only God; however, when we live from our deluded ego states we perceive a sense of separation and in that lie we can choose to serve something other than Love. Do you choose to serve God, the Divine Love which is the Allness and Oneness of Everything or do you serve the illusion, the lie, the Ego which plays the same shadowy illusions in your mind day in day out making the things you fear seem real so that it can keep its foothold of control. So again I reiterate it all begins with a choice—which master each person serves is up to the individual. You live, move, and have your being in Christ consciousness or in seeming separation from it because you choose the illusion over truth.

A student of mine once asked me about this illusion of separation and I gave this analogy: Imagine you are working 60 hours a week to keep a roof over your head and food on the table for you and your family and then one day a lawyer shows up at your house and tells you that you had a great uncle that left you half of his estate. The lawyer then tells you that as a result of this you now are worth 25.6 million dollars! However, due to fear of the change in lifestyle, the change in housing, friends, job, etc. you postpone signing the necessary papers. You don't tell your spouse or your kids and you keep this secret and continue to go to work at a job you hate, where your boss continues to threaten to fire you, where your spouse must work as well so that you don't end up homeless or hungry. Why would anyone choose to continue to live their life based on the illusion of scarcity and poverty when abundance and prosperity is their birthright? This individual has millions and yet continues to overwork because of fear. He continues to be a victim or circumstance because of fear. He continues to suffer because of fear. And he denies his family the material, emotional, spiritual abundance that he has access to; all because he is afraid of the unknown changes! That is precisely where many of us are standing, at the crossroads of freedom or fear. This is a place that everyone human being will make one day find themselves. Many shirk from this and do their best to not make the choice believing that by avoiding making the choice they somehow avoid having to choose; however, not choosing IS choosing!

The journey of the spiritual warrior is about making that choice and continuing to make that choice everyday of their lives. After having made the choice, living one's life from that place of power must occur on a daily basis. From this place of power each person is called to invoke their divine birthright. Ernest Holmes said,

> "High Invocation is when we invoke the Divine Mind and that this is why some of the teachers of olden times used to instruct their pupils to cross their hands over their chests and say; 'Wonderful, wonderful, wonderful me!' definitely teaching them that as they mentally held themselves, so they would be held. Act as though I am and I will be (Holmes)." [sic]

It was this high invocation that allowed Jesus to perform what history has called miracles. Jesus knew beyond any doubt who and what he was. Jesus also knew who and what his disciples were. He knew who and what the multitudes were. He knew what mountains were. He knew what water was, he knew what disease was, he knew what death was and he knew what life was. Because he knew the truth, he was able to access the Divine, to use Spiritual laws and principles to "change" what seemed unchangeable. Jesus did not claim the divine power for himself. He made it quite clear that the power he had access to was a power accessible to all. John 14:12 states, "Truly, truly, I say to you, He that believes on me, the works that I do shall he do also; and greater works than these shall he do; because I go to my Father." Because Jesus went to the Father, meaning he was in communion with the Divine which was the Source of him and his abilities, he had access to the "miraculous." When, through faith in his teachings and his living example as one who walked the walk, anyone who believes him, that person will do as he did and "go to the Father." From that place of At-One-Ment, that individual can also boldly and authentically proclaim as Jesus did in John 14:10, "I am in the Father and the Father is in me . . . Rather it is the Father in me who does His work."

Authentically, as an empowered spiritual warrior each person will then take their rightful place as a child of the Most High and from this place they will have the ability to feed the hungry, clothe the naked, provide health and healthcare for all humans, provide quality education, bring peace where there is war, love to all, and satisfy the spirit that desires to know its place in God. This can be learned and put into practice by way of the three-fold method: Thought, Word and Deed. Think it. As has already been discussed, thoughts are important for it is from the thinking is life shaped. Having thought it, speak it. Invoke through the creative power of the divine word what has been thought. Utilize your creative power to speak a thing and decree a thing. And having invoked it, the person must do it. The person must put into action what they have thought and what they have spoken. This is walking the walk and the hard part for many is that sometimes the deed portion is to do nothing. It is a form of inactivity. "One of the ancient sayings is that 'to the man who can perfectly practice inaction, all things are possible' (Holmes)." While that may sound like a direct contradiction it is merely a linguistic convenience to attempt to put into words something that is better experienced than theoretically explained. Think about it this way using my analogy of the farmer. The farmer cannot make or force his crops to grow. He must allow them in their own time according to their divine gestation period to unfold and grow accordingly. All the while the crops are doing their thing, he continues to water, weed, and farm and in due time he reaps what he has sown.

God cannot be coaxed, convinced, bribed, or manipulated. Many people having prayed, visualized, treated, meditated, and visioned a desire will say they have let go and let God, however upon closer inspection it is clear that they are attempting to "make" it happen in their time. Inaction is the actionless action that many martial artists refer to it which can be seen in nature when you see the lioness standing motionless in the bush as a herd of gazelle race past. She, while being motionless is in fact engaged and active in the task of observing and hunting! She is patiently awaiting the opportunity to do what she is there to do, feed her cubs. The Reiki practitioner does not "do" anything to the recipient except allow Reiki to move through them. The spiritual warrior does not "do" anything except allow "the Father within" to work through them. The doing on the part of the spiritual warrior is participating in their spiritual practices; the prayer, the treatments, the meditation, the living of life. As I mentioned before, "Treat, then move your feet." Having done your spiritual work let go and let God. Go about the living of life as one who knows and knows that they know.

Detach from the outcome. Oprah tells a wonderful story about how she detached from wanting a role in "The Color Purple" and that once she surrendered and let go to the point that she could bless the actress who potentially could get the role, the very role she prayed for, presented itself to her in the character of Sophia who was married to Harpo which is the reverse spelling of Oprah. Talk about signs from God (smile)!

"God can dream a bigger dream for me, for you, than you could ever dream for yourself. When you've worked as hard and done as much and strived and tried and given and pled and bargained and hoped . . . surrender. When you have done all that you can do, and there's nothing left for you to do, give it up. Give it up to that thing that is greater than yourself, and let it then become a part of the flow."

**Oprah Winfrey

The implications of truly living the life of the spiritual warrior are immeasurable and without limit. Living from a place of abundance not lack, health not disease, peace not war, love not hate, light not darkness, and God, not the devil, is living not only in heaven but it is living as heaven. You become a living breathing heavenly BE-ing. As each person lives from that consciousness, the race mind or mass consciousness begins to shift higher and higher, more and more until eventually the default setting of the race mind becomes one of love rather than the current setting of fear. This is important to understand because it is not simply man that has a mental atmosphere. "Every business, every place, every person, everything has a certain mental atmosphere of its own. This atmosphere decides what is drawn to it (Holmes)." By changing the mental atmosphere or mental equivalent, the person changes not only what is drawn to them but they change the vibration, the tone of the environment. This is what shamans, ministers, and spiritual adepts do when they bless a house; they are shifting the energy of the place. If one person no longer attracted hostility ever again that is amazing, but imagine if 10 billion people stopped attracting hostility towards themselves, what kind of affect does that now have on the world? If a few thousand could meditate and affect the crime rate in DC one summer, imagine if every man woman and child in America began their day in prayer and meditation for the world! Simply sitting with that feeling of global peace, prosperity, and love!

The spiritual warrior is one who not only attracts peace, love, joy, health, and the full expression of the Divine, but she gives them as well; they exude from her naturally. It is time for each person to surrender their addiction to fear. If anyone must be addicted to anything, let it be an addiction to the Divine, to love, to the full expression and expansion of God.

Ester Nicholson performs a song called, "I Believe This Belongs to You." The song so eloquently identifies what living an authentic life looks like for the man or woman who stands in their truth living from that place of the divine.

> I once had a powerful story I used to carry around.I thought it was you all this time that held my spirit down. But now I know the truth of who I came here to be. You are my angel in disguise, and not my enemy.
>
> So I thank you for the part you played. In the dance we had to do. I give you back your own true love. I believe it belongs to you. I will lift you up and do what I can do. I feel your heart, I know your pain, I have been there too. I will hold you high while you do what you have to do.
>
> I give you back your freedom now, I believe it belongs to you.

This is how each of us is called to live. Live from a place of love and compassion. The Dalai Lama said, "If you want others to be happy, practice compassion. If you want to be happy, practice compassion." Until each of us takes the responsibility for our own peace of mind and the raising of our own frequency of love, we will continue to look outside of ourselves for that which is within. There is a beautiful Hindu myth that tells of a "Suitable Hiding Place" for that which man seeks.

> An old Hindu legend says there was a time when men were gods. But they abused their divine powers so much that Brahma, the master of all gods, decided to take these powers away and hide them in a place where they would be impossible to find. All that remained was to find a suitable hiding place.
>
> A number of lesser gods were appointed to a council to deal with the issue. They suggested this: "Why not bury man's powers in the earth?" To which Brahma replied, "No, that will not do because man would dig deep and find it."
>
> So the gods said, "In that case, we will send their divinity to the deepest depths of the ocean."
>
> But Brahma replied again, "Sooner or later man will explore the depths of the ocean and it is certain he will find it and bring it to the surface."
>
> So the lesser gods concluded, "Neither land nor sea is a place where man's divine powers will be safe, so we do not know where to hide it."
>
> At that moment Brahma exclaimed, "This is what we will do with man's divinity! We will hide it deep within him because that is the only place he will not think to look."
>
> From then on, according to the legend, man searched the world over; he explored, climbed, dove, and dug in search of something that was inside himself the whole time.

We spend so much time looking everywhere else for what is, has been, and will always be with us because it is the truth of who and what we are. “Seek ye first the kingdom of God and His righteousness and all else will be added unto you (Matthew 6:33).” “Nor will people say, ‘Here it is,’ or ‘There it is,’ because the kingdom of God is within you (Luke 17:21).” Once we go within and find and access the kingdom and live according to a consciousness of heaven we will have joy, peace, love, and prosperity.

I don't really think in terms of obstacles.
My biggest obstacle is always myself.

Steve Earle

CHAPTER FIVE:

LIVING THE LIFE YOU ARE MEANT TO LIVE

"Be all you can be." Many a youth after hearing the famous army slogan have made the choice to enter the military. Why? What is it about a few words strung together that makes joining the army seem so appealing? Having studied the business of advertising for a short time, I understand the power of advertising. Every word, every image, and every sound is carefully orchestrated to evoke not only a memorable image but an emotional response as well. The call to be all that you can be echoes within each person. It is a primal call to our very essence to step up and live the life we instinctually know we are meant to live. Yet, we submerge this call, deny the urge, ignore the divine discontent, and repress the emerging shift that this slogan sparks. We cannot seem to accept our greatness. Could Marianne Williamson's often quoted passage from "A Return to Love" be correct?"

> Our deepest fear is not that we are inadequate. Our deepest fear is that we are powerful beyond measure. It is our light, not our darkness that most frightens us. We ask ourselves, Who am I to be brilliant, gorgeous, talented, fabulous? Actually, who are you *not* to be? You are a child of God. Your playing small does not serve the world. There's nothing enlightened about shrinking so that other people won't feel insecure around you. We are all meant to shine, as children do. We were born to make manifest the glory of God that is within us. It's not just in some of us; it's in everyone. And

> as we let our own light shine, we unconsciously give other people permission to do the same. As we're liberated from our own fear, our presence automatically liberates others. (A Return to Love: Reflections on the Principles of "A Course in Miracles")

When you read that, what do you feel? Do you feel the expansiveness of your being or do you feel constricted and a wanting to withdrawal? What does it mean that our light is what frightens us? Why would that be what we fear? One afternoon when I was teaching American Sign Language at Arundel high school and conversing with a few of my students, I was asked why I had so many superhero posters on the walls in the classroom? I took this as a perfect opportunity as a teachable moment to explain the role of responsibility and power. I started off by asking if anyone had seen the movie Spiderman. After several had said they had seen it, I asked if they remembered when Peter Parker said, "Whatever life holds in store for me, I will never forget these words: "With great power comes great responsibility." This is my gift, my curse. Who am I? I'm Spiderman." Which are quite similar to those found in Luke 12:48 "When someone has been given much, much will be required in return; and when someone has been entrusted with much, even more will be required." After quoting Peter Parker, who was quoting his Uncle Ben, I asked the students what they thought he meant by this. A few said that he had a responsibility to help people now that he had super powers. I then asked if they saw any parallels in their own lives and that of Spiderman. A few said that they knew there were times when they could have helped someone and they didn't, where they could have stood up and they didn't, where they could have done better and they didn't. I told them that is what being responsible means, knowing what you are here to do and doing it. It is living your life in the fullest and best way possible. I told them that the superheroes, Superman, Spiderman, Silver Surfer, The Phoenix, and all the others represent the qualities that are within each of us. They are the essence of who and what we are and that the posters remind me to live from that place where I offer my gifts, my super powers to the world as the superheroes do.

For me, the gifts we have access to are far more powerful than we tend to realize, imagine, or acknowledge. I remember when I first heard the passage, "Jesus answered them, "Is it not written in your Law, 'I have said you are gods'?" I was blown away! I was a student at Carlow College (now Carlow University) and was taking a course in religion to satisfy my Bachelor degree in Art Education requirements. If I recall correctly, the course was "The Human Experience of God." While I had been a Christian and had perused the Bible in a not so disciplined manner, I had not encountered that passage to my recollection. Something shifted in me that day. The professor asked us to read the passage silently to ourselves. This was followed by the class hearing it as the professor read it aloud. And finally, he asked the class to read it aloud together. I cannot fully explain what I experienced in that moment. What I do know is that something in my consciousness shifted, something was transformed and changed the course of my life. I wanted to know more about this claim Jesus was making. Was he saying that we were gods? Was he simply making an analogy? Was he saying something totally different? I began to read, seek, and ask anyone and everyone that I thought might offer insight. I asked the nuns at Carlow, I asked some of my Jewish friends what was the meaning of the Old Testament reference that Jesus was quoting Psalm 82:6 "I said, 'You are "gods'; you are all sons of the Most High." I spoke to rabbis, priests, ministers, professors and I read critical analysis after exegesis after essay in search of an answer. And after getting all of my data from my many sources I sat and processed it and I noticed something quite interesting. There were two clear groups of people, those who vehemently said the passage is figurative and meant something other than what Jesus was saying and those who said it means what he said plain and simple, it was not a parable, it was Jesus being direct with those who questioned him.

Then it dawned on me, if I was made in the image and likeness of God, does it not stand to reason that I am like my father. I mean humanly speaking, if I am made in the image and likeness of my parents and the DNA within me is the combined genetic material of all my ancestors cumulating in me then why would I not be made of the spiritual DNA of my Creator. At that time I still saw God as out there and separate. None the less, I reasoned that if in the image and likeness of God I was made, then God and I share similar traits, qualities, and attributes. My father and mother were human and so am I; therefore, if my Heavenly Father is Divine, so am I! This was the beginning of my evolution into metaphysical Christianity though I did not know it at the time.

The life we are meant to live is the life of the Divine! Everything we do is to mirror that knowing. The way we cook, get dressed, cut the grass, and the way we poopie scoop while walking the dog are all divine activities when seen through the lens of "you are a god!" Sacred actions are no longer relegated to prayer and meditation; everything literally becomes a sacred act. So the challenge now becomes how do you access that awareness so that you live from that state of being? This is what Rev. Dr. Martin Luther King Jr. was teaching to the group of students at Barrett Junior High School in 1967, six months before his assassination.

> I want to ask you a question, and that is: What is your life's blueprint?
>
> Whenever a building is constructed, you usually have an architect who draws a blueprint, and that blueprint serves as the pattern, as the guide, and a building is not well erected without a good, solid blueprint.

Now each of you is in the process of building the structure of your lives, and the question is whether you have a proper, a solid and a sound blueprint.

I want to suggest some of the things that should begin your life's blueprint. Number one in your life's blueprint, should be a deep belief in your own dignity, your worth and your own somebodiness. Don't allow anybody to make you feel that you're nobody. Always feel that you count. Always feel that you have worth, and always feel that your life has ultimate significance.

Secondly, in your life's blueprint you must have as the basic principle the determination to achieve excellence in your various fields of endeavor. You're going to be deciding as the days, as the years unfold what you will do in life—what your life's work will be. Set out to do it well.

And I say to you, my young friends, doors are opening to you—doors of opportunities that were not open to your mothers and your fathers—and the great challenge facing you is to be ready to face these doors as they open.

Ralph Waldo Emerson, the great essayist, said in a lecture in 1871, "If a man can write a better book or preach a better sermon or make a better mousetrap than his neighbor, even if he builds his house in the woods, the world will make a beaten path to his door."

This hasn't always been true—but it will become increasingly true, and so I would urge you to study hard, to burn the midnight oil; I would say to you, don't drop out of school. I understand all the sociological reasons, but I urge you that in spite of your economic plight, in spite of the situation that you're forced to live in—stay in school.

And when you discover what you will be in your life, set out to do it as if God Almighty called you at this particular

> moment in history to do it. Don't just set out to do a good job. Set out to do such a good job that the living, the dead or the unborn couldn't do it any better.
>
> If it falls your lot to be a street sweeper, sweep streets like Michelangelo painted pictures, sweep streets like Beethoven composed music, sweep streets like Leontyne Price sings before the Metropolitan Opera. Sweep streets like Shakespeare wrote poetry. Sweep streets so well that all the hosts of heaven and earth will have to pause and say: Here lived a great street sweeper who swept his job well. If you can't be a pine at the top of the hill, be a shrub in the valley. Be the best little shrub on the side of the hill.
>
> Be a bush if you can't be a tree. If you can't be a highway, just be a trail. If you can't be a sun, be a star. For it isn't by size that you win or fail. Be the best of whatever you are.
>
> http://www.drmartinlutherkingjr.com/whatisyourlifesblueprint.htm

Is this how you are living your life? Are you doing whatever it is that you are doing to the degree that Shakespeare wrote, Michelangelo painted, Leontyne Price sang, or Beethoven composed? Are you, at the end of the day as you lay your head on the pillow, pleased with a day well lived? Are you left with a sense of pride for how you lived the day? Has the day brought you joy not only in the living of it, but in sharing of your gifts that have brought light to someone and as a result a life has been elevated?

> "On this path effort never goes to waste, and there is no failure. Even a little effort toward spiritual awareness will protect you from the greatest fear." **Bhagavad Gita

If we are going to talk about living an authentic life, seems like a good place to begin would be to talk about what I mean by authentic. Simply put, being authentic is being an original not an imitation or copy. As an authentic individual you are living *your* life. You may ask or wonder what I mean by this question; after all how someone can live anything but their life? Anyone who copies another person's life in order to escape their own life is living a lie. People who compete with the Joneses are living a lie. People who operate out of a carefully built and maintained façade are people who are living a lie. You cannot be who you are meant to be while also deceiving yourself and others into believing you are something else any more than you can walk on the beach while standing in your hotel room. I am sure you can think of times when you wanted people to think highly of you and so you may have padded your resume or embellished a story about how you met the President. It is the classic fish tale where you make your fish out to have been much larger than it actually was. We somehow believe that to tell the truth lessens the other person's estimation of us. This is something the ego dreads! The ego wants to always be on top, applauded, and esteemed. If you come across as ordinary, the ego cringes. Keep in mind that there is a distinction between telling a story with embellishments to entertain and embellishing as a lie to somehow appear better. I am warning against the one that is ego driven to boost a false sense of pride.

I remember when I began to think about acting and getting my own television show, many people said that I could be the next Oprah or the next Dr. Phil and while I understood what they were saying, I had to reframe their statements by saying that I want to be me. There can never be another Oprah or another Dr. Phil. Even Oprah tells how she was able to succeed by realizing that she could not be Barbara Walters and that her job was to be the best Oprah she could be. That is living authentically. Living in comparison with others is not living authentically. Being your best in each moment is what you are called to do.

Now a brief word from our sponsor via a fable of sorts to, address what it means to be your authentic self. A long time ago, an eagle's egg from high atop a mountain rolled down the mountain and onto a nearby farm. Though the egg was larger than the chickens' eggs, the farmer, thinking nothing of it, placed the egg in the hen house with the other eggs. One day several of the eggs began to hatch, including the larger one. All of the newly born chicks chirped for food. As the hens fed the chicks, the larger one though different, was fed just the same. As years went by, all of the young chicks were now approaching adolescence.

For several years, as they grew older they noticed the eagles flying overhead. This one particular day, one of the flying eagle's also noticed them below but it was one in particular that caught his attention. The eagle flew to the ground. Fearing being eaten, the chickens ran for cover. Though they ran, the eagle that had grown up with them remained still. In moments, the eagle that had just been in the sky was now standing face to face with the youngster.

"Wow! I wish I could fly as you do."

"What do you mean? Have you been injured?"

"No, I am a chicken and we can't fly."

The older eagle looked on, puzzled.

"You are no chicken."

"Yes I am. This has been my place of birth and I have been here always."

"You may have been born here, but you are not stuck here. You are an eagle who believes he is a chicken and I tell you today that if you change what you believe, then you will fly as high and as fast as I can."

"How do I change what I believe?"

"Close your eyes, see yourself flying high above the ground. See yourself as free from the confines of gravity. When you can see yourself flying as clearly with your eyes open as you do with them closed you will be free to fly!"

Everyday for a month the young eagle closed his eyes and saw himself flying but once he opened his eyes he remembered he was a chicken.

One day the farmer walked by and asked the daydreaming eagle why he was concentrating so hard.

"I was told by an eagle that I too am an eagle and not a chicken and so I am trying to believe I can fly."

"Why do you believe you are a chicken?"

"This has been the only life I have ever known. Why would I think otherwise?"

"When I first found your egg, I must admit I thought it was one of the chicken's eggs that had rolled out of the coup but once you were hatched, I could clearly see that you were an eagle, as did all of the other animals on the farm. None of us ever took the time, for various reasons, to tell you were an eagle though. So if flying is what you want then let go of what you think you are and embrace what you know you are!"

With those words, the eagle closed his eyes and saw the earth drop below him . . . once he opened his eyes, wings outstretched and waving, he was flying!

Each of us has an inner knowing that we are free, but out of fear and complacency, we settle to be something and someone we are not. We become trapped somewhere we don't have to be, doing things we are not meant to do.

P.S. That eagle, now older and more skilled, went back to the farm several years later and taught some of the chickens, pigs, cows, and horses (those that would listen) how to be free—How to defy gravity!

He taught them that no matter what you are, where you are, or who you are—You can be free. Believe you can fly and the sky becomes your playground!

This fable, much like the story of Jonathan Livingston Seagull, teaches us that we are what we believe we are. We are as earth bound or skyward as our thoughts take us. The thing that separates the ordinary from the extraordinary is that little EXTRA. That extra is something that each of us has access to. There are those who would look at Nick Vujicic and they would see a man to pity. He after all has no arms and no legs, surely he deserves our pity. Yet, Nick travels the globe teaching and preaching, he plays golf, surfs, swims, and does many things that the rest of us only dream about. For more info check out his website at www.lifewithoutlimbs.org or Google him and see some of what he has had to overcome and be encouraged that if he has done it, so can you! As he said before the inmates at Solano Prison, "there is hope until you give up." So my words to you . . . don't give up!

Vow now to be your true authentic self, to do whatever you need to do to make that happen.

Like the mother who finds within herself super human strength to lift a car and free her child from the wreckage, so to must you find the strength to face your shadows, face your fears, face the mountains and face the very darkness and not only shine a light to dispel it, you must become the light itself! When you are, as the old folks would say, "sick and tired of being sick and tired," you will do something about the situation. Have you truly had enough to make the changes in your life that you need to make in order to live authentically? Note, I use the word need as a linguistic convenience not as a judgment. It is important that we distinguish the need to, should, and have to statements and to not use them to further condemn us, thus keeping us in the rut of mediocrity. When you notice you are saying things like, I should know better, I need to get up and exercise, I have to lose weight, and I must change, you know that you are using them to judge yourself. You are using them like arrows being fired from the bow of incrimination. This is where Don Miguel Ruiz's first of the Four Agreements comes in handy—Be impeccable with your words. Say nothing that need not be said.

I remember the old TV series Kung Fu with David Carradine and in the first episode the series premiere, while working on a railroad, a younger Chinese man criticizes Kwai Chang Caine for his silence and Caine responds by telling him, "If one's words are not better than silence, one should keep silent." Simply meaning that many times we allow that infamous illness called diarrhea of the mouth to overcome us and we blather on and on like an irritating mosquito buzzing about. "The tongue can bring death or life; those who love to talk will reap the consequences (Proverbs 18:21 NLT)." As many a grandmother can be quoted, "That's why God gave you two ears and one mouth, so you can listen more than you talk." Sometimes it is best to just shut up.

Remember earlier in the book when I mentioned thought, word, and deed? When I was studying the Japanese art of Ninjutsu while in high school, I was exposed to a Buddhist concept where I practiced certain *mudra* hand symbols referred to as *kuji-kiri* while also vocalizing or speaking certain *jumon* or *kotodama* or better known as *mantras*. Later I was again exposed to these concepts when I began studying Aikido since the founder of Aikido Morihei Ueshiba is said to have been a devote practitioner and believer in the power of *kotodama* and then I was exposed to the concept again when I began practicing Reiki which uses *kotodama* as well. This practice centers around the belief that sounds (words) have power. So in high school, I learned that the ninja would set his intention (thought), invoke a mantra (word), and perform an mudra as a physicalized representation of the intention already being done (deed). So you see, there is spiritual support for this mindfulness of one's words in all four corners of the world. I digress slightly, so back to the point I wanted to make about—thought, word, and deed . . .

> The thought manifests as the word;
> The word manifests as the deed;
> The deed develops into habit;
> And habit hardens into character;
> So watch the thought and its ways with care,
> And let it spring from love
> Born out of concern for all beings . . .
> As the shadow follows the body,
> As we think, so we become.
> Buddha, *Dhammapada*

STEP ONE: Change Your Thoughts

If you actively, mindfully, honestly, and compassionately analyze your thoughts, you will be able to identify those that do not serve the authentic you. If people could see or hear your thoughts, what would be made known to them? Are these things that uplift? One of the opening scenes of the Louise Hay film "You Can Heal Your Life" introduces the viewer to a woman. It is that woman that we follow throughout the film. We are following her as she makes the journey to authentic living. So, in the beginning of the film we are given access to her thoughts and we can hear the tirade of negative abuse she inflicts upon herself. When her life takes the initial turn, we are also given access to the thoughts of others on the street and we notice one woman in particular whose thoughts are quite different from the others. This one woman's thoughts are about how great the day is, and how wonderful she feels. Why was she the one different one? Why wasn't it the norm for the masses to feel amazing, think about greatness and affirm how good life is? What is your first thought at the beginning of a new day? "Oh God it's morning," can be said with dread or excitement. Do you see in optimistic terms or in pessimistic terms? Do you think of the glass as half full or half empty? Before you go defending you right to be a realist, as many people do; proclaiming that they are only thinking about the worst case scenario in order to be prepared for the worst while they hope for the best . . . take a moment to consider the impact your thought have in creating that worst case scenario.

Your thoughts lay the groundwork for what you are expecting. I mean would you take that job if you expected your boss to harass you? Would you put your child in that daycare if you expected them to neglect her? Would you encourage your son to join the football team if you expected them to haze and bully him? No, no, and no!! You would not . . . ! Then why say you prepare for the worst, BUT hope for the best? Can you truly hope for the best while planning for the worst? I mean I understand that faith is the substance of things hoped for and the evidence of things not seen. Faith is an expectation in the invisible, it is a power that says though I do not see the job, the cure, the new house, or the acceptance letter to college, I have faith that there is a power at work back of that which is seen that is in motion and working according to a divine order. So the hope that is used here is a hope that expects the best and a hope that expects the best would operate based on that expectation. The faith filled person is not going to have faith in getting healthier while also arranging their budget to pay for all the possible medications that someone with that diagnosis *could* or might be prescribed, would they? Who would expect a diagnosis of health while at the same time plan for the worst when they go to the cardiologist by speaking to a funeral home director about possible arrangements just in case the Dr. gives them bad news? What is it that you expect to happen in your life? What do you place your faith in? By the way the glass is neither half full nor half empty—it is FULL! There is no "empty space" because that seeming space is filled with vibrating molecules, atoms, and energy!

STEP TWO: Watch Your Words

So you say you are having a difficult time catching your thoughts? Watch your words then since they are your thoughts given voice. What do you notice coming out of your mouth? Do you praise or criticize? Do you gossip and spread rumors? Do you tell others what your opinion is even when they have not asked for it? Do you use your words to tear people down or to build them up? The more you pay attention to what you say the more you will begin to identify those little passive aggressive statements used to control others; which you really cannot do anyway. You will be able to identify when you are using your words to manipulate, cajole, ridicule, and even seduce. You will see if your words are passive and weak or assertive and strong. Do you have certain phrases that you repeat like, "My kids are going to be the death of me. I can't do anything right. I am such a klutz. I am so sick and tired of my boss I don't know what to do. Life sucks and then you die." There are billions of others that can be heard on any given day if you tune your ear to hear them.

People's complaints can be quite revealing and you don't have to be Sherlock Holmes to decipher them. Look at your own complaints. What do they say about you? Do you complain about your weight, your hair, the weather, gas prices, the economy, the President, the judicial system, or education in America? What thoughts are you adding power to by reciting your complaining mantras daily and putting them out into the world? What would happen if you stopped complaining? Do you think you could do it for one day? I challenge you to do it . . . one sentence at a time one hour at a time for one day. Do you notice that when you are with certain people you are more prone to complain or gossip? Why? Why can't you control your own mouth? Begin now to take responsibility for the words that you speak. Begin now to take back your power and to assist you in doing so, think about the truth in the words of this song "Our Thoughts Are Prayers" by Lucille K. Olson and the words of Unity co-founder Charles Fillmore.

Our thoughts are prayers, and we are always praying.

Our thoughts are prayers; listen to what you're saying.

Seek a higher consciousness, a state of peacefulness,

And know that God is always there,

And every thought becomes a prayer.

Our thoughts are prayers, the tools that we create with.

Our thoughts are prayers that Spirit resonates with.

Seek a higher consciousness, a state of mindfulness,

And know that God is always there,

And every thought becomes a prayer.

"Pronounce every experience good, and of God, and by that mental attitude you will call forth only the good. What seemed error will disappear and only the good will remain. This is the law, and no one can break it."

** Charles Fillmore, Talks on Truth (Unity Village, MO: Unity School of Christianity, 1926). Page 107

STEP THREE: Just do it

Just do what? Live your life in a manner that supports your authenticity. Talk the Talk and Walk the Walk! Begin and end your day with prayer. And I am not referring to that begging and beseeching that we were taught to do. I am referring to praying affirmatively like Unity and Religious Science teaches. Pray as Rev. Linda-Martella Whitsett teaches in her new book "How to Pray without Praying to God, Moment by Moment, Choice by Choice," this teaches how to pray from a consciousness of God and not to God.

What does that mean you ask?

Let's start with Matthew 6:6

AKJV

"But you, when you pray, enter into your closet, and when you have shut your door, pray to your Father which is in secret; and your Father which sees in secret shall reward you openly."

The Message

"Here's what I want you to do: Find a quiet, secluded place so you won't be tempted to role-play before God. Just be there as simply and honestly as you can manage. The focus will shift from you to God, and you will begin to sense his grace."

I included two different translations to merely give you more than one way to understand the point of shifting one's focus by getting away to a quiet place. I emphasize this because it is not the physical location where you go to pray that matters; it is the spiritual location that matters. When you go inward you are going to that place of spirit and you are not seeking to commune with anything that is outside of you. You are bathed in the realization that you and God are one and it is from that consciousness that you realize there is nothing to pray for. If God knows what you need before you ask (Matthew 6:8) do you really need to ask? Suppose your mom is going to the store and she writes a list of things to get and before she leaves you look at the shopping list. You notice several things on the list that make you laugh and you think to yourself, mom really knows me. She added things to the list that you were going to ask for and even included some things you forgot you needed like shampoo or toothpaste. Having seen the list and knowing that your needs are being met as your list of desired items is getting bought, why would you ask her to get them? Are you asking her in order to "make sure" she remembers? What if she never forgets anything on the list, do you still mention it? No, you have faith that she is going to do what she is going to do, what in fact she has always done—provided for you, her child. Why is it so much more difficult for us to have faith in and to believe in the power of the Divine to likewise tend to us? This is why Jesus said in Matthew 6:25-34

> 25 "Therefore I tell you, do not worry about your life, what you
> will eat or drink; or about your body, what you will wear. Is
> not life more than food, and the body more than clothes?
> 26 Look at the birds of the air; they do not sow or reap or
> store away in barns, and yet your heavenly Father feeds
> them. Are you not much more valuable than they? 27 Can
> any one of you by worrying add a single hour to your life?
>
> 28 "And why do you worry about clothes? See how the flowers
> of the field grow. They do not labor or spin. 29 Yet I tell you that
> not even Solomon in all his splendor was dressed like one of
> these. 30 If that is how God clothes the grass of the field, which
> is here today and tomorrow is thrown into the fire, will he not
> much more clothe you—you of little faith? 31 So do not worry,
> saying, 'What shall we eat?' or 'What shall we drink?' or 'What
> shall we wear?' 32 For the pagans run after all these things,
> and your heavenly Father knows that you need them. 33 But

seek first his kingdom and his righteousness, and all these things will be given to you as well. [34] Therefore do not worry about tomorrow, for tomorrow will worry about itself. Each day has enough trouble of its own.

So rather than praying to God from a consciousness of separation where you pray based on fear, worry and doubt, it is far more empowering to pray from the place of your divinity where you affirm your needs already being met.

> "I tell you the truth, you can say to this mountain, 'May you be lifted up and thrown into the sea,' and it will happen. But you must really believe it will happen and have no doubt in your heart. I tell you, you can pray for anything, and if you believe that you've received it, it will be yours. (Mark 11:23,24 NLT)."

He does not say pray that you will receive it, pray that you might receive it, pray that you are receiving it. He is very clear and says pray believing that you have received it. Praying from that place you are affirming the truth not praying based on appearances. How do you pray in this manner? Let me give you a few examples of affirmative prayers or mind treatments as they are also referred to in the New Thought practice.

Dr. Ernest Holmes, founder of the New Thought practice of Religious Science or Science of Mind, developed the technique called 'Spiritual Mind Treatment" and he defines it as follows:

> "Treatment is the art, the act, and the science of consciously inducing thought within the Universal Subjectivity (which is in us as subconscious mind) for the purpose of demonstrating (answered prayer) and that we are surrounded by a Creative Medium which responds to us through a law of correspondence. In its more simple meaning, treatment is the time, process and method necessary to changing our thought (both conscious and subconscious)."

Treatment as an art form which develops a concept within the mind of those who use it, by establishing a belief through the inspiration of the indwelling Spirit of Life, that It desires to give us whatever we require, be it health, wealth, love or happiness.

The science of treatment is realizing there is a law involved, a principle of how Life as Mind works and unfolds, and that we understand the mechanics of this law. Thus, we can specialize it to bring forth the desired purpose for which the treatment (often called affirmative prayer) is being set into motion for that specific good.

Anyone, at any age or any faith can give an effective spiritual mind treatment. The law, which is impersonal as to who may choose to use it, will work for one and for all. The method of operation of this law in comprised of five easy steps. They are Recognition, Unification, Realization, Thanksgiving and Release.

The Recognition step allows the one praying to affirm that, above all, there is only One Life and that Life is God. This step celebrates all that God is—the infinite, awe-inspiring nature of Life.

The Unification step allows the one praying to affirm their oneness with God. It is this awareness that all that is God's nature is our nature and that the creative process of the Law is the creative process we may direct for our benefit.

The Realization step allows the one praying to release from their consciousness any limiting thoughts which are not in alignment with oneness with God, and to accept, claim and declare the new and empowering thoughts aligned with God's nature that is impressed upon the Law.

The Thanksgiving step allows the one praying to fully accept and feel the fulfillment of receiving that which is given us by

God. It acknowledges that prayer is answered by way of realizing that God gives us what we desire.

The Release step affirms the faith of the one praying that the Law acts upon the thoughts impressed upon it. The one praying can let go of any need to will or concentrate since they have changed the thought which is acted upon by Law which responds with mathematical certainty and reliability.

Treatment as affirmative prayer requires a degree of understanding of how and why prayer works. This is the key to demonstrating answered prayer and every person should employ its method of operation, for this is how it works and is waiting on all people to work it!

(For more in-depth information on prayer and spiritual mind treatment as a form of prayer, refer to Chapter Nine in The Science of Mind textbook by Dr. Ernest Holmes.)

The 5 STEPS in order

Recognition—Unification—Realization—Thanksgiving—Release

Easiest way to remember: **R.U.R.T.R** which you can memorize by saying **R U Ready To Receive** (are you ready to receive?).

The simplest and shortest Spiritual Mind Treatment

1. **There is only One Power**
2. **I am one with that Power**
3. **I know it is**
4. **Thanks**
5. **Good-bye**

Expressed in another way:

1. I **RECOGNIZE** there is only one Power (Mind, Field, Energy, God, you choose the word that resonate with you)
2. I **UNIFY** myself with that Power, I am one with it
3. I **REALIZE** that this is the only and absolute truth (I realize that in the Mind I am Health, I am Abundant etc . . . what you want to treat for)
4. I give **THANKS** for knowing that Truth
5. I **RELEASE** these words into the Mind knowing their power and that it is already done, and so it is

(http://www.prospirity.com)

Affirmative prayer is understood, in Unity, as the highest form of creative thought. It includes the release of negative thoughts and holding in mind statements of spiritual truth. Through meditation and prayer, we can experience the presence of God. Prayer and meditation heighten our awareness of truth and thereby transform our lives.

Prayer is valuable not because it alters the circumstances and conditions of your life, but because it alters you.

Unity teaches that it is helpful to pray with the belief that we have already received all that we need. In this view, through prayer the mind is renewed and the body transformed. The awareness that we are conscious creators of our lives, has the power to make the bridge between the old Christianity where we are "sinners" to the new understanding that we are "learners."

The Unity school of Christianity holds that prayer is not a way to inform God of one's troubles or to change God in any way, but rather, prayer is properly used to align with the power that is God

(http://en.wikipedia.org/wiki/Unity_Church#Affirmative_Prayer

So placing such a powerful invocation out into the universe, into the Quantum field you are attracting to you the very essence and manifestation of what you have affirmed. It is like the abracadabra incantation which is thought to have originated from the Aramaic language which when translated means, "Create as I say." Your words create as YOU say. God said, let there be light and there was light. You said, I hate my job and it was so! Say it and bring to your experience more of what you are speaking about. If that doesn't encourage you to change your speaking habits, I'm not sure what will . . . So let's go to the other ways in which you can just do it.

Your body temple is the vehicle by which spirit moves through this physical life. I do not believe that the spirit is housed within the body; I believe that the spirit being an expansive essence without limit or bounds is not within the body but rather the body is within the spirit. I envision it like the Energetic Composition of the Body. We are multi-dimensional beings composed of several levels of energy, vibrating at different rates. From lowest vibration to highest, the seven levels are as follows:

- ❖ The Physical/Etheric Level
- ❖ The Emotional Level
- ❖ The Lower Mental Level
- ❖ The Astral Level
- ❖ The Higher Mental Level
- ❖ The Christ or Buddhic Level
- ❖ The Spirit Level

The various levels are various vibratory rates of the entire being that we are and are possibly only a few of the aspects known that indicate the spirit as energy that surround, penetrates, supports, and binds us together. OK so back to the body. Regardless of where the soul or spirit is located, your body temple is the sacred physicalization which you use to interact within this physical world. As such, it deserves to be tended to with care and holiness as any sacred dwelling would be. You cannot proclaim to be a spiritual warrior while spending over half your day plopped on the couch in front of the television eating half a gallon of ice cream. Well, actually you can claim it; however, you are not acting in a manner that demonstrates the sanctity of your body temple. Exercise, proper nutrition, healthy amounts of sunlight, rest, fresh air and clean water are important components to honoring your body. Why do many men care more for their cars than they do for their bodies? Your Chevy will be of no good to your corpse! And to the ladies, love the shoes but what about your health?

Confession time, I love baked goods. Oatmeal cookies, chocolate chips, brownies, apple pie, etc. and I still enjoy eating them however, I do so in much greater moderation than I once did. Not because I judge it as bad or even unhealthy, but because I feel the need to balance them with healthier more nutritious foods. Will I ever stop eating them all together? Maybe, then again maybe not; I will make that decision within each moment as it arises. There is no need to fret, worry, or judge myself for enjoying desserts. I mention this confession because they was a time that I did just that, I judged and tormented myself for eating them and for gaining weight over a 20 year period from 190 to 220lbs. I allowed my self image to become clouded by the judgments of others. "Wow Ray, picking up some weight huh?" "I like the thinner more fit ray better." "Any plans to get back in shape?" Comments such as these and my acceptance of them actually created the conditions for me to gain more weight! It wasn't until I began to love myself just as I was that I began to exercise, eat healthier, and go to a more desired state of fitness where my body was tended to as the sacred temple it is.

Many people do not like to exercise or they say they do not like to exercise. To that I say, fine, but it depends on how you classify exercise. Exercise does not have to be going to the gym to work out. Exercise can be yoga, walking, dancing, swimming, bike riding, playing Frisbee, softball, or martial arts. I love how Xbox has created the Kinect system and an interactive video game "UFC Personal Trainer" that can assist a person with working out at home. Technology can be amazing! I'm still looking forward to the Star Trek Holodeck experience! I digress once again . . . So as you can see, exercise is not only possible, it can be enjoyable. The other things I mentioned like nutrition, water, adequate rest and sunlight are equally doable. It may take baby steps which is fine because you will do what you can do as you feel able and ready to do it. It is your body after all and you have to make the decisions regarding it. Note this is not about being the perfect body type or dress or suit size. This is about enabling your body temple to move with ease, comfort, health, and joy. Why do you not put sugar or soda or the grease from fried chicken in your gas tank? Clearly you don't because it messes up the engine. Get my point? I am not condemning the eating of any of those foods, after all did you not just read my dessert confession, what I am saying is that as you eat be mindful, be respectful, and as you feel comfortable do so in moderation.

Just as your body is to be cared for, so to must your mind and emotional self be cared for. This is probably best done through the practice of compassion and the medium of meditation. Some refer to prayer as you talking to God and meditation as God talking to you. That is a cute way of looking at it; however, I think meditation is when you go into the silence and as we have established, God is not some entity outside of you, nor is God a "being" that communicates with you, God is the Isness, Allness, and Beingness of Everything! It may be better to see God not as omnipotent but as Omnipotence itself, Omniscience itself and Omnipresence itself rather than as qualities attributed to some kind of deity. So in meditation we enter the silence where we dissolve into the Oneness of God. I see it like there is an ice cube that is placed into a bowl of warm water. Meditation is taking that solidified mental stagnation that tends to accumulate in our minds and letting it dissolve into the warmth of the water. It dissolves and is returned to the natural state of oneness where there is no ice cube and water, it is all water! And this process happens without any forcing, urging, pleading, or work. It simply happens with a natural flow, with ease and grace. There is no struggle in the ice. It does not resist melting. It does not fear losing itself. It simply changes form and joins the rest of the water. Meditation offers us that dissolution of our mental junk, allowing us the opportunity to enter into the flow. In the flow we do not resist, we are not burdened with attachments, resentments, or worries. We simply go with the flow and return to Source!

Meditation does not have to be complicated or time consuming! Ideally you want to spend time in the silence rather than think of it as microwave ready—30 seconds and "ding" you are done! Meditation comes in many shapes and forms so it can fit your needs and personality. It can be sitting still, quieting your mind and breathing, taking a more formal meditation class, listening to a guided meditation CD, practicing a moving meditation style like Tai Chi Chuan, even gardening or painting can be found to be meditations if you are in "the zone" so to speak. If you are in the moment fully present and not investing in the chatter in the mind, then you are meditating.

In addition to meditation, studying things that will assist your growth and evolution are quite helpful. The things you study can range from self help and spiritual texts to biographies about people you admire like Colonel Saunders the founder of Kentucky Fried Chicken or Tina Turner or George Lucas. A lot can be gleaned by seeing how others have overcome life's obstacles, shifted their lives, and moved their mountains, as they accomplished their dreams. Spiritual study can also be attending workshops and seminars, the learning of a language you have always wanted to learn or how to play the guitar or flute. The study can be anything and everything that is in accord with living from your authenticity!

Taking classes and engaging in various forms of study can lead one to engaging in a word that when people hear, many envision church. That word you may wonder is fellowship. However, what I am referring to is a little more encompassing than that though it includes church fellowship as well. By fellowship I mean that you align yourself with other like minded individuals on a regular basis. As I said, that might be at church, it could be at a Reiki share, a spiritual meetup group, a Mastermind group, a book club, or anything where those you are around you are of like mind and energy. It is important to have a group of people who understand you, support you, and are with you on this journey as awakening spiritual warriors as they hold you accountable as you just do it—walking the walk and talking the talk.

Being willing and able to serve is also something we are here to do. How do you serve your community both local and global? Do you volunteer time to an organization that offers light to the world? Could you be someone who takes the time to read to one of our seniors or support them while they go shopping? Could you be someone who gives love to animals that have been neglected and abused? Could you be someone who tutors children so that no child is ever left behind? Could you hold the door open for someone? Could you offer a smile to everyone you see today? How can you be of service to the community? And while giving money is one form of giving service, what I am referring to is some kind of face to face person to person interaction where you are giving of yourself, giving your gifts as part of your sacred service. That is a perfect segue to the next thing I encourage you to do.

Love! Just do it! LOVE, Love without limits, without bounds, without requirements, without regrets, without restriction—love unconditionally! The ways in which you can express love are as numerous as the stars in the heavens; pick a few thousand and put them into practice. If you allow the pure love of the Divine to be all that you are, then all that you are will be love; love in the flesh! You will be a living breathing physicalized expression of love in human form. Service is a form of love expressing. Give love to others though affection, hug to express love, kiss to express love, laugh to express love, give a handshake to express love, tell people that you love them. Love the Earth through your appreciation of the sky, the clouds, the trees, the soil; love it all! Love yourself! If you truly love yourself you cannot help but to love everything else as part of the Oneness. Oh and part of loving is forgiving.

Just do it . . . Forgive whoever you are angry with. Forgive your parents for what you feel they did wrong to you. Forgive your ex-boyfriend, ex-girlfriend, ex-wife, ex-husband. Forgiving those who you find most difficult to forgive are the ones you want to forgive the most! Forgive the neighbor that molested you, forgive the person who raped you on your way home from class, forgive the mugger whose aggression put you in the hospital, forgive the man who shot your son, who stabbed your daughter. Forgive them not for their sake but for your own.

By forgiving, you release that person's continued ability to cause harm to your mind and emotions. If we were at a cook-out and I took a red hot charcoal brick out of the grill and placed it in your hand, how long would you hold it? Why would you let it go so fast? Ahh because to hold it any longer damages your hand and it hurts! For everything that has been done to you in your life, it is the same as that hot coal in your hand. Holding onto it never hurts the coal, only the hand! Holding onto the anger bitterness resentment never hurts the perpetrator of the wrong; it only hurts the one holding onto it!

And if I may get a little metaphysical about this forgiveness thing; there are many metaphysicians like Louise Hay that say that resentment if held long enough will begin to out picture in your body temple as dis-ease, most notably cancer. Allowing that resentment to eat away at your mind and heart internally begins to create in your physical self an ill that will do the same kind of harm you have allowed to happen within. Now that is a powerful thing to contemplate. My own father transitioned as a result of cancer which makes me wonder if my father in fact harbored some resentment that out-pictured as cancer. And even deeper are the Metaphysical Absolutists who believe that everything that happens in your life happened because you were in vibrational alignment with it. In other words, if you are vibrating out of fear of being mugged, through the law of attraction you are manifesting and attracting a mugger of some sort to realize your fears in your experience. That does not mean you are to blame for what happens to you! Understand that as I say it again—That DOES NOT mean you are to blame for what happens to you. You are not to blame for the rape, the illness, the home invasion or the loss of your job.

I no longer perceive accidents or random happenings as possible because to do so, for me, would mean that everything is random or at least potentially random. If that is the case there is no divine order and there is far too much order demonstrated in the universe for it to be random. I believe in the synchronistic and the coincidental happenings in life and what I mean by that is, when we are in sync, in vibrational alignment with something we notice the manifestation in our lives. We notice how things "coincide" when in alignment. Is it a coincidence that I was thinking of my mother and she called me? Or even more "random" (smile), is it coincidence that I was thinking of a old student that I had lost touch with after leaving Pittsburgh in 2000 and just as I was thinking of them they sent me a message on Facebook? Is that random or is there some energetic vibration that put us in sync where my thought of her and her message to me coincided at that moment? Is it random that I was driving to pick up Tracy and had a very minor fender bender on the way to the metro to get her? Some would say yes it is random while others would say if there was within my consciousness a hanging thought of "car accident" and that I was on some level a vibrational match with car accidents manifesting in my physical experience. With that in mind it makes me even that much more mindful of the thoughts I hold in consciousness because what I allow to fill that space is what I am also allowing to be attracted into my experience.

If we agree that God is all there is and that under that premise we are God as well, in the same way the drop of ocean water has within it the fullness of the essence of the ocean. The drop is not the ocean itself but it does have the "DNA" of the ocean, correct? Likewise, the sun is expressing itself in the stream of heat and light that it gives off. The beam is not the sun but it shares the essence of the sun. You are not "God" but God is you! Nothing can happen outside of the realm of God and we co-create with God or as some phrase it, we create using the creative power of God as us. So you see there is a vast amount of "metaphysical mathematics" involved in the creating of our experiences. One additional equations in the mix is the idea of soul contracts where you agreed before being born to have certain experiences and that you also agreed for example to have alcoholic parents so that you could learn compassion. Colin Tipping as I mentioned earlier in his book "A Radical Incarnation" outlines how and why we incarnate as we do and how people such as President Bush and Saddam Hussein had soul contracts with each other to play out the roles that they played in order to bring about the catalyst for change that we all are feeling and moving towards.

Regardless of which idea you choose to believe and live your life based upon, the point I was making was that it is not your fault, you are not to blame, and the power to forgive is yours. Forgive them all and forgive yourself! Releasing the need to continue to harbor anger towards yourself is also very important. You cannot truly forgive another until you can forgive yourself, much like you cannot love another until you can love yourself because you cannot give to another what you do not have to give. You cannot give someone a glass of apple juice if all you have is orange. You cannot squeeze an orange and get apple juice. You cannot give love if you harbor animosity, anger, hatred, and resentment. Do you find yourself blaming you for the kind of men you date, the jobs you lose, the women you marry, or the behavior of your children? Let it all go and forgive yourself. Like everyone else, you are doing the best you can in every moment and if you knew better and could do better you would do better, so relax and forgive yourself! Learn and grow and make the necessary changes rather than allowing yourself to continue to repeat old patterns, which anger, resentment, bitterness, and unforgiveness force you to repeat. Ultimately, when we fully awaken, we will realize that there is nothing to forgive. If you are unsure of how to forgive, there are therapist, counselors, ministers, life coaches, and more who can assist you in the art of forgiving.

Last but not least, on our path of Just Do It, is the wonderful skill of "Acting as if or faking it until we make it." I think explaining the art of acting as if is best done with examples. Suppose you do not feel confident and you want to be more confident, I would ask you how do confident people act? What kinds of things do confident people do? Once you answer my questions I would tell you to begin doing those things that you said confident people do. This is what came first, the chicken or the egg kind of paradoxical concept. Do you have to have the money before you can act like a prosperous person? Do you have to have the perfect marriage before you can act like someone whose spouse is loving and whatever else you consider perfect in a marriage? Do you have to lose fifty pounds before you start to act like a thinner healthier or sexy person? No you do not have to wait! You can begin today to embody not only the inner the attitude of that which you desire but the behaviors and outward attitude as well. Let's examine that weight loss example a little more in depth to clarify what I mean.

Suppose you are morbidly obese and you are asked how does a thin healthy person act and you respond by saying they exercise, eat right, wear better looking clothes, they smile and laugh and are social people. Would you need to lose any weight at all before you could embody any of those things you listed? Exercise does not mean running laps around central park. Exercise can be something you do in your room and from your bed if you are bedridden. Acting as if does not mean jumping off some cliff and doing huge drastic changes, rather it is first embodying the mental, emotional, and spiritual ambiance of what you desire and then allowing the physical to fall into sync with the already existent mental equivalent. With that in mind, now can you see how exercise, eating right, wearing or having a better attitude about how you dress, your ability to smile and laugh and be social, loving yourself, and forgiving yourself are all things you can do before a single pound is shed?

Everything starts internally. Every building, automobile, tool, TV, CD, DVD, piece of clothing, and on and on and on are all physicalized thought. Someone thought of these things and then invented them bringing them from the unseen realm of mind into the physical realm. Acting as if does the same thing. Begin by embracing the essence of what you desire to manifest and act as if you already have it. Many people use vision boards and visualize filling their minds with images of what they desire and as the mind is filled with it, the person's mood and attitude shifts and as the internal atmosphere shifts, the external experience will do likewise.

Want a bigger house? Begin to sense, see, and feel the house you want as if it were here now! How would you feel in that house? Feel that now! Do not spend time cursing the small one bedroom apartment. Spend your energy loving and being grateful for your space now, by moving around it as if it were already what you desire!

"You can't have what you want until you want what you have."
** Anonymous

Want prosperity or financial wealth? Begin now to carry yourself as a financially prosperous person. That does not mean the soap opera version of rich—selfish, greedy, stuck up. It means you have no reason to talk about scarcity and lack. It means you tithe to a person or institution where you are or have been spiritually fed. It means walking and talking like a person of prosperity. It means changing how you feel about money, changing your negative thoughts about money which repel it to more prosperous thoughts which attract it.

No matter what you desire to attract or manifest, it is possible. There is no such thing as "luck." Many people hit the lottery for millions of dollars and yet after a year or two are more in debt than before they won the money! Why is this so? They did not shift their consciousness. They were living from poverty and scarcity consciousness rather than from abundance and prosperity. Make a commitment to yourself to literally Be the change you want to see. Become the very thing you want to be.

"Luck is what happens when preparation meets opportunity." **Senaca

CHAPTER SIX:
PRACTICALLY PERFECT?

From childhood on to adulthood we are exposed to quote after quote, phrase after phrase and witty remark after witty remark about how imperfect we are.

> Have no fear of perfection—you'll never reach it.
> ~Salvador Dali

> Perfection is not attainable. But if we chase perfection, we can catch excellence.
> ~Vince Lombardi

> No one is perfect . . . that's why pencils have erasers.
> ~Author Unknown

> Only in grammar can you be more than perfect.
> ~William Safire

> Gold cannot be pure, and people cannot be perfect.
> ~Chinese Proverb

> When you aim for perfection, you discover it's a moving target.
> ~George Fisher

> Once you accept the fact that you're not perfect, then you develop some confidence.
> ~Rosalynn Carter

> There are no perfect men in this world, only perfect intentions.
> ~Pen Densham, Robin Hood: Prince of Thieves

> They say that nobody is perfect. Then they tell you practice makes perfect. I wish they'd make up their minds.
> ~Wilt Chamberlain

As you can see there are many ways in which people have commented about being perfect and these are but a few of the thousands we have been exposed to over the centuries. An interesting and entertaining perspective on the whole idea of being perfect shows up in the Broadway musical, "Mary Poppins." The show has a scene with Mary singing a song called "Practically Perfect" where she is telling the children about herself as sort of an introduction song. While Mary Poppins is a fictional character, the symbol or archetype she represents reminds each of us the truth of her words which are that each of us is in fact "practically" perfect. Much like the metaphysical debate I proposed in the last chapter with regards to the absolutist view, this idea of perfection also has a multifaceted point of view and like certain optical illusions, what you see changes depending on where you stand and look.

Paradigm one: The concept of "perfection" which I am speaking of in this chapter will be foreign and quite challenging to grasp or believe. For those who perceive the existence of good and bad, righteous and unrighteous, holy and unholy, or God and the devil, the paradigm of duality will keep them teetering on a scale that must by its very nature, judge something as one or the other; they cannot have certain absolutes. For them there is a force of evil that affects this world and for them mankind was born with the concept of Original Sin.

Paradigm two: Not only does the typical concept of duality not exist, but the concept of God as a "Being" also does not exist. This paradigm has God not being an Omnipotent Being but being pure Omnipotence, pure omniscience, and pure omnipresence itself. This view holds God not as someone who loves but as Love itself! In this paradigm there is no dualistic perspective; there is only God and therefore there is only good.

"Somewhere along the way in your life you have to make some pretty big decisions. You must decide, for yourself . . . Is there a "God"? If so, Who or What is this thing you call The Divine? What is Its purpose? What does it want, need, or require? What is your true relationship with It?" **Neale Donald Walsch

Now within this second paradigm I have found those that have two different points of view.

View one: The true essence of our being is, was, and will forever be divinely perfect. It can be nothing else! However, while in the body temple there are things we will do, or say, or think or feel that can be classified as less than divinely perfect. We make mistakes and occasionally mankind acts in ways that are not divine.

View two: Everything in the universe whether we see it or not, whether we understand it or not is in fact—perfect! Everything is perfect which includes those things we would call heinous or evil. Everything is perfect because this is a divine universe in the mind of a Divine God and there is nothing that happens outside of the figurative hand of God. If we agree on the premise that everything is God then everything is good which means even those things we judge as bad, "serve a purpose." This second view is what I believe Colin Tipping is referring to in his books "Radical Incarnation" "Radical Forgiveness" and it is the basis of his Radical Forgiveness program. As I understand it, we forgive everyone of everything because in the divine grand scheme of things and there is therefore nothing to forgive! Everything and everyone is precisely where they are meant to be, doing precisely what they are meant to be doing and it is all happening according to a divinely orchestrated (for lack of a better word) Soul Contract which we all have signed before manifesting or incarnating in the flesh.

I must agree that this is a "radical" concept not only to grasp but to put into practice! Based upon this concept, the abuser and the abused agreed to the roles prior to being born. Likewise, the rapist and the raped, the Nazi and the Jew, the Klan and the slave, the terrorist and those being terrorized . . . ! All of us are playing the roles in this performance we call life. We act and interact with one another according to the divine script that we ourselves as creators of our experience have and are writing. We determine what lessons to learn and from that set the intention into motion attracting to us the vibratory matches in people and situations to offer us the "classes" from which we learn our evolutionary lessons.

So let's go back a step for a brief moment . . .

If we agree with the premise that everything is God, then where is there room for evil? If evil does not exist, then there is only good. We may not be able to see the good in the moment; however, as many have said, hindsight is 20/20; meaning that when we are able to look back on a situation after having learned some valuable insight, we see that the situation was a gift of sorts that helped us to develop and grow. Of course it is difficult to see the ravages of a hurricane, flood, earthquake or tsunami and see it as "good" however, it is not impossible. For one thing, if we can also agree with the premise that there is no such thing as death, then those who we say died in the wake of the tragic natural disaster have in fact not died; they returned to the Oneness of God. So if there is no death, then the perspective of the tragedy and the suffering begins to change. Of course we continue to console the grieving, feed the hungry, and mend the wounded just as Jesus the Christ did; however, we do this holy work from a higher consciousness where we begin to see beyond the physical limitations. We begin to see the perfection that is back of the situation.

I like to compare it to how Glinda the good witch tells Dorothy to go to Oz in order to find her way home; yet Glinda knows full well that Dorothy already has the ability in those red slippers to go home now. Glinda sends her on this hero's journey because Glinda knows that in order for Dorothy to rise in consciousness, she must embark on this journey of self. She knows that every journey is perfect and that everything and everyone that is encountered is part of the divine plan of Spirit; there is no where that God is not. Everyone is precisely where they are supposed to be and everything is happening precisely as it is supposed to happen. I know it is quite challenging to embrace something so foreign, when we are conditioned to accept concepts such as duality, accidents, random and evil. Rebelling against oneness, perfection, and unity becomes common place. When a child dies, we say they died before their time and yet I wonder if that is even possible. Is it possible for someone to die, transition, change form before it is his or her time? This implies that something can happen beyond the perfection and divine timing of God. We often talk about the will of God as if God, being that great man in the sky who has already mapped out a blueprint that we are to follow. A plan where we do what He wants us to do. Let's take that idea for a second and suppose that God does in fact have a will for us . . . can something truly happen beyond or outside of the will of God? If something can happen outside of the will of God, then God is limited and cannot control everything.

I find that particular view of God quite limiting as well as being quite damaging to us as it keeps us locked in a state of fear and victim consciousness where we are forever bound to the dictates of our embedded theology. I know there are many who do not like the idea of God being likened to a Genie and I agree that to substitute one kind of giant being for another does not serve our evolution of consciousness. The idea I want to point out regarding the Genie is what the Genie says to Aladdin, "Your wish is my command." That statement in many ways is what God says to each and every one of us. It is the will of God that we create what we desire to create. God does not limit what you or I create. If I want to create a life of misery and pain, then I have that right and power to create according to the thoughts I chose to hold in mind. If you want to create a life of love and prosperity, then you have that right and power to create according to those thoughts you hold in mind. It is done according to each one of us based upon our thoughts. God's will is many ways is our will even when we are creating amiss we are creating and are thus masters of creation.

So you see we are perfect not only in the essence of our spiritual nature, but we are perfect beings doing exactly as we have chosen to do using our divine abilities to create according to our thoughts words and deeds. "Ye therefore shall be perfect, as your heavenly Father is perfect." This is where many of us in our duality based thinking go astray. We misunderstand what it means to "be" perfect. In the being aspect there is nothing to "do." What does a rabbit *do* to *be* a rabbit? What do you *do* in order to *be* a man, a woman, a child, a parent? There is nothing you can do. This is where you simply sit and be still and know.

We dance round in a ring and suppose,
But the Secret sits in the middle and knows.
**Robert Frost

I do not claim to understand why people like Charles Manson or Hitler do what they do; nor do I understand why phrases like "going postal" have become somewhat commonplace in our vernacular to describe any number of people who in a fit of rage have harmed or killed another. I do not know why a student would choose to go from classroom to classroom shooting classmates and teachers. What I do hold onto is the belief that despite their actions, they are children of God as well. Despite their actions, they are doing the best they can do in any given moment. Despite their actions, they are worthy of love. In any moment there is a choice between a grievance or a miracle. This is what lesson 78 of The Course in Miracles reminds.

> "Perhaps it is not yet quite clear to you that each decision that you make is one between a grievance and a miracle. Each grievance stands like a dark shield of hate before the miracle it would conceal. And as you raise it up before your eyes, you will not see the miracle beyond. Yet all the while it waits for you in light, but you behold your grievances instead (Course in Miracles Lesson)."

Now there is a certain group of people who seem to have a hard time experiencing the miracle. As they would have it, grievances are far easier to experience because they feel very strongly about having things be done or looking perfect. Some of us, perfectionists, are so obsessed with being in control and having things be what we deem to be perfect that we are actually losing sight of the inherent perfection around and within us. Our misguided sense of the perfect is only able to see the flawed and imperfect. Due to this obsession with making the imperfect perfect, we end up in a vicious merry-go-round where we will never be satisfied or happy because we are attempting to do something that is already done. For the perfectionists, perfection is an elusive mirage that does not exist and yet hours upon hours of life energy are spent on this illusion they has chosen to believe. The perfectionists hide behind a myriad of excuses why something cannot be started, or finished, or done as they expect. Excuse after excuse continues to cloud their vision keeping them blind to the truth—they feel out of control and are doing their best to hide their feelings of inadequacy by pushing even harder to be perfect.

Somewhere the perfectionists have agreed to believe that they are not perfect, that they are inadequate, and that they must do things perfectly in order to be accepted and receive love. They then go on this elusive quest for something that does not exist; not the way they believe it does. For example, there is the person who believes that she will start her own business as soon as the conditions to do so are perfect. What does that mean? For this person the day to start that business is always tomorrow. She will start when the kids grow up and go off to college. She will start when she and her husband have enough money saved. She will start when she takes another class or reads that book on starting your own business. She continues to push and push until she wakes up one day realizing that all elusive perfect time never arrived. She now lives with the regret of not having simply done it!

"Whatever you can do or dream you can, begin it.
Boldness has genius, power and magic in it."
**Goethe

There is perfection all about us when we simply take the time to be aware of it. The homeless man is perfect as is your desire to house and feed him. The terrorist is perfect as is the love you bring to quell his hatred. Do not fight against or resist your perception of evil, rather fully embrace and express that which is love. The more time you spend seeking to avoid the bad, the more time you are inviting the bad to visit you. What is there to judge when you know it is all good? What is there to call imperfect when it is all God? So let's spend some time meditating on the perfection that is not only all around us but that which is within us as well.

"Greater is he that is within me, than he that is in the world (1 John 4:4)."

MEDITATION ON PERFECTION:

Sitting or laying comfortably in a manner where you are able to release the tension within your body, become aware of your breathing as you continue to breathe naturally.

With each inhalation be aware of your abdomen rising and with each exhalation be aware of your abdomen as it falls.

Simply be aware.

After you have done this several times and as you feel ready to, say aloud as you exhale "I am perfect." Notice what emotions or thoughts arise as you say this powerful affirmation. Do not judge the thoughts or feelings; simply listen to them as if listening to a news reporter making a comment. Notice the quality of the thoughts and feelings . . . meaning do you feel good when you say it or do you feel bad. Do you notice thoughts that contradict the affirmation or thoughts that agree with it?

No matter the thoughts or feelings, repeat the affirmation several more times. "I am perfect." "I am perfect." "I am perfect."

Then add on to it, "I am perfect exactly as I am right now." Again notice your thoughts and feelings. You may notice an accuser providing evidence to the contrary to demonstrate how imperfect you are. Listen to the accusations and dispel them by repeating the affirmation again. "I am perfect exactly as I am right now." This time as you say the affirmation, I want you to put your imagination to use and imagine what it feels like to be perfect. What emotions and thoughts do you feel when you imagine what perfection feels like?

Hold onto those thoughts and feelings as you repeat the affirmation several more times. "I am perfect exactly as I am right now."

Hold fast to the idea that no matter what has happened in the past, no matter what you do, have done, are doing, or will do, nothing can change or alter the truth that you as a child of the Divine are perfect. You are in every moment doing the best you can do and as you learn to do better you will do better. As your consciousness expands so too will your thoughts, words, and deeds.

"I am perfect exactly as I am right now doing the best I can do in each moment. I am that, I am!"

Repeat the affirmation several more times as you come to the end the meditation. "I am perfect exactly as I am right now doing the best I can do in each moment. I am that, I am!"

Return your awareness to your breathing and the sensations of your body while still holding onto the power of the words you affirmed.

As you continue to repeat the affirmation as your daily mantra you will begin to notice subtle shifts in how you encounter events in your life. You will begin to see things in a more expanded awareness rather than through the blinders that once narrowed your vision.

WHATEVER MOUNTAIN IS IN YOUR WAY, IS PERFECT

So if I ask what is the obstacle you perceive to be in your way? What is blocking you, holding you back, and hindering you? Are your childhood experiences holding you back? Is the balance in your bank account holding you back? Is your boss, spouse, or are your parents blocking you? What is the mountain that is in the way of your success, happiness, love, joy? What would you tell me? Some of the things I have heard from coaching clients, students, friends, family, and congregants are:

- I'm too old
- I'm fat
- I'm too skinny
- I don't have enough money
- I am too tall
- I'm too short
- I'm black
- I'm gay
- I'm a female
- I don't have a degree
- I was raised in a single parent household
- My parents were alcoholics (or drug users)
- I was raped (or molested)
- Politicians are crooked and the President lied
- I'm an ex-convict; no one gives me a chance
- I'm from the projects
- I didn't graduate from high school
- I will do it as soon as I lose 5 pounds
- As soon as I_________ then I can_________

I could go on and on with the reasons people give for why they are not living their best life right now! There are more than enough reasons why you can't do something if you give yourself permission to believe in those reasons. You grew up and may have at one time believed in the Tooth Fairy, Santa Claus, the Easter Bunny, the Boogieman or any number of "fictitious" childhood fairytales and yet at some point in your life you decided to stop believing in them and you made a choice to believe in something else. Here you stand again at the crossroads of choosing. Do you choose to believe in and give more power to the Boogieman that tells you what you can't do, how unworthy you are, how fat you are, how ugly you are, how damaged you are? Or do you choose to invest in, believe in, and give power to the truth of who you are, what you are and what you can do?

There was a time when flight was impossible and yet Orville and Wilbur Wright did the impossible and gave us the airplane. How many modern day marvels do we take for granted that a mere ten or twenty year ago would have been believed to be impossible? Galileo Galilei was placed on house arrest by the Catholic Church for stating the not only impossible but the blasphemous when he said—The Earth is not the center of the universe; the Earth and the other planets revolve around the sun. Many believed that Gandhi's hunger strike was pointless. Yet this single man's resolve and passion brought peace to his nation. His example also changed the face of America as is seen in the influence of Rev. Dr. Martin Luther King Jr. and the civil rights movement. Every leader, inventor, author, artist, and teacher begins with the idea of what some have called impossible and rather than embrace the limitations they embrace the possibilities. So yes you have some perceived hell that is offering you resistance. Yes you have a perceived mountain blocking your way. Yes, you have some perceived injustice, illness, and impossibility standing before you and it is providing you the perfect opportunity to use it to step into your power, shift your perceptions, and become, not all that you can become, but all that you already ARE!

Let's take a symbolic and metaphysical look at a good old bible story that by the end will assist you in getting up and over your own obstacles.

Twice a day for 40 days, the champion of the Philistines, a "giant" by the name of Goliath, would go out between the lines and he would challenge the Israelites to send out a champion of their own to engage him in single combat.

However, no one would ever accept the challenge and go to fight him because King Saul and all the other Israelites were simply terrified of the giant Philistine warrior.

King Saul, weary of the taunting by the giant devises a plan. In an attempt to recruit someone, the King promises to reward the man who defeats the Philistine. The King will give his own daughter's hand in marriage to the man who defeats Goliath as well as grant him riches, and will make his household exempt from taxes in Israel. A young boy by the name of David steps forward and accepts the challenge.

King Saul, looking at this small young boy and refuses to allow this boy to in essence commit suicide. David however convinces him and the King reluctantly agrees to allow this boy to go into battle. In an attempt to help David, who is not a soldier, prepare for the battle, the King offers his own armor. David declines the King's offer and takes only his slingshot and five stones that were chosen in a nearby brook.

On the battle field, David and Goliath face each other. Goliath stood there confidently wearing his armor and holding his sword and shield facing young David who wore a simple tunic, carrying, his staff and slingshot.

"The Philistine cursed David by his gods," but David replied: "This day the LORD will deliver you into my hand, and I will strike you down, and cut off your head; and I will give the dead bodies of the host of the Philistines this day to the birds of the air and to the wild beasts of the earth; that all the earth may know that there is a God in Israel, and that all this assembly may know that God saves not with sword and spear; for the battle is God's, and He will give you into our hand."

David hurled a stone from his slingshot hitting Goliath in the center of his forehead. The Philistine falls face down to the ground; David, using a sword, cuts off Goliath's head and the battle was won.

Facing such insurmountable odds it would have been quite easier for the young boy to do as so many others had done, shrink in fear. Yet he decided to face the obstacle head on in courage and faith knowing God would be with him. 1 Samuel 17:37 "The LORD," David added, "who rescued me from the power of both lions and bears, will rescue me from the power of this Philistine." In faith David stepped out to do the impossible. He stood face to face with his obstacle which towered over him; as all mountains seem to do. He faced it, though he wore a tunic and Goliath was in full armor. He faced it, though Goliath wielded a sword and he had a mere a slingshot and five stones. He faced it, though he was no soldier and Goliath was an experienced in battle. Despite the seemingly impossibility a young inexperienced shepherd boy defeating a seasoned soldier covered in armor, holding sword and shield, David defied the odds and did the impossible. The sword carrying mountain, Goliath, was defeated by a young shepherd boy slinging stones! How perfect can you get? That is the blueprint for each of us as well . . . Thought/Word/Deed

1. David hears the threats of Goliath and is amazed that the Israelites are afraid. He makes up in his mind that he will face the obstacle. He sees beyond the illusion and holds in his mind the Truth.
2. He states that he will accept the challenge. When the King begins to give reason why David can't go into battle against this Philistine, David reaffirms precisely why he can do just that. David replied, "The lord who saved me from the paw of the lion and the paw of the bear when I kept my father's sheep, will deliver me." The king said "Go, then, and the Lord shall be with you." David has already won in word as he has already affirmed victory! He speaks his Truth and invokes the same Divine power that you have access to.

3. Lastly, he physically goes into battle armed with his slingshot and stones. He defeats Goliath and removes his head just as he said he would do upon winning the battle. He put the truth into action.

Sounds simple? Yes it does. On paper is seems quite simple while in the land of 3D flesh and blood the giant looms over us! Slaying Goliath was a task that only David because Goliath was David's mountain, David's walking talking physicalized hell and only David could remove it from his life. Each of us must take charge of our lives just as he did. David saw the mountain and rather than cower in fear as the others did, he stepped forward and removed it. In that moment he truly was the master of his fate and captain of his soul and he, invoking the power of the Divine, brought the mountain down! It is time to put principle into practice and bring whatever mountains you face down to the ground.

CHAPTER SEVEN:

CARNEGIE HALL?

There is an old joke that I think is a perfect way to start this new chapter . . . The joke begins with the line, "How do you get to Carnegie Hall?" and then the punch line, which replies, "Practice, practice, practice."

Metaphysically speaking that is precisely how we get to Carnegie Hall which is the equivalent to living the life we are meant to live. To the traditional musician or vocalist, Carnegie Hall represents the pinnacle place where one's years of hard work finally pay off as the performer goes on stage to do what she loves to do. Likewise, we are alive, on the stage of life to play our lives to the best of our ability and play the song we are all called to play . . . Love!

Each moment as was said before is a choice between a grievance or a miracle. It is important to grasp the increment of time used by the Course in Miracles author—each moment. We are not expected to do it all—all at once but rather in each moment, each present now moment you make the choice and doing this takes practice. This is one of the reasons I love the New Thought Ancient Wisdom traditions, they refer to the spirituality as being a sort of practice, it is something you continue to do. Like a piano player, you continue to practice your craft even after you have become a master pianist. What professional musician or vocalist gets to the point that they no longer practice? Now the level of practice or what is practiced clearly changes, I'm sure Yo-Yo Ma no longer plays Mary Had A Little Lamb as many young cellists have, however he does still practice playing the cello or piano or guitar for it is in playing that one's skills not only remain sharp but one gains greater and even greater skill. This is the true meaning of Kung Fu—diligent and persistent work and it is in doing our spiritual kung fu so to speak that we continue to evolve, becoming the best Christ or Buddha we can be!

What does that mean? Being the best Christ you can be. This is the state of being where you are living from an awareness of not only who you are but what you are. There are many who interpret Christ as a person rather than as a title. That word, Christ, while used synonymously or interchangeably for a Jesus (Yeshua) is more accurately used as a title and a state of consciousness. Christ is the Greek word for the concept of an anointing or that of being anointed. Many refer to one who is anointed as being chosen, such as when a person is anointed to become a pastor. Now this Greek word which means to anoint was translated from the Hebrew word used for messiah, which again means anointed one or one who is anointed, such as a king or a high priest very well would have been during biblical times. In the minds of many people however, Christ is used solely for the personage of Jesus. I however encourage each of us to expand this paradigm to understand that if we are to live according to the lessons taught by Jesus then we must realize that the Christ nature is also our nature. I know that I have repeated many of the same scriptures and many of the same concepts and I am about to do it again (smile). Understand that I am doing it for emphasis so that the lessons can be absorbed; just like when I teach American Sign Language or martial arts or acting, repetition gets the vocabulary, the movement, and the concepts in mind and body. OK so as I was saying, Christ is our nature and it must be so otherwise how could we do miracles like Jesus? (. . . will do what I have been doing.) And how could we do miracles that are greater than those of Jesus (He will do even greater things than these . . . John 14:12) unless the anointing, the Christ was also a part of and in fact the truth of who we also are?

"Don't you believe that I am in the Father, and that the Father is in me? The words I say to you are not just my own. Rather, it is the Father, living in me, who is doing his work. Believe me when I say that I am in the Father and the Father is in me; or at least believe on the evidence of the miracles themselves. I tell you the truth, anyone who has faith in me will do what I have been doing. He will do even greater things than these, because I am going to the Father. (John 14:10-12)."

Jesus could do the miracles because as he said, he was in the Father and the Father was in him right? Meaning that God was in him and he was in God. To which he then says that anyone who has faith in him, in his teachings, will do what he has done and even greater; therefore the Father must also be with them and they with the Father right? So the Christ consciousness or Christ nature must be within us as it was with Jesus. The primary difference it that Jesus fully knew who and what he was and the Christ was fully realized in him where as it is not fully realized in us because of our current level of awakening.

Speaking of awakening, the term Buddha, like the term Christ is a title and state of consciousness, not the formal name of a person though also like Christ; Buddha has become synonymous with Siddhartha Gautama. Buddha meaning awakened one or the enlightened one is a title for the first awakened or enlightened being in an era and as believed by most Buddhist traditions, Siddhartha Gautama, while not the only Buddha, is regarded as the Supreme Buddha of our age, similarly I would say, as Jesus would be believed to be the Supreme Christ of our age. Whether you perceive the Christ as your inherent nature or you prefer the idea or concept of Buddha as your inherent nature is a matter of semantics or preference as far as I am concerned because I believe that the two words are synonymous and interchangeable. An interesting sidebar note, which I will address in greater detail in the next book is the idea that Jesus' missing years place him in India where he learned, studied, and practiced the teachings of the Buddha. This is why many of their teachings are identical in concept. Some examples are:

> (Buddha had withdrawn to a forest hut at Kosala in the Himalayas for solitary reflection.) Then Mara, The Evil One, knew the thought that had arisen in the Enlightened One, so he went to the Buddha: 'O Lord, may the Enlightened One reign as King, may the Perfected One reign with justice, without killing or ordering killings, without being oppressive or serving oppression, without suffering from pain or causing pain to others.' The Buddha answered: 'What doest thou have in mind, O Evil One, that thou speakest thus with me?' Mara responded: 'The Enlightened One, O Lord, has assumed the fourfold might of miracles. If the Enlightened One so wished, he could command the Himalayas, the king of mountains, to become gold, and the mountain would become gold.' The Buddha turned him away: 'What would it help the wise man to own a mountain of gold or silver? Whosoever has recognized the cause of suffering, how should he succumb to desires?' Then replied Mara, the Evil One: 'The Enlightened One knows me, the Perfected One knows me,' and, grieved and discontented, he went away (*Marasamyutta* from the*Samyuttanikaya* II 10).

> Then Jesus was led into the wilderness by the spirit for trial by the accuser. He fasted for forty days and was hungry. The accuser said, 'If you are the son of God, tell this stone to become bread.' But Jesus answered, 'It is written, "No one lives by bread alone." 'Then the accuser took him to Jerusalem and placed him at the highest point of the temple and said to him, 'If you are the son of God, throw yourself down, for it is written, "He will command his angels to protect you", and "They will carry you with their hands so that your

foot will not strike a stone." 'But Jesus answered him, 'It is written, "You shall not put the lord your God to the test." 'Then the accuser took him to a very high mountain and showed him all the kingdoms of the world and their splendor, and he said to him, 'All these I will give you if you will do obeisance and reverence me.' But Jesus answered him, 'It is written, "You shall reverence the lord your God and serve him alone." 'Then the accuser left him (QS 6).

(http://www.johnworldpeace.com/budjesus.asp)

Man does not purify himself by washing as most people do in this world Anyone who rejects any sin, larger and small, is a holy man because he rejects sins (Ud 33:13).

Evil is done through the self; man defiles himself through the self. Evil is made good through the self; man purifies himself through the self (Dh 12:9).

Do not ye yet understand, that whatsoever entereth in at the mouth goeth into the belly, and is cast out into the draught. But those things which proceed out of the mouth came forth from the heart; and they defile the man.

For out of the heart proceed evil thoughts, murders, adulteries, fornications, thefts, false witness, blasphemies. These are the things which defile a man; but to eat with unwashen hands defileth not a man (Matthew 15:17-20).

(http://www.johnworldpeace.com/budjesus.asp)

And lastly these additional ones:

Jesus: "Do to others as you would have them do to you."
Luke 6:31
Buddha: "Consider others as yourself."
Dhammapada 10:1

Jesus: "If anyone strikes you on the cheek, offer the other also." Luke 6:29
Buddha: "If anyone should give you a blow with his hand, with a stick, or with a knife, you should abandon any desires and utter no evil words." Majjhima Nikaya 21:6 (http://www.beliefnet.com/Faiths/2000/02/Jesus-And-Buddha-The-Parallel-Sayings.aspx)

The reason I have made sure to even mention this is because many people go through their day blind and unaware of their True nature. Remember the story of the eagle raised by chickens; he never knew his full power as an eagle until many years later when he learned what he truly was. It was then and only then that he was able to do what he had previously believed was impossible—to fly and soar above the ground, to defy the bounds of gravity!

Who do you believe you truly are? What do you believe you truly are? How do you change your belief into something more empowering aligned with Truth? Well, first off all do you have a spiritual practice? What does that even mean—to have a spiritual practice? Basically a spiritual practice has to do with the principles, beliefs, paradigm that you live by. For example, Unity has five primary principles:

1. There is only one Presence and one Power active as the universe and as my life, God the Good.
2. Our essence is of God; therefore, we are inherently good. This God essence, called the Christ, was fully expressed in Jesus.
3. We are co-creators with God, creating reality through thoughts held in mind.
4. Through prayer and meditation, we align our heart-mind with God. Denials and affirmations are tools we use.
5. Through thoughts, words and actions, we live the Truth we know.

CHILDREN'S VERSION

1. God is all good and active in everything, everywhere.
2. I am naturally good because God's Divinity is in me and in everyone.
3. I create my experiences by what I choose to think and what I feel and believe.
4. Through affirmative prayer and meditation, I connect with God and bring out the good in my life.
5. I do and give my best by living the Truth I know. I make a difference!

(http://unity.org/association/aboutUs/whatWeBelieve/unityPrinciples.html)

I especially like the simplicity found in the children's version of the above principles. For more on the Unity principles I suggest the book The Five Principles: A Guide to Practical Spirituality" by Rev. Ellen Debenport as an excellent resource. I also like the breadth and depth that Ernest Holmes goes into in the "What We Believe" principles of Religious Science.

> The manifest universe is the body of God; it is the logical and necessary outcome of the infinite self-knowingness of God.
> We believe in the incarnation of the Spirit in US, and that all PEOPLE are incarnations of the One Spirit.
> We believe in the eternality, the immortality, and the continuity of the individual soul, forever and ever expanding.
>
> We believe that HEAVEN is within US, and that we experience IT to the degree that we become conscious of It.
> We believe the ultimate goal of life to be a complete emancipation from all discord of every nature, and that this goal is sure to be attained by all.

We believe in the unity of all life, and that the highest God and the innermost God is one God. We believe that God is personal to all who feel this indwelling Presence.

We believe in the direct revelation of Truth through our intuitive and spiritual nature, and that ANYONE may become a revealer of Truth who lives in close contact with the indwelling God.

We believe that the Universal Spirit, which is God, operates through a Universal Mind, which is the Law of God; and that we are surrounded by this Creative Mind which receives the direct impress of our thought and acts upon it.

We believe in the healing of the sick through the power of this Mind.

We believe in the control of conditions through the power of this Mind.

We believe in the eternal Goodness, the eternal Loving-kindness, and the eternal Givingness of Life to all.

We believe in our own soul, our own spirit, and our own destiny; for we understand that OUR LIFE is God.

(http://www.unitedcentersforspiritualliving.org/Philosophy/phil_beliefs.php)

Daily living with these principles in mind is what it means to "practice" the principles. It is seeing each situation and choice through the filter of the principles. For example, you are watching the news with a friend and you see the

Republican presidential hopeful Michele Bachmann make a comment about the hurricane being God's way of warning politicians and the country. Your friend says she believes it is the devil not God causing the hurricanes. You, being someone who practices principle would see that it is neither God nor the devil causing the hurricanes because there is no God in the sky needing to judge or teach humans a lesson nor is there some enemy of God called the devil who punishes humans. You would find a sense of peace in knowing that there is one Presence and one Power that is active as the universe and as your life, God the Good! This is what it means to practice the principles.

How does one do this however, how does one practice such principles, especially in the midst of economic woes, wars, global disasters, senseless murders, illness and disease? You do as the psalmist suggests in Psalm 121:1,2

> 1: I will lift up my eyes to the hills—From whence comes my help?
>
> 2: My help comes from the LORD, Who made heaven and earth.

What you do is shift your perspective, you change your mind, you change your thoughts, and you elevate your consciousness. You make a choice not to look at the event as it appears to be. You hear reports of the economy going to hell in a hand basket and that a second depression may be underway, as a result, you feel fear beginning to overtake you. Your spiritual practice encourages you to first acknowledge that right here right now you are fine and have nothing to fear in this present moment. From that place you can also affirm that simply because "they" are reporting one thing does not make it so. How many times has the news reported something based upon the truth (spiritual truth) and not on how something seems and of course on ratings?

How much of the ratings game is meant to instill fear rather than peace? How possible is it that you can be fine despite the economy? Is it possible to live well at this time? Are others doing it? Can you? As you go through asking a variety of questions you will begin to develop the confidence and faith that demonstrates that you can live with joy peace and love despite what the naysayers may say. You have effectively shifted your gaze from the ground to the skies. This is what our spiritual practice consistently asks us to do. Do not look at the problem, meaning to not obsess over the problem; shift your gaze to God, to the Christ within, which is the solution. This reminds me of something motivational speaker Les Brown says, "If you fall, then fall on your back because if you can look up, you can get up!"

We live in a culture that teaches us to focus on the problem, to worry and fret about the problem, yet we would do well to often be reminded of Einstein's wise words, "You can't solve a problem with the same mind that created it." You must raise your consciousness above that of the problem if you are to solve it.

Look at someone who is depressed. Notice their posture and manner of moving about. What do you see? Are they slouched over, looking down to the ground, rounded shoulders, and dragging their feet? I remember when a therapist I was seeing several years ago to help me work through my mourning process after my father's transition. She told me to change my posture to change my mood. At first I thought the woman was a fool (smile). However, I had already been on my spiritual path for some time and understood what she was saying and besides I trusted her so far with other school related therapeutic advice, so why stop now? I left her office one day and began to slowly make some minor changes. I changed how I walked, how I stood, and I changed how I interacted with people and something miraculous happened. I began to notice some major differences in how I felt! Just by looking up at the sky gave me access to a more elevated sense of joy. By smiling at a cashier in the store gave me access to a greater sense of happiness. And it didn't even matter if she smiled back! I was making a conscious choice how I was going to meet the world on my terms and it was empowering. Did I still miss my father? Yes! Did I still mourn? Yes!! However the "suffering" that I was enduring was no longer a part of my healing process. I was free to mourn and yet remain joyful and love filled in the midst of my mourning! May sound odd, however, I was able to find a sense of peace that I had never felt before and as you will read later, that was a major turning point in my life. So by changing our physical posture and behavior we are able to change our emotions as well; add to that a change in thought patterns and beliefs and we have the makings of a miracle!

Determining your Spiritual Practice Paradigm

No one can tell you what you believe. Beliefs are like fingerprints, each person has his/her own unique set. Though your parents and teachers and ministers and friends have told you things over the years, it was *you* who decided to believe them or not. As each piece of information comes before you, you weigh it on the scale of your former beliefs which might already be off kilter but none the less it is the tool you use. Suppose someone comes to you and asks what you think of the guy running for President. You will answer based upon all of the information you have taken in and weighed about this person and then and only then do you have an answer that is subjectively based on your beliefs. You may not like him because of how he looks. He might remind you of Frankenstein and because you can't get past how he looks, you can't hear what he says. You have judged him through your filter as being unworthy of being President because you do not like how he looks. Never mind the fact that he might be able to end world hunger and war, you don't like how he looks! To do this means that somewhere you hold a belief about people's appearances equating with their value and effectiveness.

This belief may have come from your 5th grade teacher who said something about the girl sitting next to you not becoming class president because of how her hair was cut and you took that statement and established a belief about it and then lived your life weighing things against that belief. The good news is that if you made the choice to believe it then you can make the choice to believe something different!

We each make up our minds to follow the religion in which we were raised. My parents were Christian so I became Christian. If I am born in a Hindu part of the world, most likely I will practice Hinduism just as I would practice Islam if born to a Muslim family and Buddhism if born in a Buddhist family and so on. There is absolutely nothing wrong with that. The potential dilemma comes when we believe our way is the ONLY way and so we condemn and judge and in many parts of the world, kill others for being different. These blasphemous outcasts are judged as wrong, sinful, and unworthy of life!

Many people never question their faith and that also is fine. As I said before, in the absolute, it is all good. As is those who do decide to question, to investigate, and inquire a bit deeper, what is this that I believe and why? If I say that I am a Christian, what does that mean? If I say that I am a Baptist or a Pentecostal Christian, what do either of those labels mean? Many people leave one church for another because they no longer believe what is being preached at one location, they have changed their minds. Again, you will read my story a little later about how and why I left a more fundamentalist or traditional Christian faith to become a New Thought Ancient Wisdom metaphysical Christian minister, teacher, and practitioner, as well as, an interfaith/Interspiritual minister. In essence, I changed my mind because I out grew the limitations I found in the dogma of scarcity and fear consciousness.

It is time to consciously make choices that will empower you and assist you in this journey you have incarnated to take. It is time to decide what to believe, why to believe it and how to put it into practice. This is what it means in James 2:14-26, "Faith without works is dead." If you are not a living manifestation of your faith then your faith is dead, it is fruitless, and barren.

Why have a faith that you are not living?

This is an interesting question because in reality each of us is in fact living according to what we have faith in. Having faith in a government system of improper use of power will result in your living one way where as having faith in a government system of democracy will result in your living in a different way. Faith in lack and scarcity will out-picture in your life as someone fearful, hoarding and competing to get what you can because there isn't enough for everyone versus living with a faith in an abundant universe where there is plenty for all out-pictures as peace, sharing, and compassion.

It simply does not matter what you believe in—it will show up as your life in expression. There is no way around that! The question then becomes yet again—are you satisfied with what it showing up? Are you satisfied with how you feel on a daily basis? Are you living a consciously aware life and are you living from the higher consciousness of the Christ? If you find yourself unsatisfied, suffering, discontent, struggling, angry, confused, bored, in the dark, and in a place where you know the real you, the authentic you is not being expressed, then it is time to put into practice a new series of beliefs and faith; because as you believe within so it will be lived on the outside.

Are you willing to accept that you are the Christ? Is that too much for you to receive? If it is too much why is that so? Do you feel that you are somehow unworthy? Not spiritual enough? That the Christ is only a title or consciousness for Jesus? Pay close attention to what I am about to say to you AGAIN so you get this!

The Aramaic Bible in Plain English says in John 14:12 "Timeless truth, I tell you: 'whoever believes in me, those works which I have done he will also do, and he will do greater works than these, because I am going to the presence of my Father.'" Jesus or Yeshua, as he was called in his original Aramaic language, is saying that he did a series of works and than those who believe can not only do the works he did but can do even greater works. And earlier in chapter 14 we see how it is that we can do this.

8 Philippus said to him, "Our Lord, show us The Father, and it is sufficient for us."

9 Yeshua said to him, "All this time I am with you and you have not known me Phillip? Whoever has seen me has seen The Father, and how do you say, 'Show us The Father'?"

10 "Do you not believe that I am in my Father and my Father in me? The words which I am speaking, I am not speaking from myself, but my Father who dwells within me, he does these works.

Yeshua (Jesus) tells them plainly that he and God are one. By seeing him you are seeing God. He continues to say that it is God who does the works and not he himself . . . therefore if He is telling us in verse 12 that we can also do these works, he is clearly saying that God also is in us and does the works through us as he has done through Jesus!

The kingdom of heaven is within, it is not in some far off skyward place . . . seek first the kingdom and all else will be added to you. When we know our divine birthright as brothers and sisters of Jesus, just as divine as him, then we are able to make use of the faith of the mustard seed and move the mountains in our lives. It is here that the Goliaths fall to our feet. It is here that we raise the dead in consciousness and dead in spirit. It is here that we give sight to the blind. It is here that we feed the multitudes and it is here that we heal the sick and infirm, and are fully present with the I AM that is us!

I am an avid movie watcher and I always tend to look at them from the metaphysical perspective and while I enjoy the movies I am also watching for what the movie is teaching me about me. Regarding this idea of beliefs and what is happening in our mind, I am reminded of a particular scene that I love in the last of the Harry Potter books (and movies). This scene shows this mysterious heavenly place where Harry now dead, has a chat with is teacher, mentor and friend Dumbledore—

"Tell me one last thing," said Harry. "Is this real? Or has this been happening inside my head?"

Dumbledore replies, "Of course it is happening inside your head, Harry, but why on earth should that mean that it is not real?"

Profound!! . . . Why do we, like Harry assume and believe that the thoughts, ideas, images that happen in our minds are somehow not real? According to many quantum physicists and spiritual masters, that which is happening in our minds is *more* real than what we call real! So it is of paramount importance that we become conscious creators of our lives because as has been said already repeatedly—Our thoughts are things! What are your thoughts creating today?

Creating A Spiritual Practice

Your spiritual practice is what you do on a daily basis to align yourself with your true self, your true nature, your Highest Self the Christ / Buddha, which you are. Do you pray? If so how do you pray? I ask this because there are more effective and less effective ways to pray. We will discuss that a little more in depth momentarily. Do you meditate? Do you exercise? Do you treat yourself to treatments like a massage or Reiki? Do you read spiritual and inspiring materials? Do you creatively express the divinity that you are by being of service to the community? Do you read inspiring and empowering books? Do you fellowship with other like minded people? What do you do to embody and align with the God of your being?

There are millions if not billions of ways that you can practice spirituality. I say billions, which is a lot, because anything you do while in a state of mindfulness is a spiritual practice! Cooking while being present and mindful makes preparing the meal a spiritual practice because you are present and consciously aware of all you are doing. Your mind is not on work while your body chops carrots. Washing the dishes can be spiritual, doing the laundry, writing a letter, cutting the grass, it all can be a spiritual practice; even having sex while being mindful is a spiritual practice. "WHOA!" I can almost hear some of you gasp when I put sex and spiritual practice in the same category! I know, I know, and yes—I know. Believe me I do! So much of our culture, our religious dogma, our domestication, and mainstream puritanical beliefs prohibit to a large degree still hold sex as an immoral sinful act which should only be done for procreation, in the confines of marriage, and for many should not be enjoyed too much. In light of that limiting belief about sex, it most certainly cannot in any way shape or form be considered a spiritual act.

For those who are more "traditional" in their belief, let's look at this for a moment. Did God create us? Yes. Did God create us with genitals? Yes. They came from somewhere! Do genitals feel pleasure? Yes. Therefore does it make sense that God created our sex organs in the manner in which they were created which feel pleasure then God knowingly created us to enjoy sex? Enough said and I rest my case. Sex, like money can be used in less conscious ways or more conscious ways. It can be satisfying to the ego or to the soul. Before we judge it and condemn it as less spiritual, I share these words worthy of remembering. Dr. Rosenthal said, "What isn't spiritual? We're spiritual beings. Everything we do is spiritual, including pooping in the morning! That's very spiritual." Sex therefore is also spiritual. How you practice it is the key. Whether consciously as an act of union expressing love, compassion, and joining of energies or through abuse, rape, degradation, manipulation, or simple gratification is your choice.

We tend to fear sex and so we judge it as wrong, sinful, and evil and it is precisely because of this fear that our culture is proliferated with images of sexuality, pornography, and a multitude of what we consider sexual perversions. It is also why, out of fear and ignorance that many still consider homosexuality a sin. Our religious institutions have made not only homosexuality as sin but it is also sinful to engage in sex before marriage and even then there are certain sexual practices that are still forbidden. I am not debating the morality of premarital sex or anything else I have mentioned. What I am saying is that rather than letting someone dictate what is and is not healthy for you, you should decide what you believe and why and live accordingly. Is sex evil to you? Is it a sin to you? Can you find the spiritual in sex? Those are questions you have to answer for yourself. I simply point out that sex can be spiritual when practiced from the paradigm I am speaking about.

Something closely related to the taboos of sex is the naked body, which is something that encourages lust and so we judge nudity as evil and sinful. If it is evil, what about Adam and Eve, as the story states, were created nude! Clearly God did not see nudity as a problem. If God didn't see it as a problem, where did this issue come from? It was those early church forefathers who had the problem with it and labeled so much of our humanness carnal, taboo, and sinful.

Sex, eating, cooking, driving your car, taking a plane ride, and taking a walk through the middle of Times Square can all be as spiritual as sitting in a meditative state in an ashram or Zen garden all by yourself. The state of mind you are in while doing these things is what determines the level of consciousness and awareness and level of spiritual practice. You could be sitting at your altar, your candles lit and your nostrils taking in the sweet incense that is burning as you quietly sit in a meditative stance. Outwardly, you appear to be engaged in a deep meditation and yet if your mind is busy with a "To Do" list of what all needs done when you complete your 30 minutes of meditation, were you even meditating at all? You are not present, you are not aware and you are not connected to the Source of all that is if you are scattered mentally.

See everything as part of your practice and you will notice huge changes in your life! I can't remember where I heard this but I always love to hold it in mind since I am someone who at times has experienced or exhibited mild road rage tendencies (smile); confession time again I guess. The quote basically says, "If you ever want to know how spiritual your teacher is, get in the car and take a ride with them and you will see just how spiritual they are." In other words, in the simple act of driving, the spiritual master will show you just how spiritual he or she is by how they behave while driving!! You might want to take the bus if we ever hang out . . . Just kidding ☺

You might be wondering though why I experience road rage—One of my pet peeves is when people do not obey the laws. It sometimes bothers my ego when I see people changing lanes without using turn signals, exceeding the posted speed limit in excess (80 in a 55 for example), and driving while texting or talking on the phone (holding the phone versus hands free). I realized that by allowing my ego to get upset, the "I" that "I AM" was relinquishing my power. I was then co-creating by default through my complaint more of the very thing I was complaining about. What you resist persist! It is only when I am more mindful and aware of what I am doing as the operator of the vehicle that I find greater peace. I either manifest more people driving as safe and mindful drivers which I affirm that I will see when on the road or I am no longer emotionally invested when I do see the occasional speeder or non-light using lane changer. In those moments, driving the car becomes a spiritual practice for me because I am spiritually aware and mindfully practicing that awareness from my higher self instead of ego.

This is why I emphasize that *everything* you do, when done from that state of mindfulness, spiritual awareness is part of your spiritual practice . . . even going to the bathroom. Thank you, Dr. Rosenthal for that reminder.

CHAPTER EIGHT:

WHAT NOW? CHOP WOOD CARRY WATER. . .

So now that you have reached that state of Enlightenment . . . (smile) . . . Now what do you do?

Hmmm, do you go out and put an end to world hunger, do you multiply fishes and loaves; do you raise the dead, walk on water, fly around the world like Superman patrolling the planet and ending wars and famine? Ok so that would all be cool and nice if it is what happened after enlightenment and funny thing is that in a way you are going to be doing that however, it will be more through your everyday activities as the ancient sages used to say . . . Before enlightenment—chop wood, carry water; after enlightenment—chop wood, carry water.

Before you start telling me, as some of my students have done, that you have no wood to chop or water to carry, let's put this in modern day terms.

Before enlightenment—drop kids off at soccer practice, pick up dry cleaning. After enlightenment—stop off at post office and fix dinner.

There you have it. There is no magical floating off to live high on some ethereal mountain once you become enlightened. Your life continues, on the surface, as it has. One major difference is that you realize now that every action is part of your spiritual journey. Before, during and after this thing called enlightenment, which is simply waking up to the Truth and living the Truth that is now known, you live your life. Before you awaken, you live your life and after awakening you live your life. I will reiterate this point again in case you missed it the first time . . . do not expect bells and whistles! I have had moments of being awake and I believe that those moments could have lasted longer had I not expected things to change in some magical way.

Somehow, I expected to feel differently. I thought maybe my physical strength would increase or maybe I would suddenly have a halo or golden aura that all could see like in the old Renaissance paintings of Jesus and the saints. Silly? Yes, I know, but growing up with the desire to become a superhero, I developed an image of what would happen when I became "enlightened." Ironically, it was that very image that kept me asleep in many ways.

What I found years later, was that like waking in the morning from a night filled with dreams, I simply awake and once awake I go about my day as a man who is awake. I do not expect the illusions of last night's dreams to show up while I am awake. The goblins, faeries, unicorns, dragons, and such of my dreams do not follow me to my waking consciousness. I don't get on an elevator and see the zombies from my dreams buying coffee or the vampires and mermaids getting in line at the grocery store. Likewise, upon awakening or becoming enlightened, the illusions of life do not follow me. I have the ability to see and live according to the Truth, all the while still going about my daily life doing laundry. The difference is that now I do laundry as a man who is awake.

What does it mean to be awake, to live awake, and to embrace your ordinary life knowing that it is extraordinary?

Waking up occurs when you have an experiential knowing of the Truth. "Then you will know the truth and the truth will set you free (John 8:32)." You will KNOW. It is that knowing that makes the difference. It's like the old G.I. Joe cartoon characters used to say, "Knowing is half the battle!" And like Oprah is fond of reminding and teaching others, "When you know better you do better." So you see it is quite important to know experientially versus just intellectually. There are many theologians who know *about* God but they do not *know* God. It is one thing to know *about* the people or the faith of Islam, Buddhism, or Judaism but until you know someone personally there is a closeness, a personal, and compassionate intimacy that is missing.

When you really think about it there are certain concepts that no matter how much you describe to someone, they will never know until they experience it for themselves. For example, try describing chocolate to someone who has never tasted it or seen it. They have only heard of it. No amount of describing will ever give them the experience of tasting chocolate. How do you describe a sunset to a person who is blind? They know what a sunset is intellectually and can attest to the shifting in temperatures as the sun goes down however; the visual beauty that so many speak of is missing experientially. Think about how many things we take for granted on a daily basis that are purely experiential and cannot be described.

And then we come to a huge concept that people are killing others over and are committing suicide in the name of . . . and denying people their rights of life, liberty, and the pursuit of happiness because of their intellectual understanding of this word "God." Three simple letters can in no way shape or form encapsulate the Isness and Allness that is God!

The *word* sunset does not contain the beauty, the awe, or the total majesty that you feel when you see a sunset. There have been people who say that they have had a spiritual experience when taking in the beauty of a sunset; this is what it means to know a sunset versus to know about one. Yet there are many people who expect something different when it comes to God. Many people demand a form of reverence for their concept of God which is based on the intellectual understanding of the word God. Their demands are based upon their understanding of a word that is used to label something that cannot be labeled. It is not possible for that word or that label to satisfy anyone spiritually any more than the word food can satisfy a starving child. In order to have hunger satisfied, the person must experience food by eating, thirst by drinking, a sunset by seeing . . . these must be experienced. Likewise, God must be experienced!

This whole concept of knowing experientially versus intellectually reminds me of one of my biggest religious debates which occurred many years ago. This debate was sparked by a comment during a bible study when a friend made about Tia Turner after seeing a movie called "What's Love Got To Do With It," which was about Tina's life. After seeing the movie, my friend called Tina Turner, of all things, a "devil worshipper." At that time, while I clearly knew who she was and I was familiar with her music, I wasn't really familiar with many of the details of her life, so I asked my friend what he meant by his comment. He said that she left her Christian roots to become a Buddhist which made her, in the eyes of the church, a devil worshipper. Still unclear of the details, I asked if he knew why she made the decision to change her faith. My friend couldn't answer; so I made it my business to go see the movie. He told me to be sure to pay attention to a scene where she was chanting or something. So I found when the movie would be on cable again and I made sure to watch.

After watching I found myself oddly conflicted. At that time I was what I would call a moderately conservative or fundamental Christian; which years later I would see was because I felt a need to fit in and be absolved of my sins, rather than because I believed in every aspect of the dogma of the religion. Anyway, after viewing the film, I felt a sense of pride that she found the strength to live her life on her terms and where I saw strength my friend and many of the others at the bible study found betrayal, blasphemy, and demonic forces at work! And the more I argued the more they held their grounds with blind faith, unwilling to even listen to what I was saying. I left not only that Bible study group but I also left those friends. I tell you this story because for me it illustrated at that time of my life how limited many people are about the concept of God. It's as if God is a formula that can be explained as simply as 2 + 2 = 4 or God is some pretty trinket that can be kept in a nice neat little box and pulled out each Sunday for people to see. I had a realization that this power we call God, was what Tina Turner experienced on the path called Buddhism, and for someone else the path would be Hinduism, for another Islam, and another Christianity, and even within the Christian journey there are the Baptist, the Catholic, the Methodist, Lutheran paths as well as the many others. There is no one road, no one path that all are expected to walk. God is far more than our human experience can fully grasp. We must evolve from our myopic point of view about God and stop looking to the heavens for some kind of Zeus or Odin type of anthropomorphic deity who is jealous, judging, biased and temperamental, God will never truly be experienced or known for as long as we hold that limited point of view. If you look at the world through the peep hole in your door, how much of the world are you really seeing and can you judge the world based upon such a limited view? And can you dictate to me what I should do when what you see from your door and what I see from mine are in fact different?

Waking up begins by realizing and understanding that God is within each and every one of us and in everything. I always mention over and over again how much I love George Lucas' description of The Force in Star Wars when Jedi Master Obi-Wan Kenobi describes the Force as "an energy field that surrounds and penetrates living beings and binds the galaxy together." His description is quite close to the truth of God and is far closer than the old white haired man in the sky concept; though it is still not all encompassing or experiential. For the Jedi to use the powers offered by the Force, they had to learn to experience it. Another powerful scene which I briefly mentioned earlier from The Empire Strikes Back shows Jedi Master Yoda teaching Padawan Luke Skywalker. Luke is being asked to use the Force to levitate his X-Wing aircraft from the Dagobah swamp.

After seeing the X-Wing sink deeper into the swamp, Luke woefully says, "Now I'll never get it out."

"So certain are you. Always with you what cannot be done. Hear you nothing that I say?" "Master, moving stones around is one thing, this is totally different."

"No! No different! Only different in your mind. You must unlearn what you have learned."

"Alright, I'll give it a try," he responds. Yoda quickly responds, "No, try not! Do or do not, there is no try."

Luke closes his eyes and extends his arm and the craft begins to stir in the water and begins to rise, Yoda looks on with an expression of gleeful expectation, however, Luke's attention is disturbed or he doubts again and the craft sinks back into the water deeper than it was before he began. Luke winded, falls to the ground and says, "I can't, it's too big."

"Size matters not. Look at me, judge me by my size do you?"

Luke shakes his head.

"As well you should not, for my ally is the Force and a powerful ally it is. Life creates it, makes it grow. Its energy surrounds us and binds us. Luminous beings are we not this crude matter. You must feel the Force around you; here, between you, me, the tree, the rock, everywhere, yes. Even between the land and the ship."

Luke stands and walks away saying, "You want the impossible."

Yoda sighs, closes his eyes and raises his hand. His face showing a sense of calm focus as the X-Wing begins to stir in the water and rises higher and higher until it is above the swamp and being guided onto dry land. R2-D2, toots and whistles ecstatically with excitement calling out to Luke. Luke stands to see what R2 wants. He stands in amazement to see the ship being lifted, guided, and gently placed upon the ground by his master who is using the power of the Force. Luke touches the ship as if it were a dream or illusion standing before him.

Luke, in shock says, "I don't, I don't believe it."

To which Yoda responds, "That is why you fail."

Luke was unable at that time to let go and fully experience the power that was available to him. He was still stuck in the ego state of impossible, can't, and the other judgments of what should be. It wasn't until later in his training that Luke was able to, as we are so fond of saying, let go and let God or in the world of Star Wars let go and let the Force be with him. Until then he was not able to fully make use of the power available to him. This is waking up.

Waking up is the process of seeing beyond the physical and illusions of the material manifest realm. You see God in every man, woman, and child, you see God in both the friend and the foe. Mother Theresa and Hitler both are divine! Mother Theresa used her divinity on purpose and Hitler misused his. Think about it in math terms, both were math geniuses however Mother Theresa used her skills to get the best possible answers to benefit all and Hitler who was living from his ego, did not care and came up with the worst possible answers. Waking up is seeing that like snowflakes are individualized manifestations of water and show up with their own uniqueness as individualized manifestations of the Divine, each of us, share the same common element of our source. Snowflakes are all water and in this instance we are all God!

Waking us is seeing the reality of lack and scarcity yet knowing that what is real does not make it truth. The reality of lack and scarcity are illusions and while they may be based on facts in this manifest physical world, they are not based on truths. The fact was that Luke's ship was in the swamp. The fact was that the ship weighed a certain amount of weight as did Luke. The fact was that the size of the ship was larger than that of Luke. The fact was that Luke lacked the required amount of belief to do what Yoda was telling him to do. However, the Truth was that the ship could be moved. The fact that was Yoda, despite his size knew it could be moved and demonstrated this truth to Luke. The fact was that Lazarus was dead and buried; the truth was that there is no death and so Jesus raised him from the "dead."

Have you ever been to a magic show? You see the magician cut a woman in half and though it appears real you know it is an illusion! Like the magician's trick, everything in this physical manifest world is an illusion. It is not what it appears to be. You think the chair you sit on is real? For the quantum scientist, the chair is made up of mostly empty space yet for us it seems quite solid. Then there is the perplexing concept of time. Time seems real and limited, finite and seems to go in a linear manner yet the truth is that time is infinite and time is more spiral or fractal as Greg Braden describes in his book "Fractal Time" and not linear at all. So this concept of time being linear, limited, and fleeting is a man made construct to make living and planning more convenient. Yet, we get lost in this illusion by obsessing with the past and worrying about the future. Our freedom comes when we can wake up and dispel the illusions and remain in the present. It means you continue to use your day planner or blackberry to plan your appointments and your "To Do list," however; you are not bound to and enslaved by the calendar, the clock, or the never ending list of things to do. You realize that you can at any moment step out of time and embrace the power of the now.

"Life is now. There was never a time when your life was not now, nor will there ever be."
**Eckhart Tolle, The Power of Now

"To be free of time is to be free of the psychological need of past for your identity and future for your fulfillment"
**Eckhart Tolle, The Power of Now

So yes you do the same daily activities you would normally do, go to work, go on vacation, do laundry, cook dinner, buy new clothes, and get the car repaired; the difference is that prior to waking, you did them from an unconscious default setting of being asleep. You did them on autopilot and from the consciousness of the illusion being real where you may have believed that if you did not get something done on time, the world would end. You catastrophized many experiences and suffered as a result. Awake, you now know that you are in charge and you determine what gets done and when and why. You realize that though your boss may place a demand upon you that is unrealistic due to the time constraints, when you are in a place of calm, you find that you actually have "more" time and you get more things done rather than always feeling like you are racing against the clock. Even more empowering is that you realize that if you no longer desire to live under the dictates of your boss, you have the option to leave and work elsewhere or even start your own business. These are options that the sleeping person would never consider due to the fear of the unknown.

Awake you no longer shop for clothes or cars or computers or other material trappings of the world because of what your ego says you need to somehow validate you. Awake you no longer engage in the petty dramas of one person's ego as it attempts to spar with you; you have nothing to prove or to defend. You cannot be insulted. You cannot be offended. Awake, you communicate and move through life with a fluidity and a calmness as you know that all things are happening just as they are meant to happen. Awake you know that you, like the master teacher Jesus, have the ability to see beyond a disease, illness, sense of lack, or scarcity and seeing and knowing the truth you can align with the Divine One Source and in alignment God energy moves through you to affect and in essence shift the vibration of the illusion and bring health, wholeness, healing and abundance to the situation.

So if our call is to live as men and women who are awake, the question again is how do we wake up?

When you engage in those spiritual practices I mentioned in the previous chapter, you will wake up. It is not a question of IF you will wake up; waking up is inevitable for all of us at some point in this life experience or some other. The spiritual practices are less like an alarm clock telling you that the time for waking has arrived; they are more like a gentle nudge from a parent letting you know that it is time to get up. The first nudge you may only roll over. The next nudge you may open your eyes, yawn, nod your head but as soon as they leave the room you are sleep again. The third time it's almost like you sensed it and you wake before they nudge you again and this time you get up and start your day. It can also be likened to lucid dreaming where you know you are asleep and dreaming and because of this knowing you can affect the surrounding and experiences within the dream and then in time can actually tell yourself to wake up and you do!

Will you ever fall asleep again? More than likely you will. Most of us do, however, we do not have to fall back into that deep sleep where we are completely oblivious as the proverbial shit hits the fan. What is preferred is that if sleep is inevitable then let it be short cat naps, here and there. There will be times when someone cuts you off in traffic and you react from that place of illusion, ego, sleep and then there will be those times an irate cashier cannot disturb the calm sea of your consciousness no matter how much they raise their voice and tell you that you cannot have the shirt for the sale price because the sale ended yesterday even though the sale sign is still up.

When we build our daily practice to include meditation, prayer, visioning, and we engage in mindfulness and exercise our awareness regularly, our momentary cat naps will become more like power naps because even when asleep we are awake on some level . . . like in the movie The Matrix. Even when Neo was plugged into the machine system and his body was in effect asleep or inactive, his mind, his consciousness was wide awake and aware!

From the newness of this "awake" life you also realize that nothing in life is "ordinary." You begin to see the uniqueness and specialness in everyone and everything. You greet each person with a consciousness of *"Tashi Delay"* which is a Tibetan greeting meaning "I honor the greatness in you." Or Namaste, which has many translations such as, "I recognize that within each of us is a place where Divinity dwells, and when we are in that place, we are One." You see God in all! And when you see God in everyone and everything, you understand that everything is extraordinary. The rain falling on a spring morning inspires a sense of wonderment and awe as does the autumn leaves changing color, the smell of the morning air on a cold cool summer day, the daily activities like cutting grass, washing dishes, vacuuming the floor; *all* then become sacred events filled with the presence of God. In this place you are living a sacred life!

CHAPTER NINE:
MOUNTAIN OR MOLEHILL

Many times as a child I heard some adult admonishing someone not to make a mountain out of a molehill. It wasn't until maybe middle school that I finally remembered to investigate further and so I asked a teacher I had at the time, Mrs. Kukic, and she explained to me that it meant to take something small and blow it out of proportion like getting a paper cut and running around screaming that you are bleeding to death, you need the ambulance, and stitches. Though her analogy made us both laugh, it made the saying quite clear to me and made it clear in a way that also made me uncomfortable.

I had been a person who was guilty of doing precisely that, 'blowing things out of proportion." If a friend, other classmates or even a teacher gave me an "off" look or said something that I could interpret in a negative way, I seemed to always tend towards the negative and made it out that the person did not like me or even hated me. And to illustrate what I mean by something I could interpret negatively suppose I was in art class and the teacher was going around the room and when she reached the table where John and I sat, she said to him, "Very Nice John" and to me she said "Nice Job Ray." I would hear that because mine was not *very* nice like John's mine was merely nice it was the same as being bad! And so went much of my young childhood process of self-criticism, judgment, and self loathing! I had become quite the architect when it came to taking that molehill and making it into an elaborate mountain.

Based upon things that I hear when I coach or counsel people on spiritual matters, or when I simply engage in conversations or over hear people talking, people seem to like making their problems larger than they are. Again, it's like the fish story, when the men would come back and talk about the one that got away. It was always such a huge whale of a beast that got away in comparison to the average sized one that they caught. While this type of banter is playful and not harmful since all generally know what is in fact happening, there is the flip side where we do a similar thing which I call the error of "What If!"

There are many people who will sit and practice how a phone conversation MIGHT go in order to make sure they are in control or that they know ALL of the possible outcomes so they can ALWAYS be prepared for the worst. If the best happens, great, but if the worst happens they want to be prepared in advance. So they "*what if*" all possible sides of a conversation to be prepared and in control; which is only an illusion of control and is one sided because most people never *what if* the positive.

Negative: "If I call and ask them for a different delivery date, what if they say Monday is the only day, I will say this and then what if they say no, I will say this and what if, what if what if . . .!!"

Positive; "If I call and ask them for a different date, what if they say they can accommodate whatever I need?"

In what world is this negative form of *what if* healthy and or necessary? Why can you not simply converse naturally and in a relaxed manner accepting the flow of events as they come? So many of us want to have a firm grasp of control on every single aspect of life and that simply is not possible nor is it a healthy pursuit. It is time for us to begin to quiet our minds and realize that the boulder we are faced with is in reality a pebble that can be easily tossed aside. We need not endlessly wrestle with our obstacles as Sisyphus did; we can shed the chains and be free of the mountain any time we are ready.

I make this being free thing sound so simple don't I? I know I do and it is because I learned the hard way that it is simple! And the funny thing is that it is something I am still learning with each new experience and what it brings me to learn about myself. With each experience I have the option of seeing it through the eyes of love or the eyes of fear. And I mean each and every experience.

The person you love no longer wants to be married to you. Do you see with eyes of love which will first accept what was said without judgment or retaliation of any kind including trying to convince them otherwise? Simply accept what they have said with no resistance to it. It is what it is. The old Taoist story about the farmer illustrates this point about non-resistance. Enjoy.

So you know, Taoism refers to a philosophy that emphasizes living in a state of harmony with the Tao which is the source and essence of everything that exists.

Once upon a time there was a Taoist farmer. One day the Taoist farmer's only horse broke out of the corral and ran away. Each of the farmer's neighbors, all hearing of the horse running away, came one by one, to the Taoist farmer's house to view the corral. As they stood there staring at the empty corral, the neighbors all said, "Oh what bad luck!"

The Taoist farmer replied, "Maybe it is, maybe it isn't."

About a week later, the horse returned however it did not return alone. It returned, bringing with it an entire herd of wild horses, which the Taoist farmer and his son quickly corralled. The neighbors, once again hearing the news, this time of the corralling of the horses, came to see for themselves. As they stood there looking at the corral no longer empty but filled with horses, the neighbors said, "Oh what good luck!"

The Taoist farmer replied, "Maybe it is, maybe it isn't."

One day the son, while marveling at the beautiful stallions, decided to begin to break them one by one. One of the horses bucked and threw him violently to the ground. The son broke his leg and as a result became quite ill. Each of the farmer's neighbors, all hearing of the son's injury and consequent illness, came to see for themselves, to view the son lying unconscious in bed. As they stood there staring at the young man, the neighbors all said, "Oh what bad luck!"

The Taoist farmer replied, "Maybe it is, maybe it isn't."

While all of this was happening, beyond the farmlands, at that same time in China, there was a war going on between two rival warlords. The warlord of the Taoist farmer's village was one who was involved in this bitter war. In need of more soldiers, he sent one of his captains to the neighboring villages to enlist young men to fight in the war.

When the captain came to take the Taoist farmer's son, he found the young man with a broken leg and delirious with fever. Knowing there was no way the son could fight in his present condition, the captain left him there. A few days later, the son's fever broke and he was awake and no longer delirious. The neighbors, hearing of the son's not being taken to fight in the war and of his return to good health, all came to see him for themselves. As they stood there, each one said, "Oh what good luck!"

The Taoist farmer replied, "Maybe it is, maybe it isn't."

It is neither good nor bad; it simply is and again as Shakespeare said, there is nothing neither good nor bad but thinking makes it so. Meaning it is your thinking that determines if something is good or if it is bad, not the thing itself.

Eyes of fear go on the defensive. What will I do if they leave me? I can't be alone! You can't leave me! I won't let you! Please stay, why don't you love me? What did I do wrong? Love accepts that it may very well be time for the person to move on and as nature abhors a vacuum, their absence in your life opens you to a new mate or new possibilities that you were not open to while in that particular relationship. Love allows you to be free. Yes you will miss the person and may mourn and feel lonely, however, because you see it through the eyes of love, you will find peace far sooner than the person clinging with a death grip due to fear. Fear will keep you bound to the corpse of their memory, bound to the guilt and shame of the relationship not working out and how and why it didn't as you point the finger of blame; blaming both yourself and blaming them for what should have or what could have been!

We can do this with the less frequent events, as well as, what I am going to call the regular everyday events, like shopping where someone bumps into your cart or steps in line in front of you and you go off into all the reasons that person is rude, has offended you, needs to pay attention, has some nerve, etc. Is that being seen through the eyes of love or those of fear? Even if the person was deliberately getting in line in front of you, why react with anger which is a side-effect of fear? "Sometimes letting things go is an act of far greater power than defending or hanging on." ** Eckhart Tolle

The racism that created segregation was responded to by the civil rights movement which Rev. Dr. Martin Luther King Jr. was involved as were many others. I however want to specifically address him and a man who influenced his non-violent method of protest, that man being Mohandas K.

Gandhi. Both King and Gandhi believed that injustice could be overcome with compassion and love as they responded to injustice not with violence but with peace. Eckhart Tolle reminds us that, "Anything that you resent and strongly react to in another is also in you." To resist racism from the position of the ego indicates that racism or prejudice exists within you. There is a much healthier, holistic, and spiritual solution that is permanent rather than some of the social bandages in place and that solution is—Love.

"Nonviolence springs from love, cowardice from hate." **Gandhi

"A coward is incapable of exhibiting love; it is the prerogative of the brave." **Gandhi

"Where there is love there is life." **Gandhi

"Love is the strongest force the world possesses, and yet it is the humblest imaginable." **Gandhi

"Whenever you are confronted with an opponent, conquer him with love." **Gandhi

They eyes of love allow you to keep the molehill a molehill which in turn keeps you in a place of serenity and peace and from that consciousness you are far better equipped to see the situations or events in life as a mature and enlightened creator rather than an immature unenlightened reactor. As I said before it really does not matter what the event, you can see it for what it is or you can blow it out of proportion and make it an insurmountable mountain. The adolescent girl who sees a pimple the day of her prom can react as hysterically as the person who is told their flight is delayed, and as strongly as the person diagnosed with cancer. In perspective we can clearly see which one potentially warrants the hysterical reaction however in the moment each of these people responds based upon how they will perceive the mountain. Even something as unwanted as a diagnosis of terminal cancer or what my father was diagnosed with when I was about eight years old, Amyotrophic Lateral Sclerosis (ALS or Lou Gehrig's disease) can be taken calmly and dealt with from a sense of calm, a consciousness of love and of well being rather than from fear. It is quite possible. My father overall maintained an optimistic attitude and persisted though he was given two to four years to live and I will talk more about that particular situation later in the book in the chapter entitled "My Story", for now I mention it to say that it really does not matter what the doctor says and I say that for two reasons.

One: There have been countless times that a doctor gave someone the prognosis of how a disease will advance and claim a person's life and yet the person was cured, healed, and lived life disease free or lived well past the prognosis because the disease either went into remission or moved far slower than the doctor anticipated. Either way, the doctor's word was not the final say in the matter.

Two: There are those who do die as a result of the disease and yet for those who see death not as an end but as a new beginning, for what the caterpillar calls death the butterfly calls life. This second point of view is a more enlightened way of living, but it is by far the more empowering as well for there is no resistance and no attachment to the prognosis of what the doctors have said. If you heal and live, then you heal and live and yet if it is time for you to make the transition from the physical, back to pure potential in the Divine, then so be it.

As Byron Katie said, "The only time we suffer is when we believe a thought that argues with what is." She goes on to say that, "When the mind is clear, what is, is what we want." Meaning we realize that this disease, the bad marriage, this disobedient child, being laid off from work, is what we want to experience! On the physical ego level of consciousness of course, it is easy to disagree with this idea and we resist it by saying there is no way we would ever want such a thing in our lives . . . who wants to be sick!? Yet, time and time again cancer survivors have said that having cancer was the best thing that could have happened to them for it taught them how to live and love. Or for the woman who says getting divorced was the best thing to happen to her because it taught her how to forgive, how to live free, and how to live and independent life knowing that they she need not be dependent on a man. "Within each experience there is an opportunity for our growth as we realize that we are the creators of our own experience" as my friend Laura Shepard is fond of reminding those she teaches and coaches.

Laura likens our lives or experiences to a pot of soup and within each person's pot there are various ingredients that make up the soup and that even when both you and I have a pot of chicken noodle soup my ingredients will vary from yours. Mine may have less pepper and yours may have more meat never the less it is still chicken noodle soup. Each of us has within our consciousness various "ingredients" or beliefs that shape who we are and how we live out our lives. Those people who make mountains out of molehills have a belief, an ingredient in their consciousness, their pot of soup that inclines them to do this and for them it serves some purpose that offers them more opportunity to wake up. When they take the time to be more aware, their underlying beliefs begin to surface and they can see what is working for them or against them. From this kind of heightened awareness you see why you created the disease, dysfunction, or despair that is showing up in your experience. And so you know, Laura extends your circle of experience to include anything you hear about or see. For example, if you hear about the earthquake in Japan, it means that on some vibratory, energetic, level you created or resonated with the experience because it has shown up on your radar so to speak. Everything that shows up in your experience is there as a result of some co-created demonstration. Not only that, but it is also showing up for a reason—nothing is random or merely coincidental. Deep huh? Yeah I know. It took me some time to grasp that concept but the more I listened to the teachings of Abraham-Hicks, which Laura credits with helping her to shift her paradigm from a person who practiced depression for years to the person she is ever becoming, the more I got the concept and could apply it to my life consciously. Meaning I can look at various experiences and see how and why I manifested or attracted the experience. I am able to better connect many of the dots, and though there are some dots yet to be connected, I trust the process.

What does it serve you to make a mountain out of a molehill? Does it elicit sympathy and pity from others? Does it feel like you have more control? Are you able to get more support from people? If you were not getting some emotional energy from it, you would not do it. Spend some time asking what is the lesson, the gift in blowing things out of proportion? What is the mountain there to teach you? Once you have your answer you will be able to let the boulder shrink down to pebble size and dismiss it. There is great wisdom in the often quoted phrase, "Don't sweat the small stuff; It's all small stuff."

God grant me the serenity to accept the things I cannot change, the courage to change the things I can, and the wisdom to know the difference.

Reinhold Niebuhr

If there is no struggle, there is no progress.
Frederick Douglass

My daily experience, as of those who are working with me, is that every problem lends itself to solution if we are determined to make the law of truth and non-violence the law of life.

Gandhi

CHAPTER TEN:
THE CREATOR IS YOU

In the last chapter I mentioned a concept that stated that you are the creator of your experience and knowing that you are the creator does not mean that as you look at the seeming obstacles in your life, you are able to see how or why you *created* these obstacles. For a more in-depth discourse on the creation process be sure to read the next volume in this series on living a sacred life; the Journey of the Spiritual Warrior. So as we begin this portion of the text I am asking you to simply read and rather than resist the idea, take it in as though it is 100% true. After that you can then decide if it works for you or not and choose to ignore or take some of it and apply it to your own life. OK? Cool . . . Let's begin.

As I have mentioned, your thoughts as well as your words have creative power in creating your experience however, there is something that has more determining power than either of those separately or together. Know what it is? Ok, I'll tell you . . . Your feelings!

Your feelings are the prime substance that not only create but provide ample evidence of what you are creating and what you will continue to create. Meaning if you look to how you are feeling in any given moment, you will have a clear concrete blueprint that shows you what you are creating more of. Feeling angry, then you know you are sending more energy out to the Universe and the Universe will answer your call and give you more to be angry about.

Feeling joy, then the Universe will aid you in manifesting more to be joyful about. While that does seem simple, it is not quite as simple as that because it is a prolonged feeling that is responded to; not the occasional or sudden feeling of anxiety because you are stuck in traffic today and feel anxious because you are late for a major appointment. Now if you feel that anxiety or road rage daily, then you are paving the road with more to have anxiety and rage about. It is the ongoing, consistent, repeated feelings that leverage more power towards the manifestation of like vibration.

> "We have told you that your thoughts are magnetic. But we want to add a point of clarification here: although every thought has creative potential, the thoughts that do not bring great emotion with them are not bringing the subject of your thought into your experience with any sort of speed. When it comes to thoughts that you feel strong emotion about—whether it is positive emotion or negative emotion—the essence of those thoughts is being quickly manifested into your physical experience. And that emotion that you are feeling is communication from your Inner Being, letting you know that you are now accessing the power of the Universe . . .
>
> If you want it and expect it, it will be yours very soon. However, it is not often that you have achieved a balance where your wanting and your expecting are equal. Sometimes your wanting is very high, but the belief is not there at all. For example, in the story of the mother whose child is trapped beneath the automobile, she does not believe that she can lift that heavy vehicle off of her child, but her wanting to is so extreme that she does. On the other hand, there are many examples where your belief is high, but your wanting is not. The creation of an illness, such as cancer, is that sort of example where your belief in it is very keen, while your wanting of it is not.

Many of you find yourselves in what we would term a negative workshop many times a day. As you are sitting at your desk with your stack of bills besides you, feeling tension of even fear because there is not money to pay them, you are in a negative workshop. For as you sit there giving thought to not having enough money, you are in the perfect position for the creating of more of what you do not want. The way you are feeling about that is the signal from your Inner Being saying to you that what you are thinking is not in harmony with what you want.

(Abraham through Esther Hicks, from the book, The Law of Attraction http://spiritlibrary.com/abraham-hicks/my-inner-being-communicates-through-emotion)."

When you do the math, thought plus feeling equals creating you gain a different kind of perspective to this creation process. Thinking of health while feeling the fear of illness will manifest neither healing nor a cure. Ideally, aligning your thoughts and your feelings for approximately 17 seconds of uninterrupted focused concentration will magnify your creative power exponentially! Meaning, if you feel anger as a result of road rage and you are thinking about how stupid these people are consistently focused for as little as 17 seconds on the stupid people on the road and you cuss and swear and complain about them, you are adding more fuel to the fire so to speak and you are actually manifesting more similar experiences to complain about.

"If you can hold a thought, just a simple thought, for 17 seconds, without contradicting it, another thought like it same shape, same size, same vibration, same tone, by law of attraction another thought like it will come to it. And at precisely the 17 second point, these two thoughts will join one another, they coalesce and when they do that there is an energy that is expended, it is like a combustion point. And when these two thoughts join and combust, you can feel a measure of enthusiasm or interest bubbling within you. And in that moment of 17 seconds, these two thoughts that were same become one bigger, more evolved, faster vibrating thought (http://spiritlibrary.com/abraham-hicks/only-17-seconds-away-from-your-true-desires)."

This is why Myrtle Fillmore taught that we should never speak what we do not want to see demonstrated in our lives. And this is why the Bible says according to your faith it is done unto you. If you are complaining about stupid drivers then what you are in fact saying is that you have placed your faith in stupid drivers who do not know how to drive; Eric Butterworth said of our faith, "We all have plenty of faith, it's just that we have faith in the wrong things. We have faith in what can't be done rather than what can be done. We have faith in lack rather than abundance but there is no lack of faith. Faith is a law."

An important thing to remember is that there are many times we will say one thing but feel something different. Our feelings always weigh more on the cosmic scale of creation. If you tell someone you love them but the feeling is one of distrust and insecurity, it will be the feelings that the Law of Attraction will respond to far more than the words which are empty and void of meaning when weighed against the emotions. And remember that emotion is broken down to mean energy + motion = emotion! Your emotions are energy in motion and like energy attracts like energy. Angry energy attracts more angry energy, fear attracts fear, hate attracts hate and love attracts love and joy attracts joy! And there are many times you may not know your deep underlying domesticated and ingrained beliefs; however, your feelings will show you what you believe even when your thoughts may not be clear. Look to the feeling! How are you feeling about a person, place, event, situation, job offer, etc. the feelings will tell you far more than your surface mind, your egoic mind, or your rational mind can. Feelings are tapped into the intuitive mind and are visceral and more truthful.

Therefore, if you start there you have a clear indication what you are in fact creating and what needs healing so the obstacles in your life can be removed, dissolved, transmuted, and overcome.

Do your feelings lie? No. Are our feelings always right? If by right we mean appropriate or aligned with Source, No. There may be mothers who are jealous of their daughters, fathers jealous of their sons, siblings who hate one another. These feelings are not in alignment with Source; however they do clearly indicate where the person is energetically. And like any traveler knows, once you know how far off course you are, you can recalculate and re-chart your course to get to where you desire to be. Do you want to feel jealous? Do you want to feel hate or anger? Do you enjoy feeling that frustration and anxiety? Many people hold on to those negative emotions because they become comfortable and controllable and so people become complacent to remain miserable. Misery loves company and so that energy will continue to bring more misery to you. Great thing is that you can at anytime you are ready, shift the energy, change your life, and create something different.

The moment you stop seeing the boulder before you as an obstacle and see it as an opportunity, the shift occurs. The easiest way to do this is through prayer and meditation because in that place the limitations and appearances of the material world fade away and it becomes easier to see and thus feel the joy, freedom, and love in every situation. This is the daily task of the Lightworkers, the Avatars, the Bodhisattvas, the Shamans, the Spiritual Warriors of the Universe to hold a higher consciousness, a consciousness of Truth and Love despite the appearances and occurrences in the world and from this elevated consciousness create as they desire.

> "You're always getting a perfect vibrational match to what you predominantly give your attention to. But you've got to

> make the best of it. You've got to vibrate slightly different from where you are if you are going to improve where you are. You can't keep taking score of where your business is or your relationship is or your body is without continuing to create it as it is. To make improvement, you've got to reach for a different thought." (Abraham Excerpted from the workshop in Tampa, FL on Saturday, December 6th, 2003 http://www.abraham-hicks.com)

I will add that having read and listened to Abraham for a while now and I believe that the reaching for a different thought is also the reaching for a different feeling as well as different words to speak about your experience. If you want something different you have to believe, think, feel, and speak differently.

Iyanla Vanzant has spoken often about how her welfare consciousness sabotaged her television show and continued to manifest limiting outward experiences to mirror her inner most thoughts and feelings. Until she did the inner work, the outer could not change. Each of us must do the inner and I stress INNER work if we desire to see an outward change in our lives.

> "Take your Inner Being everywhere you go. If you take your Inner Being to the party, it's going to be a good party! If you take your Inner Being, the food that you eat will be received perfectly by the cells of your body. Every word that comes out of your mouth will be beneficial to everyone who hears them with their ears—or with their vibration. Don't go anywhere without your Inner Being. That's what "Allowing" is. Always having your Inner Being present. And then, anything else that happens is always orchestrated perfectly by Law of Attraction."
>
> (Abraham Excerpted from the workshop in El Paso, TX on Saturday, February 17th, 2001 http://www.abraham-hicks.com)

CHAPTER ELEVEN:
DIVINE ORCHESTRA

I grew up in the Star Wars era when George Lucas first released episode four of the saga. One of the first things I did as soon as I left the theatre was to go to the record store to buy the movie soundtrack. Yes this was the pre-CD era. Each time I listened to the John Williams compositions for the film I was transported to that galaxy far, far away. I love the way the orchestra weaved the threads of sound, to evoke a tapestry of images and emotions. Those musical pieces continue to be a source of inspiration to me and I listen to them quite often. The orchestra itself is made up of individual people each of them playing various instruments and all having a particular place to be and a role within the creation process. The orchestra of life is no different. Each person has a role to play in the divine theatre called earth and on this stage of life we are each here to play the part we incarnated to play; to that end everyone has a soundtrack accompanying their story.

For some, their story is like an Hitchcock suspense, for others a George Romero zombie horror, for others a Bradbury sci-fi thriller, and for others a Tyler Perry dramatic comedy and for some a Shakespearean tragedy. There are a myriad of genres that a story can be classified by. Whether yours is a romantic comedy or action adventure or even a fantasy is entirely up to what you have chosen to create. The key is to remember that each person wields the pen and crafts the life of his choosing; Stephen King cannot blame Toni Morrison for altering his stories, Dan

Brown cannot blame Dan Millman for changing his stories. In reality, no one is at fault, no one is to blame, not even you because as I have reminded you several times—Each person is doing precisely the best that they can do in any given moment of time. Within each interaction we create the opportunities for blessings or curses, and the funny thing is that even the curse is a blessing in disguise for the enlightened creator. Divinely speaking, no note is ever truly out or tune. That is what this book has been about, seeing that the obstacle before you is in reality not an obstacle but a stepping stone. Whatever it is that stands before you and seems so overwhelming that you cannot possibly get over it or around it is in reality not a curse but a blessing that is there to aid you in waking up, growing, and evolving to the place where your true inner self shines forth in every moment.

No one is in control of the life you live and once you realize, are ready, and are willing to assume your responsibility as a spiritual warrior, you will begin to recognize the face of God in everyone you meet and hear the melody of the Beloved Creator in every situation and circumstance that comes into your experience, you will count it all good as it is all God! Our challenge is to actively engage in the part we are here to play; to take up our instrument and play the music we are gifted to play. With conscious awareness we return our gaze to the heavens and the obstacles in life shrink before us to the pebbles they actually are and we realize that the actual problem is our belief that there is a problem! What a cool paradox! Have you ever heard The parable of the 84 problem? It is another cool story that illustrates my point, so again sit back and enjoy. ☺

Once a man travelled quite far and sought the Buddha for help with his life's problems. When the man finally found the Buddha he presented one of his problems and waited for the Buddha's solution. Much to his surprise, the Buddha simply replied that he could not help the man with that problem.

The man, somewhat perplexed, presented a second problem to which the Buddha replied once again by saying that he could not help the man with that problem.

The man growing increasingly confused and frustrated presented the Buddha with a third problem he was having in life. And again to his third problem the Buddha replied as he had to the first and second problems.

Having become quite impatient the man spoke, "How can you be the Buddha, the perfectly Enlightened One, and not be able to help me with my problems?

The Buddha smiled as he replied, "You will always have 83 problems in your life. Some will go and when they do, others will come to replace them. I cannot help you with those problems."

The man was now even more frustrated and confused, he asked the Buddha, "Then what can you help me with?"

The Buddha replied, "I can help you with your 84th problem."

The man, who was growing weary, asked, "My what? What is my 84th problem?"

With great wisdom the Buddha said, "That you want to get rid of your 83 problems."

We raise our eyes and begin to see all with eyes of love and know that in this divine orchestra the Holy Composer and we are One and that in truth there are no problems, there are no mountains, there is no separation; God and you are One!

"As you become more clear about who you really are, you'll be better able to decide what is best for you—the first time around."
**Oprah Winfrey

It is up to the individual what he will ask of the universe, what he will believe, and what he will receive. It is given to the individual in precise measure that which the individual allows. It is God's good pleasure to give the kingdom, but it is up to the individual to receive it. On "Master Class" on the Oprah Winfrey Network, Dr. Maya Angelou said,

> "If a human being dreams a great dream, dares to love somebody; if a human being dares to be Martin King, or Mahatma Gandhi, or Mother Theresa, or Malcolm X; if a human being dares to be bigger than the condition into which she or he was born—it means so can you. And so you can try to stretch, stretch, stretch yourself so you can internalize, '*Homo sum, humani nil a me alienum puto*. I am a human being, nothing human can be alien to me.' That's one thing I'm learning . . . I am grateful to have been loved and to be loved now and to be able to love, because that liberates. Love liberates. It doesn't just hold—that's ego. Love liberates. It doesn't bind. Love says, 'I love you. I love you if you're in China. I love you if you're across town. I love you if you're in Harlem. I love you. I would like to be near you. I'd like to have your arms around me. I'd like to hear your voice in my ear. But that's not possible now, so I love you. Go."

There you have it! Will you dare to be greater than the conditions that seem to hold you captive to depression, addiction, abusive relationships, loneliness and isolation, weight issues, fear, low self esteem, lack of confidence, poor self image, scarcity and poverty, or illness and disease? All of these can be blessings rather than curses if we but lift our consciousness to the Truth. Lift our eyes to see with love and the mountain becomes manageable the boulder can be carried and the molehill remains a molehill and the pebble remains a pebble! We no longer make the small into some catastrophic event and we see beyond the fog of the illusions and the lure of the ego that has hypnotized us for oh so long!

In 2011 I hosted a radio show "Living a Sacred Life" on voiceamerica.com the 7th wave network, and I did my best to creatively and with a hint of entertainment softly remind all listeners, including myself, that our birthright is to live a divine and sacred life. Each day is an opportunity to live that sacred life and that the choice always rests within our hands. Nothing can disturb our peace of mind unless we allow it to do so. Likewise, nothing can remove the holiness from you or your life. And even when you cannot see the holiness, the sacredness, or the blessings they are there! Your lack of awareness of, acknowledgement of, or alignment with God does not belittle, erase, or remove God's presence from all that is, which by the way includes you. You are part of a divine orchestra and have gifts that can transform the world if you but chose to play the song in your heart!

As those words by Maya Angelou so poetically illustrate, it is for each person to embrace the fullness of their humanity for in so doing they embrace their divinity as well and from this place of awareness and consciousness, the empowered, self actualized, healed individual can then go forth into the world being fruitful and multiplying the miraculous in their everyday living.

All the adversity I've had in my life, all my troubles and obstacles have strengthened me . . . You may not realize it when it happens, but a kick in the teeth may be the best thing in the world for you.

Walt Disney

WHAT DID I BIRTH MYSELF INTO??

CHAPTER TWELVE:
MY STORY

Born March 25, 1966 in Pittsburgh, PA, I was the youngest of seven sons born to my mother Lois. My father, Charles had one prior son, Charles Anderson Jr., the offspring of my father's first marriage. My mother, married 3 times. Her first marriage, which was to a Givner resulted in the birth of my oldest three brothers Eddie, Leslie, and James Givner. Her second marriage, to an Allen, resulted in the birth of my next three brothers Charles, one that died at birth, and Tyrone Allen. Lastly, her marriage to my father resulted in my birth. I mention this aspect of my childhood because I believe that the birth order and the age differences played a major influence into the foundation upon which my life was structured. As the youngest, I was afforded the opportunity to see how my older brothers lived. I saw what seemed to work and what seemed not to work as well in their lives. I witnessed the good, the bad, and the ugly as it showed up in their lives and this allowed me to be more selective in some of my choices and actions; my choice to refrain from using alcohol and drugs for example. I saw firsthand how it influenced them and that provided me with motivation to avoid those particular addictions. I did however adopt other addictions. Interesting thing was that while I at one time judged them for their addictions, my own were equally as crippling though in different ways. I will address this more later. Being the youngest and nine years apart from Tyrone seemed to also spare me from being the little brother who tagged along. I believe that had we been closer in age, I would have gotten involved in more of what he and my other brothers were into such as basketball, football, cars, etc.

I grew up in my own world as a result of not hanging out with my brothers, similar to how Robin Williams grew up entertaining and keeping himself occupied as an only child. Comic books, ancient mythological stories, drawing and painting, and martial arts became my playgrounds and playmates. A child of the early Sesame Street era, I was very aware and what my parents called intelligent every chance they got to brag to people about me. This translated into my being a very studious student in school. I was quite the avid reader and researcher at a young age. While still in elementary school, my father was diagnosed with amyotrophic lateral sclerosis (ALS) or Lou Gehrig's disease. Being the studious young man I was, I began then to investigate the meaning of this series of words. I asked questions when I could and I listened intently whenever a nurse or doctor explained anything about it. The thing that stuck most pointedly in my mind was the "death sentence" they spoke about. My father what given two to four years to live! My young mind could not grasp what that meant and so I began to isolate myself in many ways from the world. Somehow, I sought to shield myself from the pain of death, for surely if my father could become ill and die, then so could my mother, brothers, and ultimately, so could I.

Fear of death began to grip my life in a profoundly oppressive manner. Every funeral or viewing I attended with my parents, I was reminded of the fleeting nature of life. The line between life and death was so fragile and without any effort, death could come for me. I did not have to be in an accident; I could simply continue living as I was and a disease could be born within me and take my life from me. In my mind it was as if the Grim Reaper was ever stalking me awaiting the time to reap my soul

I find it very interesting how my fear of injury and death later resulted in my becoming accident prone, injury prone, and illness prone! Law of Attraction in action. As a youth I had nose bleeds, severe allergies, many bumps, burns, and bruises, developed migraines, an ulcer, and a psychosomatic allergy to fresh fruits and vegetables that as of this writing, I am finally working on healing.

Looking back, I can see clearly how my thoughts were shaping my experiences. I can also recall how my self-righteous religious judgments developed from watching several of the TV evangelists on at the time. This was where my Christian education developed and it was from those teachers that I learned to condemn, criticize, and castrate anything that was NOT Christian, which meant anything not like them. I began to judge my parents consumption of alcohol and labeled them alcoholics. I began to condemn and label my brothers as drug dealers and users of drugs. While the facts were that my parents did drink and my brothers did use drugs, the truth behind this was oblivious to me and I could not see the divine thread connecting it all. This realization of truth would not occur for many years. As I said before, despite my finger pointing, I developed my own addictions. I became addicted to sugar, to self inflicted injury and pain, to pornography, and to co-dependent / passive-aggressive relationships and behaviors.

So I think in order for the picture to be clearer, I will establish some time lines per se and address things based on the "era" of my life when they occurred. The eras interestingly enough follow my formal education: Lincoln Elementary, Reizenstein Middle School, Westinghouse High School, The Art Institute of Pittsburgh, Carlow College, Community College of Allegheny County, University of Pittsburgh, Virginia Commonwealth University, the American Institute of Holistic Theology, and the University of Sedona and lastly back to the American Institute of Holistic Theology.

LINCOLN ELEMENTARY

My elementary school years would be what I would title my "descent into hell." It was at this time that can clearly look back and see where and how I learned, through domestication, how to think in limited and fearful ways. I was indoctrinated by family, friends, teachers in school, and from TV evangelists as to who I was and what I could and could not do. There were lessons on what it meant to be black. Being black meant it was us against the white man, who could not be trusted. Being black meant that I was not as good as my white counterparts and that I would have to constantly prove myself to them. This was a lesson that was, what I will presently say for linguistic convenience, *proven* true once I went to middle school. The seeds of inferiority were planted, however, during elementary school.

The seeds of fear were also deeply imbedded in the fertile soil of my mind and heart. My father being diagnosed, as I said earlier, with ALS was a major turning point for me. The innocence that I felt before this seemed to rapidly fade into nothingness. Anger, resentment, fear, and frustration became daily companions on the playground. I began to resent my mother for not being more compassionate and caring. I resented my father for not being stronger to somehow prevent getting sick. I resented myself for not being a better son. I resented God for allowing my father to get sick and for not healing him.

I began to bury myself into my comic books where Superman, Wonder Woman, and Batman always came out on top! By fifth grade, I began to get into drawing and painting as I learned that this was a skill I possessed and it was a skill that garnered me with praise and attention. Thus began the development of my vampiric nature which began seeking more and more praise to offset the incessant chatter that told me I was inferior, ugly, stupid, and worthless; much like a cocaine addict needs more and more cocaine to satisfy the hunger. After all, I was learning from my family and other black adults that as a black child I was always going to have to fight to prove myself in a world where I was going to be judged as less than and then there were the TV ministers that preached that I was a sinner at birth, born in sin, and God hates sin and sinners!

Any one of these by themselves I possibly could have resisted. I like to think that I may have been able to fend off this negative energy, but various things both in school and at home echoed and reinforced these beliefs and feelings. As I stated in the book earlier, the ego, once allowed to control will find more and more evidence to support whatever you chose to believe. That is why I said a page ago "This was a lesson that was, what I will presently say for linguistic convenience, *proven* true once I went to middle school. The seeds of inferiority were planted, however, during elementary school", it was proven to be true because my ego was seeking validation of this false truth and so it found evidence to support its thesis of inferiority. I believed I was not worthy and so no matter how much praise or how many compliments I received, I made sure that I held onto the negative comments. I could get fifty compliments for something great and then one criticism and I would hold onto the one single criticism. This is why I called this era my descent into hell for this began my downward spiral into an abyss that could have easily killed me as I faded farther and farther into the darkness.

Despite the descent, there were elements that I know served as my torches. In hindsight I can recognize these beacons of light that would later be used to show me the way back from the pit. My martial arts studies were one such torch. And interestingly enough my desire to learn martial arts began as a response to bullying. As a youth I was bullied fairly regularly and as a result of being bullied, I asked my brothers to teach me how to fight. None would do so since they were always busy living their lives. It wasn't until I saw my first Bruce Lee movie and fell in love with Asian culture! I wanted to be Chinese or Japanese so badly that I began adopting cultural mannerisms like bowing and reading about the philosophy behind the martial arts. Later, seeing how serious I was about learning, my brother Jimmie began teaching me the basics of Karate which evolved into more in-depth studies of Kung Fu when I was in middle school. It is important to keep this in mind as the journey continues because this aspect of my life will have major impact in many ways.

REIZENSTEIN MIDDLE SCHOOL

Middle school only furthered my already deeply engrained belief in scarcity and fear based illusory living. Reizenstein was a multiracial multiethnic school and it was here that my comparisons with others took an angry and bitter turn for the worst. While being convinced that my white school mates were smarter and better equipped for learning, I was determined to do my best to excel nonetheless. As a result, I began to break from many "black"

friends and began to associate with more eclectic mixes of people. I no longer held to the homogenous friendships that I held in elementary school. I developed friendships with whites, Asians, Indians, Hispanics, Jews, Muslims, and Buddhists. No one was "off limits" for me and as a result I learned to be open minded to diversity. However, this realization did not occur until many years later after much ridicule from my black peers for trying to be white! I was mocked, teased and harassed pretty often, not by all my black friends but by many. Then there were the black students, who like me, were already in more diverse groups, and they chose to ridicule and criticize me as well.

The competition with others was a subconscious burden that I do not recall ever being openly or consciously aware that I felt inferior and needed to prove myself. There just seemed to be an inner ache that needed to be healed and at that time only co-dependent vampire like behavior gave me solace. I began to establish bonds where people "needed" me or "wanted" me for things such as study help or to draw something for them. This included classmates as well as teachers. Then there were my developing athletic and martial art skills that were proving to be a source of praise. Despite this developing skill I was not confident enough to stand up to the occasional bully that would increase my levels of cortisol, GH and norepinephrine i.e., stress hormones! Out of fear, I never opted to defend myself. I simply took the verbal or physical abuse and stuffed them in my already over packed Pandora's Box.

With all of the energy I was using to maintain façades and to keep the illusions alive, I began to develop migraine headaches. First around fifth grade the headaches appeared monthly, then by sixth grade they were weekly, then by seventh grade daily and it hit a crescendo once in high school when I passed out and had to go to the hospital after having had one migraine continuously for eighteen months! The stress of adolescence was unbearable and yet I somehow endured. I had the stress of my father's illness and approaching death, my feelings of uselessness and hopelessness, my anger and frustration towards my parents who were now fighting, arguing, and drinking more heavily, my lack of affection which quickly attached itself to my questioning sexual orientation, the stress of being alone in a crowd of friends, and lastly there was the pressure of what I dreamt was possible for me to be, do, and have but seemed only a distant dream.

While taking Spanish in I believe seventh grade, our class took a field trip to Heinz Hall to see the musical "Man of La Mancha." As embarrassing as it was, I was the only student and as I recall the only person period from our trip that cried as Don Quixote died and the prisoners sang to Don Miguel de Cervantes when he was called before the Inquisition.

That show planted an amazing seed in my consciousness, the concept of—"Dream the Impossible Dream."

I began practicing martial arts in a more intent and focused manner while in middle school. I had grown tired of feeling weak as others verbally and physically picked on me. I began taking the long way home so that I would not be the first one home. I did not want to arrive home and find my father dead in the house so I found creative ways to occupy my time and allow someone to arrive home first. One day, I went home and ravaged the Yellow Pages in search of any martial art schools in the area that I could visit and watch classes. My parents would not or could not pay for classes due to lack of income from my father being ill, which reinforced my consciousness of lack and not enoughness. Determined not to let that deter me, I took my list of schools and began visiting the ones within walking distance. I had the chance to visit several martial art schools where I sat, observed, and put pencil to paper by drawing each movement they practiced. I then went home and practiced what I had seen. Taking the long way home also afforded me the opportunity to chat with an older cousin, Kazoo, who truly looked like he could be one of those ancient full blooded Native American chiefs. It was he and our frequent conversations about our Native lineage that sparked both my curiosity in Native American shamanism and spirituality, as well as my eventual study of the art and practice of the Medicine man and Medicine woman which I quickly tied into my passion for the mysticism of the Far East. Interesting sidebar note is that years later when I would read the book "Gay is a Gift" by Salvatore Sapienza, I would find that the Native culture (as well as certain African cultures such as the Dagara tribe) held a high place of honor for the gay individual as that person was seen to be the spiritual gatekeeper.

> Gay is a gift is a wisdom the Native Americans knew centuries ago. In his book, The Hidden Spirituality of Men, spiritual writer and teacher Matthew Fox writes that "it is

> well known among Native Americans that gay persons have always been the spiritual directors to their great chiefs. Homosexuals, it seems, don't just bridge the male and female worlds, but human and spiritual worlds. A Lakota shaman tells Fox that gay people have a gift of prophecy, explaining that "if nature put a burden on a man by making him different, it also gives him a power." It is not just the Lakotas, but mostly all the Native American tribal cultures, it seems, have recognized gay people as holding special powers of the Spirit, giving them the title of Berdache or "Two Spirit." It is believed that these Two Spirits are more in tune with the healing powers of natural beauty, and that they are the true Way Showers to the Divine Spirit (Sapienza)."

Ok back to what I was saying about the martial arts. So, later, I took my first trip to a martial arts store in Oakland near the University of Pittsburgh and I began to buy books so I could study and practice the physical, mental, and spiritual aspects of the martial arts that I saw being spoken about in the television show that both my father and I watched often. "Kung Fu," starring David Carradine was a favorite of ours. We both loved not only the physical aspect of the martial arts but the mental and spiritual aspects as well. I think it was as a result of watching the series that I learned that my father had served a life sentence in jail for murder. I think he was explaining this part of his life to me by making a comparison to the David Carradine character Kwai Chang Caine who killed the emperor's nephew out of rage and revenge. My father said that taking a life is never honorable; however, what he had done was far less noble than Kwai Chang Caine. He told me that he killed a man accidentally while attempting to rob him of money. The man fell to the ground, hit his head and died. My father was convicted and sentenced to a life sentence and served close to 30 years before being paroled for good behavior. My father told me many stories about what being in jail taught him and one thing that I seemed to focus on most intently was that while in jail he became quite studious. He focused his attention on learning and improving himself in order to maintain his sanity. I am unsure how old I was when I heard the full story, the point I am making is that his story blended into my story as he taught me many lessons related to reading, studying, and self improvement. The wisdom that the "Kung Fu" series portrayed weekly was one vehicle he used to point out various lessons to me as we would discuss the moral of the stories. This again, would come to be a powerful thread connecting future events.

WESTINGHOUSE HIGH SCHOOL

High school ushered in the next phase of my evolution as an adolescent. I was approaching the final four years of school and would soon be an "adult." The prospect of being out in the world terrified me yet amid the fear of adulthood was the joy that my father had lived beyond the four year prognosis. Though the joy was tainted with mini flecks of fear as there was no idea of when to expect his death. Looking back now, I realize how illogical, as Mr. Spock would say, this idea of not knowing becoming a source of fear. I mean, I did not know when my mother would die and I wasn't afraid. I didn't know when my brothers would die and I wasn't afraid. And I didn't know when I was going to die and I wasn't afraid so what was the big deal about not knowing when my father was going to die?

Anyway, I no longer took the long way home to avoid finding him and in time I stopped consciously thinking about it though I realized years later that it was in fact still in my mind and was playing a major part in my life. My practices in the martial arts helped me to release much of the fear around his illness, at least on a conscious level. I was also much stronger and faster and therefore more confident in many aspects. The bullying was long over and not so much because I could defend myself but because I had somehow shifted to a state of mind where bullies didn't show up in my experience any more. There were no more black knights charging the castle to challenge the king; it was like they knew better and decided to visit other kingdoms instead.

By this point I began to study martial arts with others and teach my own students. In addition to Kung Fu I also began to learn and study the Japanese art of *Ninjutsu*. Initially all of my martial arts studies were to a certain degree, self-taught. I mean my brother Jimmie did teach me the basics of *Karate* however I did not formally train under anyone who had the title of sensei or teacher. And it wasn't until maybe my sophomore year at Westinghouse that I formally began learning *Kung Fu* from my cousin William who was himself a teacher of many years and then N*injutsu* in my junior year from a guy who told me he had been trained as a teacher from the *Bujinkan* Dojo in Kettering Ohio under the instruction of *Ninjutsu* master teacher Stephen K. Hayes. As I progressed and then began teaching classes myself, my backyard became my personal *dojo*, where I taught martial arts for many years, 19 or 20 years total. Many people passed through that gate for instruction. The method of study and growth of my martial arts skills was quite interesting. As I mentioned already it began with me observing countless classes, drawing the movements, and then later practicing them over and over again. At the time I did not know anything about the formation of dendrites and synapses in the brain and I was only beginning to understand the power of intuition or what many call the Sixth sense and it wouldn't be until much later that I would realize how this influenced my martial arts abilities. See, what I came to later understand was that my method of study was in fact a form of hypnosis or subliminal programming. And it was a form that I had actually used while in middle school to help me study for tests, while asleep. I would play a cassette tape of music and me reading notes for the test. Apparently, while asleep the material was being absorbed into my subconscious where it was later accessible consciously for the test. And in fact, I studied this way for many years and passed many tests as a result of this method! So it was nothing new to utilize this skill for the martial arts except now the majority of the material was visual rather than auditory. What I would do was watch and read anything and everything related to martial arts. I became a voracious student of the arts. I collected books, magazines, movies, weapons and Asian paraphernalia. This method created pathways in my brain making my acquisition of martial arts and Eastern philosophy almost as natural as breathing.

Funny thing is that a psychic once told me that he believed I was Asian more than once in previous incarnations and that was one reason that I was so attracted to the Asian culture, philosophy, and the martial arts. I later applied that same methodology of study to my American Sign Language studies and I found that those skills progressed just as the martial arts had done. I remember there were many times I feared that my students would no longer want to learn from me if they knew how I had developed a major portion of my skills, as if what I was teaching them was somehow invalidated based upon how I learned. I held this fear for a while; despite the number of times black belt teachers and other higher level students praised my level of skill and level of teaching ability, as I turned out a number of highly skilled students. One of those students Phil went on to be accepted into the American Gung Fu Association and as a result of his acceptance into the organization as a *sifu* (teacher) I was invited to join by the several of the *Sijos* (grandmasters) to join and it was then that I received the title *Sigung* (master). Ok so back to my time in high school.

Despite my increasing self awareness and control of my mind, I was still wrestling with my Christian beliefs. According to Christianity and my oldest brother who at this time was an ordained minister through Regent University incorporated in 1977 under the leadership of Pat Robertson, my practicing martial arts made me a "devil worshipper." The Eastern mysticism and philosophy that martial arts were based on was akin to worshipping the devil. As a result, my oldest brother stopped speaking to me and did not allow his children to speak to me for approximately eight years. I began to resent the church and reevaluate what being a Christian meant. This would serve as the impetus later for my spiritual awakening.

Not only was I questioning my religious beliefs, I was questioning everything about life which included one of my major mountains at the time my sexuality. By high school I had already had some minor sexual experimentation with both female and male friends. However, the three male friends were the ones that were of concern and of interest. I could not accept the possibility that I was gay. That was not an option! The idea of this began to reawaken suicidal ideations that first appeared in middle school. "There is no reason for me to be alive," was a major reoccurring proclamation as were the questions, "What difference would it make if I died? Who would care?" All I was concerned with was that the pain, confusion, self hatred, and fear would end. For several years part of my nightly prayer to a certain degree included some desire to die in my sleep and have all the pain end and those prayers didn't end until many years after high school! Though I never formally attempted suicide, I did become more reckless in my behaviors, for example, I would ride my bike, throwing caution to the wind, almost hoping to die in an *accident*. Frequent crashes and falls were interpreted as my being a brave and adventurous daredevil rather than a kid with a death wish. So I graduated in 1984 and at graduation had to face one of my largest mountains, speaking in public. I had been selected as the salutatorian to deliver a graduation speech. Three things I remember about standing in Soldier and Sailors memorial hall was that I was terrified, that part of my speech quoted Shakespeare who said, "To thine own self be true," and that when someone started to heckle me, my cousin Vaughn told them so shut up. This speech giving experience would unfold quite interestingly over the years.

THE ART INSTITUTE OF PITTSBURGH

I think this death wish was most evidently seen during my years at the Art Institute of Pittsburgh which were from July 1984 to December 1986. Let me back track a little bit. While still in Westinghouse, I had been told by a trusted teacher that my desire to go to school to learn to be a movie special effects technician would be pointless because I lacked the artistic talent to succeed in that field. I then changed my mind and decided to stay in Pittsburgh and go to the Art Institute where I could increase my skills and then later go to California to study movie making magic. That same *trusted* teacher then told me that going to the Art Institute would be a waste of time as well due to my lack of artistic skill. Rather than listening to him this time, I moved forward and applied to the Art Institute. I believe this was out of sheer spite and the desire to prove him wrong.

To say that my time at the Art Institute was racked with turmoil and distress would be as much an understatement as saying the surface of the sun is pretty warm. With each assignment given I cut myself down by reminding myself that I lacked not only the skills but the finances to purchase the top level materials and tools to be used in the classes. As a result, I began to take out more loans to be able to buy what I needed and wanted in order to do the assignments. Again I compared myself to my white classmates, who outnumbered me by the way. I was in the minority during my time there. I was also emotionally spent by this time from my co-dependent relationships with friends and family members. This wasn't fully realized until I witnessed an eleven year old cousin, in self defense, kill his mother's boyfriend. This event was a major turning point in my life as the entire series of events surrounding the court case caused me to have what I would later realize was a nervous breakdown. Due to the stress and the breakdown, I ended up writing a letter to my school advisor saying that I was sorry I could not go on. He, after reading this note, assumed

I meant that I could not go on with life and that I intended to commit suicide. The advisor, the dean, and an administrative assistant attempted to tackle me as I was leaving the school, in order to save me from myself and to prevent my suicide. As a result of their actions, someone outside of the building looking in through the huge windows saw three white men and one black male wrestling in the lobby and so they called the police to come help stop a thief from escaping. Then several police officers arrived and a large fight ensued. The Art Institute staff stepped out of the way as I and the several officers got into an interesting brawl. I knocked two officers out and threw a third into the trashcan before allowing my left arm to be handcuffed after hearing one officer say for them to hit me with the clubs. Once handcuffed though I did not understand what was happening, so again, I fought back and upon hearing the gun being un-holstered, I surrendered and was handcuffed fully and placed in the back of the truck where I cried uncontrollably having then realized what just happened.

Sometimes I look back and wonder if I did not recognize them as officers because I was that enraged and scared that somewhere in my mind I wanted them to shoot me and put me out of my misery. Having handcuffed me and placed me securely in the truck, they asked what I had stolen. The dean, shocked by the question, assured them that I stole nothing. He went on to say I was suicidal. As a result, they took me to the Western Psychiatric Institute and Clinic where I stayed for nine days. It took nine days to convince them that I did not want to commit suicide. It was there that they explained that I had a mild nervous breakdown and was displaying signs of depression. Once released, I had to go to weekly out-patient therapy sessions. In all honesty the sessions were more of a formality especially since the first two therapists talked more than they listened, received guidance from me far more than they gave it, and were of little therapeutic assistance. They did however inadvertently open the door for me to see that I had an interest to learn more about healing. So I began to read and focus more on my healing process. Part of that healing included the beginning of my release of being co-dependent and passive aggressive.

One thing that I did not mention about the Westinghouse era that I did not realize until this healing journey began was part of my motivation for having developed a close relationship with a fellow student who I sort of adopted as my brother. I felt such a void in my family with my biological brothers that I decided to adopt a surrogate older brother. Though he was biologically younger, I looked up to him as if he were my older brother. He was popular, in shape, attractive, athletic, and did I mention popular? It was also around the same time that I attempted to get closer to my favorite cousin, for basically the same reasons. Though I did honestly care about them, they were what I wanted to be and I felt that by being around them I would somehow become more like them and less like myself. As a chameleon I could cloak myself in their aura and hide myself.

Apart from seeking to eradicate me, I wanted a bond, best friend, and a brother that I could be close to and hang out with. Though this desire was half tainted by my own insecurities, it afforded me great opportunities to learn more about myself and about friendships and I thank both of them for allowing me to bond with them. I did develop a similar relationship with another friend during the Art Institute era. We became brothers and though that bond was altered greatly when he went to the military, I was adopted into his family as a brother to his siblings. His mother and I developed a very strong bond that would quickly become co-dependent and passive aggressive to the third power and as a result would turn to what I later could identify as a toxic relationship. I believe that part of that toxicity is what resulted in my developing an ulcer in my early twenties. Despite the drama and emotional, psychological, and physical pain caused by this toxic bond, I was eventually able to look back and connect the dots and see the benefit of all that I experienced while in those relationships. There truly were blessings in the midst of the darkness that I could not see at the time. Those relationships helped me greatly in my overall healing process and in learning more about my co-dependent and passive aggressive tendencies and the eventual road to empowerment, as I learned more of who and what I am as a person. The process of healing took me several years to fully integrate and there are still days that I see remnants of the co-dependency popping up in my thoughts or even in some behaviors. Now that I spot them, I can eliminate them before they lead to more negative consequences like they once did.

After graduating from the Art Institute with my Associates degree in Illustration and Graphic Design, I did a few part-time jobs until receiving a full time job working for the YMCA in Lawrenceville. As with all the prior experiences I was unable to see the pearl amid the pain until many years later. This job was a drain on my soul. I did not feel right being there. And though I did my best, it was never good enough and as my creativity was stifled, so to was my desire to even try. So I withdrew and was eventually fired and interestingly enough discovered that the women in the office disliked me and didn't want me there anyway because I was black and a male. After being fired, I eventually took a job for the Pittsburgh public school system as a substitute teaching aide and was eventually hired as a full time substitute to work at Whittier elementary in their in-school suspension room. I developed quite a rapport with the students, the teachers, and administration as well as the staff. So much in fact that several teachers suggested I go back to school to become a teacher. They suggested that I talk to the women that I was filling in for, which I did. She told me that she just graduated from Carlow College and as a result I looked into their education programs and enrolled in the art education department seeking to earn my Bachelor of Arts in Art Education certified to teach K through 12.

CARLOW COLLEGE

While attending Carlow College (now Carlow University) the process and studies of healing continued and it was while attending Carlow that I experienced a major catalyst in my spiritual studies and growth. The school was known for being a Catholic women's college and as such it was mandatory to take a women's studies course and a religion course. So to fulfill both my pre-requisites and my interests, I took several religion courses and could have declared a minor in religion had someone told me that at the time. Those courses in religion further paved the way for my evolving spiritual journey. Carlow afforded me many opportunities for growth. My experience as a student there forced me to get out of my nice neatly formed comfort zones. Several classes and professors expected a totally different level of participation that I was not accustomed to. The classes were small in number and very personal, which was one of the reasons I decided to go there. I was expected to speak out in class when asked a question, I was expected to stand up and give a speech in my public speaking course, and I was expected to do class presentations and group assignments where several of us had to collaborate. The kid who was used to flying solo was now forced to be a team player and sometimes as the captain of the team!

This was an all new game and I was learning the rules as I went. To top off the academic challenges, I was still dealing with relationship challenges, identity issues and concerns, and self worth problems, but as usual I was hiding it all very well or so I thought. Someone made it painfully obvious that I needed to address this, as she put it, "bullshit that I was trudging through so I could be free." That someone was Ruriko "June" Masutani, my Aikido Sensei. I had wanted to study Aikido for many years. Ever since I used to visit schools and observe. During those, visit schools and observe years, I wandered into an Aikido dojo in East Liberty (the neighborhood in which I lived and went to school). Sensei Masutani was the founder and heads Sensei of that school. I was not able to join, however, through an interesting series of events Sensei was offering classes at Carlow for Physical Education (P.E.) credits. I don't recall if taking some P.E. credits were required or not and it would not have mattered because I was going to take this course. Aikido opened me up to an entirely new course of inner work as I delved into the philosophy behind Aikido and how and why its founder Moreihei Uyeshiba created it, practiced it and taught it.

Aikido is about harmony and Sensei was fond of reminding me that I needed to find harmony in my life as well as on the mat. I began to find similarities in my life and my difficulties on the mat in a way that I could never have imagined. It seemed almost mystical that as I would grasp one technique, I would also grasp its application in resolving an issue in my personal life. As I found harmony on the mat, I was actually finding it in life. I began attending the classes held at the dojo which at the time was in a community center in Squirrel Hill. I stress the study of Aikido because the martial arts and Eastern philosophy played a HUGE part in my shifting paradigms as the years went on and I believe that without them I very well may have died.

My academics at Carlow were excellent. I was on the dean's list every semester. Several classes stand out in my mind as being particularly influential; some because of the course material and some because of the professor. One such class was a psychology course with Dr. Winter. I found Dr. Winter to be a straight forward no nonsense woman whose compassion and encouragement motivated me to continue when I thought I was going to drop out of school in those first few weeks. Dr. Bloss, my biology professor, was another such teacher who let me use her son's bike when I did not have money for the bus to get to school. Dr. Hopkins' public speaking course prepared me in ways that I would never have imagined for what I do now as a teacher, speaker, performer, and minister. When I began teaching public speaking at Virginia Commonwealth University, I used a lot of what I had learned from him. Karen McGann, my American Sign Language teacher who opened the door to an entirely new world and culture to me. I fell in love with both the language and the culture and have made some amazing friends in the deaf community. I will talk a little more about this a little later, so stay tuned. Some of the teachers I cannot recall their names but their influence is no less powerful and without the challenges they placed before me and the faith they had in me, I may not have excelled as I did.

Despite the excellent grades and camaraderie I had with friends, I was dealing with some hidden demons that would appear from time to time to inflict pain and suffering just to remind me that they were in fact still there. One such time was when a particular teacher and I had a confrontation centered on my expected graduation date. The change of the date was not really the issue; the manner in which I found out was what caused the conflict and my ego based anger outburst. Thankfully, Dr. Bloss was there and was able to speak sense into me before I either broke something or dropped out of school! School wasn't the only place such turmoil occurred. My home life continued to find me having fits of rage which began back in middle school when the migraines grew in intensity and reached their peak when in high school when I was examined from head to toe in search of why I was passing out in school and was having the same headache for eighteen months! The result of the search revealed that I was experiencing stress related migraine headaches. As a result of the stress, anger, and pain, I developed a destructive side. I began destroying my bikes, punching holes in walls in my bedroom, smashing my stereo equipment and records, and breaking my martial arts weapons. Carlow saw a huge reduction of such outbursts; however, when they would occur it was a storm worth hiding from.

Home and school were not the only places where I felt out of place and frustrated. I was a big brother or father figure to several neighborhood kids. Many of them were simply using me for the money I would spend on them, though a few legitimately enjoyed the family like bond we shared and one in particular, Kenny, as I would find out years later, saw me and spoke of me as his father. He later adopted me and I him and he became my first of three sons and as my first son is the first to give me grandkids as well!

After I finally graduated from Carlow I became a public school teacher. I began teaching art as a full time substitute in a middle school until a full time position opened in a high school. The entire teaching experience was ever so eye opening. Nothing I learned at Carlow truly prepared me for the actual experience of teaching; book knowledge and real life experiential hands on in the trenches experience is an all together different creature to tame. No psychology book teaches you how to deal with your adrenalin as you step in to break up a fight or have a student tell you he will kill you. Both of which happened while I was the full-time substitute and breaking up fights was almost a weekly event. Despite the dramas, I found that I bonded easily with the students and they responded well to me. Many of the *difficult* kids responded to me in ways that other teachers could not understand and many would later become jealous of.

Teachers did not become part of the drama until I took that full time position in a high school. Once there, issues began to develop pretty rapidly with other teachers and the administration. The students and I bonded even stronger than those at the middle school, there was a level of maturity where I could talk to them as young adults and many, though they still had to learn the hard way, would listen and they seemed to develop respect for me for taking the time to respect them and care about them. Anyway after several years there, the administration issues resulted in my being transferred to a new school. I was now at a new middle school which initially I thought was a good change because I had student taught there. Little did I know that the lessons I was to learn there would demand a heavy price. That price being my job. After a few short years at this new middle school, I resigned from being a public school teacher all together. The administration related issues continued as did the teacher dramas. I did not know then to look at myself since I was the common denominator and that these people and situations were merely mirroring back to me aspects of myself. Looking back now, I can see that their disrespect of me was due to my self-disrespecting thoughts and feelings. I was dishonoring myself and was keeping it buried. They were merely bringing it out in the open. They were acting out towards me what I believed about myself!

Once I resigned, I had to deal with the guilt and shame of failing. I felt that I had failed because I spent all that time and money in school to become an art teacher only to get so mad that I resigned. Having more free time, I dove deeper into the Deaf community as an interpreter and performer. Oh that's right I didn't tell you that part yet. Ok, so like I told you before, while I was at Carlow I took my first American Sign Language (ASL) class from one of those life changing teachers, Karen McGann. Well as a result of taking her class, I later formed a performance company called S.T.A.R.S. (Sticking Together Always Results in Success) and I began taking more ASL classes at the Center on Deafness. I took ASL levels one through six several times each until I had pretty much memorized the text book. Several teachers, deaf friends, and other ASL students encouraged me to enroll in the Interpreter Training Program (ITP) at the community college. After looking into it, I did just that while I was teaching during the day, I was taking evening and weekend classes up until I resigned from my full time job. I then enrolled full time in the program.

THE COMMUNITY COLLEGE OF ALLEGHENY COUNTY (CCAC)

After graduating with an associate degree from the Art Institute, a Bachelor of Arts degree from Carlow, here I was again in school pursuing a second associate degree at CCAC. I had no desire to get the degree. I was more interested in obtaining greater skills in the language and increasing my knowledge of the Deaf community; getting the degree was a byproduct of that interest. Brain Cerney would become a great mentor along this leg of my journey. As the director of the program he was a fount of information and I drank as much as I could of the wealth of knowledge he offered. As a result of his mentoring me, my ASL skills improved immensely and to this day I credit him with helping me make the major improvements that I made over the years and am still making. It was also due to his guidance that I became a freelance interpreter professionally and became a certified teacher of American Sign Language with the American Sign Language Teachers Association. Brian was also the one responsible for my performance style changing from being more English based as I transliterated songs to a more idiomatic conceptual and visual based style which deaf audiences and many hearing people who appreciate ASL love to watch.

ASL wasn't the only thing to have changed during my time at CCAC. I began my first long term relationship while attending CCAC and it was and due to a conversation at a neighborhood co-op where the bluntness and honesty of Nancy DeWitt, one of my favorite ASL teachers, convinced that it was time to come out of the closet. I had made many changes over the years in my level of self acceptance and so coming out was the natural next progression. After coming out to my friends and faculty at CCAC I came out to my family. It was a most terrifying time and for years after, I questioned if it was the right thing to do even though I knew in my heart that it was. After several years of being together, my partner and I decided to relocate to Richmond Virginia. It was the worst of times that became the best of times. I digress though. Long before we moved, our relationship endured some major peaks and valleys. There were a few times we nearly went our separate ways but each time we reconciled and fixed what seemed to be the issue. I did not realize at the time that he was mirroring back to me my own issues that needed to be healed. Had I realized that then though I don't think he and I would have been together for as long as we were; there wouldn't have been a reason.

After completing the CCAC Interpreter Training Program, I began interpreting more frequently and professionally as an employee of Pittsburgh Hearing Speech and Deaf Services. During this time I was busy building my skills and confidence. I also was spending more time developing my performance related skills with S.T.A.R.S. And I was addicted to a new found area where I could dabble, theatrical interpreting. I was also an aspiring actor sort of, and having the opportunity to learn more about this specific interpreting field sort of fed my acting bug by getting me close to the stage and to other actors. I also applied for a job at the Western Pennsylvania School for the Deaf to teach art. I was actually offered the job but due to my insecurities, I turned it down. Brian suggested that I might gain more confidence in my skills to teach deaf students if I studied Deaf Education. Returning to school and getting another degree and amassing more debt was far from what I wanted at the time, but I applied and with his glowing recommendation I was accepted without reservation.

UNIVERSITY OF PITTSBURGH

This was the shortest and most despised of all my educational experiences. There wasn't anything particularly wrong with the program or the teachers or the other students; the problem was me. I really did not want to be in the program. I was there because of fear, not because of my desire to pursue a passion. I remembered that while I was in fifth or sixth grade we had an assignment where we were asked to write about what we wanted to be when we grew up. Though I don't remember what all I wrote, I do remember writing that I was going to have ten degrees, be a teacher, karate expert, actor, director, artist, doctor, superhero, father, husband, and author. Quite a list and the teacher in so many words told me that it was nice, but unrealistic and that I should write something real and not so imaginary. Well the little rebel in me not only refused but I added a few more things on there that made it even more surreal and I think I got a lower grade as a result. One by one my education was actually aligning with those childhood goals; however, this educational choice was not and so without word to the faculty or students who I felt no particular bond with anyway, I simply withdrew and vanished.

There were a few times I wondered if Brian or my parents were disappointed yet again by my lack of follow through or lack of direction. In spite of the wondering I continued to follow some silent beckoning in my heart that had me following the things I felt a passion for. I was selling some art work to people, I was interpreting, performing, and teaching workshops on signing songs, I was learning and teaching martial arts, enjoying time with my son when he came to town from college in Hampton VA, and enjoying the good times with my partner. In 2000, he and I relocated to Richmond VA. This was perhaps one of the most difficult transitions I ever made. It was a leap of faith which opened me to an entirely new vista; the likes of which I could never have imagined. The pain of this new birth was however more than I felt I could endure many times!

VIRGINIA COMMONWEALTH UNIVERSITY (VCU)

We moved in April of 2000 and the pains of leaving my family were intense, especially leaving my father who for some time now had been wheelchair bound. I was the one who would help get him in and out of his chair or help him get on his bed if he fell or help him in the kitchen if he fell while reaching for something in an upper cupboard. Without me there who would assist? My mother was not able to serve in that capacity without severely injuring her back, so my leaving left my father to struggle and spend many hours on the floor until he gained the strength to pull himself back onto his chair. The guilt I felt was matched only by the eventual anger I felt towards my partner for what I felt was his insensitivity to my pain.

Our relationship changed taking several ugly turns as jealousy, insecurity, judgments, and my need for understanding and sympathy to help me deal with the never ending guilt. Our relationship that had endured several years quickly unraveled over a period of months and by early fall, I and the one puppy he bought me were gone. Let me back track just a bit because there are a few important events that occurred before the breakup. First one being my first job while in Richmond. I was an employee at Barnes and Noble. Even though getting to that store was a challenge due to the public transportation system in Richmond, I loved that job. It was the first time I worked a register which terrified me as it challenged my math skills which I always felt were a little lacking. According to Toni the head manager I was a very helpful, friendly, polite, and positive employee that customers were always talking about and asking for by name. Toni decided to start grooming me for a management position and my fear kicked in and I left the job. Amazing how fear continued to show up to block me and yet leaving the store and getting my next job was a great blessing; a blessing that would not have happened had I become manager of Barnes and Noble.

Event two, a student that I had been teaching for several years while living in Pittsburgh, who had helped us move to Richmond came back to Richmond one evening and in an act of violence, smashed our windows as we slept. The short version of this event was that he had a schizophrenic episode and was told that he had to remove several people from the picture so that he could go to Florida and accomplish his mission which was to free a young woman and have a child with her and after a certain number of years kill them both so that he would be able to rule the universe. That is a very brief synopsis of the story. Guess you can get the full unedited version from my biography one day. As a result of this attack, I was cut with glass in my arm, chest, feet and eye and this further added stress to my already weak psyche.

Event three, in an attempt to meet more people and get out of the house, so I would not feel so isolated and alone, I joined the Metropolitan Community Church in Richmond. After attending for a while I began interpreting there and while interpreting one Sunday a group of people came up to me after service and we chatted. One of the people told me about a new unit, a deaf unit, to open at the Virginia Treatment Center for Children. I later applied to be a behavioral specialist on the Deaf unit. One of the perks to working at the hospital was that I could take a free class at VCU. Feeling no pressure, I decided to take a class from the theatre department since learning to act had always been something I desired to learn and was a passion of mine. After several months, having taken two or three classes I was then told that the free classes had to be from certain select lists which did not include the theatre department. When I pointed out in the handbook that no such list existed, I was told that it was at the director's discretion to approve of classes or not and that if I wanted to continue to take classes, I would have to reconsider what type of classes I took. Well, that in addition to certain employees taking certain liberties to break rules like smoking on the premises and getting away with it and other administrative scheduling issues, I did my typical rebellious thing and up and quit one day with no notice. I showed up, was told the schedule had been changed; I became enraged, asked another employee to escort me out as I exited the building never to return again. Thus began my enrollment as a full time graduate student in the theatre pedagogy program under the leadership of a great mentor and friend Dr. Noreen Barnes.

This part of my education marked a major pivotal point in my life. By the time I enrolled full time I had already left my partner, lived homeless for a few days before a co-worker at the hospital let me stay with her and her partner, and after a few weeks moved into my own apartment with my Jack Russell terrier puppy, Jai, and soon to be added as the our third musketeer, a beagle named Winnie. So there I was living a life I never would have imagined I would live and I was living it alone for the first time in my life. I was paying all the bills, I was cooking all the meals or ordering out, I was cleaning the entire apartment alone, I was responsible for veterinary appointments and for everything all on my own. For someone who felt that he could never do that as a recovering co-dependent person, this was a major accomplishment and in hindsight was a huge paradigm shifting time for me as one major life changing event happened after another.

- Relocation to Virginia
- Management job training with Barnes and Noble
- A former martial arts student and friend attacks me
- Joining a church
- Working at hospital
- Enrolling in theatre department
- Break up, move out, brief period of being homeless
- Living alone (with dogs)
- Founded a new S.T.A.R.S. in Richmond
- Teaching ASL at the community college and teaching public speaking at VCU
- Joining the university gay student group
- Going to therapy to help with depression and guilt
- Studying theatre and all of the self inquiry that came with that

- Being cast in two shows one of which I was a main character who never left the stage
- Major knee surgery to reconstruct a new ACL and the physical therapy needed to learn to walk, run, jump all over again
- As graduation approached, my father passed away
- Going to therapy to help with grief and guilt
- Graduated and moved from Richmond to the Washington DC metro area to work with an all Deaf performance company—the Wild Zappers and the National Deaf Dance Theatre

There is no way to identify any one particular thing that truly marked the precise moment I changed my paradigm; however, this era was one filled with one of the greatest transformational shifts. There are a few that I would like to spend a little time going deeper into because of the impact they had on my shift.

The process of studying theatre as taught here was, for me, therapeutic and spiritual. I have no idea if it was meant to be that way or if others felt that way about the program; however, for me and my experience, each class offered a unique set of challenges that assisted me in peeling away the layers of gunk and debris that I had collected over the years to shield, deflect, and protect me. My instructors provided just the right amount of attitude, confrontation, and compassion to help me see that I was far better than I was giving myself credit for being and that I had a gift that needed to be nurtured not buried away like an old shoe in the attic. I can remember many times I fussed and complained about how unfair Dr. Leong or Dr. Simms were being over some assignment, yet I now realize that they *were* being fair and that they were pushing me to see in myself what they could see in me; they would not settle for anything less than my best. Each instructor played a unique part in the detonation and demolition of my old limiting paradigm. Due to the seeds they planted, I am tending a garden far more beautiful than what I could have imagined at the time.

Being cast in the play "The Day the Bronx Died" directed by professor Gary Hopper was yet another major life shifting experience. It was the realization of a dream come true. It marked a time when I was actually called an actor and not only that but according to reviews and feedback from others, I was a pretty skilled one. I was told it was natural for me and while I could not accept that at the time, it helped set the stage for some events that later built upon that foundation. It was an amazing test of stamina, skill, and confidence and though I was tempted to back out several times, I for some reason stayed put; thankfully so, I might add! And finally in an odd way this play helped to prepare me for what was yet to come in 2002.

In 2002 my father became increasingly more ill. The summer of that year I went home after reading a letter he had sent me in which he said, "If I could find a way to make it home soon it would be great to see me." My intuition must have read between the lines because I heard, "come home as soon as you can please." As soon as the semester ended I did just that and went home for several days over summer break. Dad and I chatted on several occasions; however, the night we sat in his room, the night before I left was the one I remember most vividly. That night, dad told me that he was tired and I joked and said, "well get some rest," though I knew what he meant; but not feeling emotionally prepared for the words he was preparing to say I tried to deflect the conversation. He continued, "You know, when I first got sick, the one thing that hurt me the most was the thought that I would not be able to see you grow up and become a man. When you graduated from high school, my dream was achieved and I was content then to die but for some reason I stayed around and I am glad that I did because I have had the chance to see you become a remarkable young man and I am very proud of you. I know that you will be fine now and so I feel at peace. I am tired of being sick and struggling and being a burden on your mother and all the arguing and frustration over the years. I wanted to see you and let you know that I am proud of you and I love you very much!" Even as I write this now, my eyes fill with tears because as much as I did not want to hear what he was saying I know he needed to say it and I wanted to honor him enough by letting him say in effect, good bye. I held back the tears, gave him a hug, told him thank you for being a great dad, gave him a kiss goodnight and filled his water jug before turning off the light and closing his door as I used to do nightly when I lived there. I left the house to get some fresh air and I walked for hours and cried and thought and cried some more. The next morning I left for Richmond. Dad's health immediately declined.

He needed several surgeries which to this day I do not know what exactly they were for. After the last surgery he said it was enough and was moved into a hospice. I had called him on one occasion, the last time we spoke and I told him I was coming home to be with him. He told me that there was no reason for me to leave school since there wasn't anything that I could do except sit there and watch him sleep. He said that I could visit during the semester break, I agreed that I would do that; however, that did not happen. On October 14th dad made his transition shedding his physical body. When I received the phone call that day from my brother Tyrone, I knew before I even picked up the phone. After talking to Tye, I went to school to inform my instructors and I began to make arrangements to go home for the funeral.

My oldest brother Eddie, who had semi-reconciled with the family was asked by my mother to be the minister at dad's funeral. It was also Eddie that secured permission from the funeral director for me to see dad before the rest of the family came to the funeral home. I cannot explain why I needed to do that but I felt a need to apologize to him for being a bad son and I wanted to do that in private. Standing there looking into the casket and my father's now empty body temple was one of the hardest things I have ever done in my life. The day of the funeral, I was overcome with guilt and grief. It took both my brother Leslie and my mother to help me walk was the procession of the family went into the funeral home. The night before, I was asked to read a poem entitled "When Tomorrow Starts Without Me" but I could not stop crying long enough to read it so Eddie's wife Karen read it. Once the funeral ended, we went to the cemetery where dad's body was laid to rest in the grave site that I had selected a day or two earlier with Eddie and one of the cemetery staff. I remember picking that particular site because of the trees which offered shade and the view of the grounds from atop that hill. I appreciated the support Eddie had offered during that time and though we do not speak at all currently, I remain thankful for that experience. Long after the funeral ended my mourning continued. It would be years later that I would find a sense of peace where I could experientially know that my father was not gone; he simply released the body that he no longer needed but his soul endured.

I graduated in 2003 and spoke at the theatre department's graduation ceremony. I decided not to go to the main college ceremony. I wanted this experience to remain intimate and personal. I spoke of dreams and doing the impossible and about friendship and support from the theatre department family. I cried like a baby, but what I said needed to be said. Afterwards David Leong, the chair of the department approached me and told me that he had no idea how similar our background experiences were. He gave me a huge hug and thanked me for being there. Many others approached me and thanked me for what I said and how moving it was for them. This marked the end of a powerful chapter.

AMERICAN INSTITUTE OF HOLISTIC THEOLOGY

Just prior to graduating from VCU, I was offered a job by Fred Beam, the director of the Wild Zappers and the National Deaf Dance Theatre. They were seeking someone with some theater experience who was also skilled in ASL and interpreting to travel with them and be their full time interpreter. I considered it an honor and so moved to Mount Ranier Maryland where I stayed with a member of the company. Living with a Deaf person gave me daily use in the language and improved my receptive skills, my ability to understand what someone was signing to me. This was quite different from when I dated a deaf girl while teaching in the public schools in Pittsburgh. Didn't mention that before huh? Yeah we dated for a few months during one of my many "what's going on with me" period of life. So this experience with a Deaf roommate was different from dating the young woman because I did not live with her and my skills at this time were one hundred percent better than when she and I dated. Anyway, I began traveling with them and interpreting for them and then eventually was given the opportunity to do a solo piece as a guest performing artist. I enjoyed the experience and the opportunity to travel each week with them to various states via van or plane depending on the performance scheduled that particular week.

It was sometime around the summer of 2003 I believe that during a visit to Pittsburgh, I visited my son Kenny. During that visit he shared with me a catalog that he received from a school in Birmingham Alabama called the American Institute of Holistic Theology or AIHT. From the time that he was around nine, Kenny and I were always having spiritual and philosophical discussions and he thought this school might be of interest to me. After some consideration, I decided that I wanted to further my spiritual studies especially since several of my professors at Carlow who taught the religion courses commented that I offered a unique and refreshing perspective on theology and the loved the enthusiasm, interest, and insights that I shared in projects and in class discussions. It was with their encouragement that I would go to members of the Jewish community and ask the rabbis questions about their beliefs. I asked about the Talmud, the Old Testament, Jewish culture and its influence on the New Testament as they saw it. I was already at that time delving into the interfaith, Interspiritual arena. I chatted with Buddhists, Muslims, Hindus, Wiccans and anyone who had a different perspective or practice of religion or spirituality. All of those experiences encouraged me to look more into studying religion and spirituality for myself and for my own personal growth and development so I found this a perfect opportunity to do just that. I enrolled in the Doctor of Divinity program majoring in Christian Theology in October 2003.

This AIHT era was a relatively quiet one for lack of a better word. What I mean by that is there were no major upheavals that forced me out of my comfort zone. I was making more choices to step out of my box, which I at times semi-consciously made, but was becoming more increasingly conscious as I was beginning to see the connective threads to my life events. I ended my time with the Wild Zappers after nearly a year and a half and before I began interpreting in the DC area I ran into some financial issues which were resolved by agreeing to model (nude) for two photographers. One was in the Maryland area and the other in NYC. I had modeled nude and semi-nude for art classes over the years periodically. That began right after I graduated from the Art Institute. I modeled for one of my former professors, the esteemed and amazingly talented Henry Koerner. I then modeled at several other places in Pittsburgh, then in Richmond at VCU in the art dept, and then for these two photographers who in hindsight, I could see were vampires seeking to use and abuse me. As a result however I did in fact learn several great lessons about myself, body image, self respect, and spirituality regarding nudity.

Not long after having left the Wild Zappers and beginning to interpret on a more frequent basis my financial situation improved and the DC area interpreting inadvertently opened a door for me to become employed as an adjunct professor at Southeastern University. I also eventually began teaching ASL through the Arlington Adult Education program and then with Prince George's Community College as well. I was keeping quite busy either interpreting, or teaching or relocating. My first four months found me living in Mount Ranier, the next four months I was living in South East DC living with a fellow interpreter, the next four months I lived in Greenbelt Maryland where I lived with the person I was dating at the time, the next four months I lived in Arlington Virginia, just a hop skip and a step from the Pentagon, where I was roommates with a great guy who was dating a martial artist friend I had met while doing the DC gay club scene. The DC gay club scene was an interesting time, will wait to share that in the biography as well. My next move was to District Heights Maryland where I remained from 2004 to 2009. While each of the previous living environments afforded lessons in themselves, this more stable move offered me a chance to connect in a totally different way with the housemates.

The home owners, a man, who was an African American man from London who was of Trinidadian descent, I think, and his fiancée who was from China. The two of them were very welcoming and sociable which I found off setting at first because the DC vibe was very cliquish yet here they were friendly and welcoming and accepting of diversity as could be seen in their diverse set of friends which reminded me of my days at Reizenstein. When I moved into their basement apartment there were three rooms available, I called them the three bear rooms as they were sized like the three bears—there was the large papa bear room over near the kitchen, beside that was the baby bear room which was right across from the bathroom, and there was the mama bear room just past the large living room area and near the basement entrance. I took the middle sized room since it seemed to be off by itself. Another guy moved in and took the larger room. We lived quite content for a few months and then the other guy moved out. The other rooms remained empty for several months until finally two gay guys moved in. One guy was black and he took the large room and the other guy from Canada was white and he took the small room. Our housemate dynamics were odd in that we all pretty much stayed to ourselves. It wasn't until both of them moved out and two new people moved in and I stopped dating the Deaf guy I had been seeing for a few months that things in the house changed. The large room went to a fireman and the small room to a young lady. I am not sure what shifted, but I was bonding with both of the other basement housemates as well as the landlord's son and stepson. I had also finally connected with his dog, Wali, who would not let me pet him for nearly a year. It was almost as if once Wali accepted me and let me pet him and play with him, that I felt at home! I began to house sit for the landlords when they left town on business or on vacation, I would be invited upstairs to watch movies on their large screen TV with them, and occasionally eat dinner and chat with them. It was a very pleasant environment.

My academic studies with AIHT were now well underway and I was learning quite a bit about the historical formation of Christianity which I had never really delved into to the extent that I was at this time. Though I had heard of Emperor Constantine, I did not know about his involvement in the Council of Nicaea. So this aspect of my studies was quite enlightening. I completed my degree in June 2007. With this degree I also applied for ordination from an ecclesial organization called the United Christian Fellowship and after submitting the necessary paperwork to demonstrate both my education as well as my commitment to my spiritual path, I was ordained by them. At this point I was fired up and decided that all of those childhood goals could be achieved.

I wanted my ten degrees especially now that I was officially, Rev. Dr. Raymont L. Anderson.

THE UNIVERSITY OF SEDONA

Awhile attending AIHT and living in District Heights MD, I founded in 2005 a new Sign Language performance company and after a few suggestions from friends I settled on the name believe and created the acronym B.E.L.I.E.V.E. (Being Empowered, Living Inspired & Exemplifying Victory Everyday). At some point while building B.E.L.I.E.V.E, I and the then vice president began exploring spirituality in the DC metro area. We eventually found and visited frequently not only two Unity churches in DC but also found in Silver Spring Maryland, Inner Visions Worldwide which is the organization founded and run by Iyanla Vanzant. We regularly attended their Wednesday evening services held by the Inner Vision ministers. After graduating from AIHT I strongly considered attending their school for coaching and ministerial studies, however after applying and getting a different call, I enrolled in the doctoral program with the University of Sedona. One thing about this program was that I had to do their prerequisites which included getting a bachelors and masters through them *before* getting to my doctoral coursework! I opted to major in Metaphysical Science which offered me a greater opportunity to study the New Thought movement as seen in Unity, Religious Science, and Divine Science. Much like the AIHT era, this time period was quite quiet as well. Yes there were rough times and baggage that I was still working on healing; however, now I had more tools to put to use and for the first time in my life I could actually say that I was truly happy and mean it!

While in the DC area I had dated a few people and was still in communication with the long time partner however after dating the Deaf guy I decided to remain single. There was something to be gained from not needing to be in a relationship or from feeling like I needed sex. I was finally able to get to know the newly developing me and I was enjoying the solitude and freedom as I learned more about who I was and what I wanted. I was rehearsing and performing with my new company B.E.L.I.E.V.E. I was teaching and interpreting consistently and paying the bills on time which turned out to be an area in need of healing as I still harbored secret subconscious fears of being homeless again. Money was an issue that I was not consciously facing as of yet.

By the time I graduated from Sedona, I was no longer living in District Height. I had moved to Bowie Maryland where I was living with Tracy, one of the members of B.E.L.I.E.V.E. who became one of my most reliable friends and newly adopted sister. Not long after moving in with her, I resigned as the president of B.E.L.I.E.V.E. due to creative differences with the board and several members and in 2010 had my first book published—Visual Music: Interpreting Songs in American Sign Language. Before moving to Bowie to live with Tracy in 2009 however, I had started working in the public school system again. This time I was teaching ASL in a high school in an Anne Arundel County school. I had originally said I would never return to public school education; however, this opportunity felt different so I changed my mind. The first year there, I must admit, was quite rough! There were issues with supervisors, other teachers, administration, and the usually adolescent behavior issues. As my stress level increased so did my weight. I almost quit that first year but something kept me onboard. Maybe it was the hope that things would get better in the second year, which they actually did. I actually enjoyed the second year and thought I would be there for the long haul; however, just as quickly as that idea began to take hold, my health began to change. I started having chest pains, dizzy spells, sore joints, and arthritis in my shoulder, migraines returned, allergies returned, and I was far more fatigued at the end of the day than I felt I should have been. I went to see a therapist to assist me in sorting through my thoughts. She helped me to not only see but to honor what my inner voice was telling me through the illnesses in my body—follow your heart not your wallet! I was contemplating staying a public school teacher for the financial security of the job more so than for my passion. It was like the University of Pittsburgh all over again except I truly did enjoy teaching and bonding with the students and formed a nice series of relationships with other teachers as well. My next two sons, Cody and James, were in fact Arundel students. In addition to adopting them as sons, I have a series of adopted nephews and nieces also as a result of teaching at Arundel.

I knew I had to face some of my long hidden demons and so I resigned to take care of those issues and some family related things that I had been avoiding. It was during those last few months at that school that I adopted Cody and James. After having adopted them, I realized how funny it is that each of my three sons sort of represents a particular aspect of my personality. Prior to resigning, I shared with Tracy my concern and the more Tracy and I chatted the more she agreed that I had to follow my heart. She was also still committed to her own dream of being my administrative assistant which she decided to be after having seen the movie "Conversations with God" in which a friend of Neale Donald Walsch became his assistant. She would schedule flights and make arrangements for him. Having begun coaching and shifting her spiritual beliefs, Tracy desired more changes in her life similar to the ones I had been experiencing in my own life. So I started coaching her more frequently as well as mentoring her with her ASL skills. We would also take trips to NYC, just hanging out as friends, going to the Unity church and Sacred Center and as a result she began to see more shifting in her life as well. Seeing this made me feel even more diligent to do my own personal work. I felt a responsibility to walk the walk that I was talking about and there were still several reoccurring issues that I had not dealt with as of yet. There was still forgiveness work to be done. There was still healing around money to be done. And there was still work to be done about my weight which had increased to about 220 lbs by this point.

I completed my University of Sedona studies, earning my bachelors in metaphysical science, masters in metaphysical science, and a doctorate in metaphysical science. I had also completed my studies with Spencer Institute and became a certified Holistic Life Coach. To compliment that, I reenrolled in Sedona to study for a Ph.D. in Life Coaching which I completed in no time since I did not have prerequisites this time. I was also ordained through the International Metaphysical Ministry University Seminary as a Metaphysical Minister and became a licensed metaphysical practitioner. It was time to put all of this material to work and I could feel some kind of divine discontent building yet again however I had one more degree to earn. Just prior to re-enrolling in AIHT, I applied to be ordained as an interfaith minister with the Many Paths Seminary and after completing their application process I was accepted and ordained with them as well.

AMERICAN INSTITUTE OF HOLISTIC THEOLOGY

This final degree was also quite easy to complete though it still took me nearly 4 years to finish. I say it was easy because I was already very familiar with the spiritual concepts. It was simply a matter of reading the texts and completing the course work as required. I enjoyed the studies though and learning so I took my time. While I was doing this, I decided to become a Reiki practitioner and so I studied with a master in Baltimore Maryland for levels one through three and then later with a master in Rockville Maryland who certified me as a Reiki master teacher. I was coaching a few clients as well as contemplating my second book, which was this one you that have in your hands. I wrote that first book in spring of 2009 after many workshop participants requested that I write a book on how to sign songs using my particular technique. And I began writing this book in spring 2011. I completed this final degree in April 2011 and with this degree also came the AIHT ordination which was through their newly formed seminary the American Interfaith Holistic Temple. The ordination ceremony happened in Stony Point,

NY during a conference held by A World Alliance of Interfaith Clergy. While there I also opted to become co-ordained as an interfaith/ Interspiritual minister with the Order of Universal Interfaith (OUnI) and I became an ordained minister within the Community of Holistic Theology (CHTh). So there you have ten degrees and five ordinations from five different ecclesiastical organizations.

With each passing chapter what I have learned and what I know for sure, as Oprah says, is that no matter how bad I sank into depression or felt worthless or wanted to die, there was a spark of the divine ever urging me onward. That spark kept me moving forward in the direction of my dreams. That spark is what gave me the ability to put my addictions in check so that I could eventually understand them and eliminate them. That spark guided me to the teachers and the lessons that would assist me in evolving to a greater expression of my true self. That spark kept me believing in the power of magic and in the influence of my heroes be it the mythical ones like Yoda, Gandalf, Dumbledore, Neo, and Don Quixote, or the flesh and blood ones like Mahatma Gandhi, Bruce Lee, the Dalai Lama, Viktor Frankl, Oprah Winfrey, and the vast sea of others whose lives have served as sources of both inspiration and knowledge. I can look back at events in my life and where I once could see only pain and desolation, confusion and randomness I now see peace, a cohesive journey, a series of divinely designed dots that have been connected with a holy thread to weave the tapestry that is unfolding as my life.

Having become a teacher of several disciplines, a leader in certain arenas, a healer and practitioner of various healing modalities, a certified life coach, minister, a father, a friend, and more, what I have seen is how the events that seemed wrong, turned out to be right and how getting lost and sent off track actually put me right on track. Were it not for the circumstances and events of my often *troubled* life, could I have become what I have become and am ever becoming?

Is it not the heat and pressure that form the diamond? And while there are events and things that occurred that I may not be able to see a direct correlation or reason for it, I trust in the power of the One Divine Source—God, and I know that no matter what happens, I always have a choice in how I respond to it. That is the power of free will; I have the choice to be in alignment with or to be out of alignment with the Divine. One day in either this life or the next or the next after that, I will finally get it and learn to align totally like Jesus and Buddha, but until then I can simply live as I choose. I can make as many mistakes as I want because in the grand design, according to what I believe is my soul contract, I am right where my Higher Self wants to be, doing what it wants to do, in order to learn and evolve into fullest manifestation of all that I incarnated to be.

And Now What?

I look back on that list of goals I set as a child and I see that many of the things on my "bucket list" can be checked off and that there are many others yet to be manifested. Having completed ten degrees, various certifications, attained a nice eclectic blend of skills and talents, what is next . . . note a few of the things below, the done (are checked) and still yet to do (are unchecked).

- ✓ Go to college and get 10 degrees
- ✓ Become a professional artist
- ✓ Sell my art work
- ✓ Become a martial arts master and teacher
- ✓ Become a teacher
- ✓ Become a workshop and seminar facilitator
- ✓ Become a philosopher
- ✓ Write and publish my books
- ✓ Collect weapons and spiritual artifacts
- ✓ Have several kids and grandkids
- ✓ Learn American Sign Language
- ✓ Learn real magic and alchemy

- O Travel to Disney World in Orlando
- O Travel to Hawaii
- O Travel to Japan
- O Travel to China
- O Travel to Sedona Arizona and the Vortexes
- O Build my dream home, Asian design
- O Learn Japanese, Spanish, Chinese
- O Open my own church and school
- O Become a Superhero
- O Travel the world especially to spiritual sites
- O Star in a major action film
- O Star in my own TV series
- O Host my own TV show
- O Produce instructional DVDs for both ASL and spirituality
- O Travel and teach, doing workshops and seminars around the world

So several items have been achieved and several more yet to be achieved and many, many, many, others have been added since childhood . . . My point with stating this is that it is important to have dreams and to live your life as someone who believes in the magic and wonder of those dreams. When you live your life on purpose no obstacle can block you, no mountain can hinder you, and no hell can frighten you. Obstacles to the enlightened are opportunities for exercise and growth. Look at the power of Gandhi and what he as one man has done. Rev. Dr. Martin Luther King Jr., Immaculée Ilibagiza, Mother Theresa, Oprah Winfrey, Steve Jobs, Nick Vujicic, Viktor Frankl, Maya Angelou, Ellie Wiesel, Helen Keller, and countless millions of others who have looked their "obstacles" in the face and said, "Step aside I have things to do!" That is the same power that rests within each of us. So I say for each of us to do as Jesus the Christ told the crippled man to do, "Take up your pallet and walk."

Get up and do what you want to do with your life; be the change!

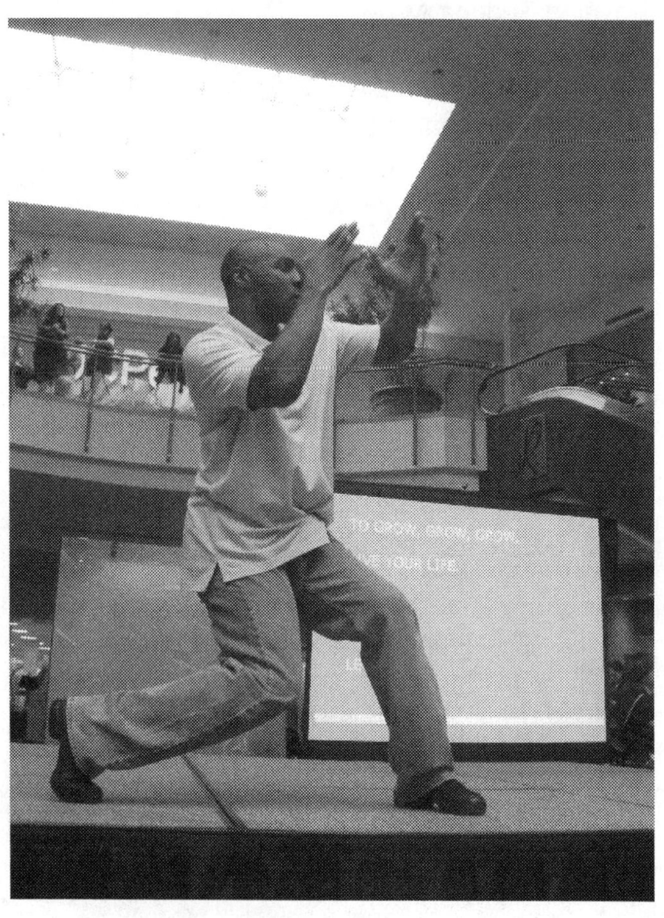

As a kid, you run around the house pretending to be a superhero, and now to be doing it as a job, I feel very lucky.

Chris Hemsworth

ABOUT THE AUTHOR:

Rev. Dr. Raymont L. Anderson is a "renaissance man" in many ways and has always been a lifelong learner. He has earned ten degrees—two Associate degrees, two Bachelor degrees, two Master degrees, and four Doctoral degrees. His eclectic academic career has opened many doors, and has aided him in transforming his own life.

As a child, he began to study various forms of martial arts including *Kung Fu*, *Karate*, *Tae Kwon Do*, *Aikido*, *Judo*, *Jujitsu*, and more and eventually narrowed his studies to *Kung Fu*, *Ninjutsu*, and *Aikido* and has since became an instructor and later, he earned the Chinese title of *Sigung* (or Master).

All of his doctoral degrees relate to religious and spiritual studies, which led him to earn the title of ordained minister within five ecclesiastical organizations including The United Christian Fellowship, Many Paths Ministry, International Metaphysical Ministry, the Order of Universal Interfaith (OUnI) and The American Interfaith Holistic Temple (AIHT). He has also earned multiple certifications and certificates of completion for various disciplines.

Rev. Dr. Anderson is also a certified teacher of American Sign Language (ASL) through the American Sign Language Teachers Association (ASLTA). He is an Artist, Actor, and ASL Performing Artist. He is the Founder, President, and Linguistic/Choreographic Director of B.E.L.I.E.V.E.—an American Sign Language Theatrical Performance Company (**www.whenyoubelieve.org**).

Additionally, he is the Founder of The Guang Dian Feng-Huang school of martial arts; Yume': The Art of Illumination art studio; and The Center for Living the Sacred: P.H.O.E.N.I.X. Fellowship and Institute, which is a place of worship and spiritual education (**www.clspfi.org** or **www.pfcls.org**).

As if this were not enough, he is also a certified Holistic Life Coach, Reiki Master Teacher and Practitioner, Tantra practitioner, seminar and workshop facilitator, freelance interpreter—specializing in theatrical interpreting, author of *Visual Music*—a text on interpreting songs in American Sign Language. Soon to arrive is his third book, tentatively called **A Spiritual Warrior's Handbook: The Art and Practice of Living an Authentic and Empowered Life**—which teaches various spiritual principles and practices to improve the quality of one's life. He was also the host of "Living a Sacred Life" an online radio program. The show segments can now be heard on http://www.youtube.com/user/CLSPFI

Should you desire more information or to contact him regarding any of the services he offers feel free to contact him by contacting both him and his Administrative Assistant at **Tracyrhymes@ymail.com** and at **raymontanderson@pfcls.org** or **raymontanderson@yahoo.com**.

Some of the services currently available:

Classes
Workshops
Seminars
Public Speaking Engagements and guest speaking
Reiki treatments in person and distance
Holistic Life Coaching
Spiritual Counseling

American Sign Language Performances for hearing and/or Deaf audiences
Mentoring

The Center for Living the Sacred is also offering specialized training for those interested in becoming skilled as a Life Coach, Minister, Reiki Practitioner, Spiritual Practitioner, and more.

YOU CAN ONLY GIVE WHAT YOU FIRST ALLOW YOURSELF TO HAVE

You already are all that you desire to be, do and have; you must awaken to this truth in order to demonstrate it in your life experience . . .

APPENDIX: WORKBOOK EXERCISES

In this section I have given you several exercises that can assist you in shifting your paradigms and help you to identify the obstacle, determine if you are magnifying it and making it larger than it really is, i.e., making a mountain out of a molehill, or is it an obstacle that is to be faced head on just as it is. Through these exercises you will be able to remove those seemingly immovable obstacles from your path by helping you to see the benefits or hidden gifts they bring and how changing your perspective changes the size, intensity, duration, and blessings in the shifting experience of the mountain to the molehill, the boulder to a pebble, and the impossible to the possible!

Exercise One: Swordplay with the 3 musk—IT-teers

*Identify it
*Non-judgment of It
*Non-resistance Of It

Exercise Two: Play the What If Game

Exercise Three: Practicing Mindfulness

Exercise Four: Shifting Paradigms

*Physical
*Mental
*Emotional
*Relational
*Spiritual
*Financial

Exercise Five: Seek and Ye Shall Find

Exercise Six: Life As If

Exercise Seven: Release into Non-Attachment

The caduceus is an ancient Egyptian symbol that was adopted into the Greek and Roman mythology as being the staff of Mercury or Hermes the messenger of the gods and god of medicine. I mention this symbol for two reasons. One because it has been symbolically tied to the chakras and our health and well being when they are in alignment and balanced and two because as a symbol of the medical profession it also reminds me of a phrase that I often found to be a sobering reminder of the work I have to do on myself—Physician Heal thy self!

Meaning: Attend to one's own faults, in preference to pointing out the faults of others. The phrase alludes to the readiness and ability of physicians to heal sickness in others while sometimes not being able or willing to heal themselves.

This suggests something of 'the cobbler always wears the worst shoes', i.e. cobblers are too poor and busy to attend to their own footwear. It also suggests that physicians, while often being able to help the sick, cannot always do so and, when sick themselves, they are no better placed than anyone else.

Origin: From the Bible, *Luke 4:23* (**King James Version**): And he said unto them, Ye will surely say unto me this proverb, Physician, heal thyself: whatsoever we have heard done in Capernaum, do also here in thy country.

The text is usually interpreted to mean that Jesus expected to hear the proverb said to him in Nazareth, and that the people there would expect him to work miracles in his hometown as he had in other places.

(http://www.phrases.org.uk/meanings/281850.html)

So this is the work we do now; the work of healing ourselves as we work through each exercise. I encourage you to take even a small step for a small step towards your goal is better than no step at all!

Exercise One: Swordplay With The 3 Musk "IT" Teers

Identify "It"

We begin our journey through identification. As any hunter will attest, you cannot hunt for something if you do not know what it is you are hunting for. If I asked you to go to the store to get me a box of *ocha*, many of you would have no idea what to get. I know there are a few of you who recognize that word to be the Japanese word for green tea and so it would be you who could actually go get the item, the others who did not know the word would have to first know what it is—identify it so it can be recognized when seen.

Begin now by identifying your "issues" or your "obstacles." Identify what you believe is holding you back, blocking you from moving forward, standing in your way. Is it a person, situation, or other type of challenge like the lack of money or lack of time? Do this now . . . get a piece of paper and write down all the things that you would label as your obstacles. What is separating you from your goals and dreams, to your joy, peace, and happiness. Without giving it too much thought, simply write.

Done? Look it over and do what Santa does . . . Check it twice! ☺ Ok so now are you done? Great job that is step one—You have identified the things that you are calling your obstacle(s). Now that you have done that we can begin to shine the healing light of love on them and move forward!

Non-Judgment of "It"

From many of the people I have coached, this seems to be one of the most challenging aspects of this process. That of not judging the obstacles and what I mean by that is precisely what it says, do not call the obstacle bad, or something to be hated, feared, or even avoided. Simply look and observe without judgment. Depending on how many obstacles you identified, I want you to take 5—10 minutes minimum with each one and read it and sit with the idea of it. Suppose for example, that I ask you to read this sentence but I want you to be sure that you do not analyze it, do not judge it, simply read it and sit with the words—"The car won't start."

Now you may be tempted to let that sentence trigger times in your life when your own car would not start and the anxiety you felt about that; and you may very quickly find yourself feeling that anxiety again as you judge the memory of a past experience or the possibility of a future experience brought about by the sentence—"The car won't start."

However, what if that sentence was spoken by a bomb expert with the FBI who just disarmed a car bomb so that the car won't start thus detonating the bomb? Does that change the level of anxiety from something negative to positive? You bet it does! Hence the reason we simply read the list without judgment. And I know someone reading this will say, "Yeah, but . . ." Yeah, but my obstacle does not have a positive side, yeah, but my issues are only negative, there is no silver lining in those clouds, and on and on the possible arguments for your limitations can go IF you allow it. All I am asking is for you to use your powers of will and concentration to read your list and not judge the words on the paper.

Nick Vujicic has no arms and no legs which is something many of us would consider an obstacle and yet he has made his obstacle a way of life and a source of power to inspire, motivate, and empower others. Viktor Frankl was a prisoner in a concentration camp where many friends and family were killed by the Nazis and yet he found strength within that gave him the will and the fortitude to survive and thrive in spite of what the guards did to him. He found the belief that while they could break his body, they could never break his spirit! Once free, he further developed Logotherapy. While it had been a new form of psychology that he formulated before the camps, it was now a solid idea that he had seen in practice as a result of several revelations while in the camps. Are these not obstacles that seem to be hopelessly negative and yet these two men took their obstacles and made them a blessing for self and for others. Even Carnegie Mellon University professor Randy Pausch, author of the "Last Lecture," who died from pancreatic cancer used his obstacle of disease to enlighten the world and leave a gift for his children and his children's children!

The most successful teachers and therapist and healers are those who do not judge the student or client. They listen with an ear of impartiality and non-judgment. What would it serve the client if the counselor believed the client was stupid? It would actually do more harm than good because what the counselor holds in her mind would eventually affect the client's therapy. Learn to be your own therapist, simply listening to the list of obstacles, impartially and without judgment.

Archimedes said "Give me a lever long enough and a fulcrum on which to place it and I shall move the world." No obstacle is too large to be moved when the right beliefs (lever and fulcrum) are in use. This starts with not judging. It simply is and as you sit with it as it is, notice how you feel and notice any ideas that come to mind about it. You may want to jot those on paper as well. Do you feel tension in your body? Do you notice thoughts of how silly this is? Put it on paper and after the task is completed, breathe and congratulate yourself on the successful completion of this step. And if for some reason you do not feel that you successfully completed it without judging it, you are invited to do it again until you can simply be with the words on the paper and those in your mind with light and love not with judgment or condemnation.

Non-resistance of "It"

When you have reached this point of the journey this is the path of non-resistance, not the path of least resistance as we are so accustomed to hearing. This is a place where you do not resist at all. It is like how Matthew 5:40 in the Bible says that if someone wants to take you to court and sue you for your tunic (or shirt), that you should give them your coat as well. The whole point is that you do not need to resist or fight against this person. Same concept here, you do not need to fight against the obstacle.

If you have money issues and you resist them, what does it change? It's like sitting in traffic and honking your horn over and over again. Does that magically make traffic move faster? Uhh no! It is a form of road rage and does not do anything except pacify your ego. As it is said in the New Thought Ancient Wisdom tradition quite often, "What you resist persists." Resist the obstacle or issues and they will continue! Frustrating? Yeah it can be if you resist what it is teaching you.

The only analogy that is coming to mind is one that involves drunk drivers who often not only survive the crashes they cause, but often come out uninjured! Now whether this is fair or not is not the karmic issue here. The point I am making is more related to the how this occurs . . . Due to their drunken state they are far more relaxed and therefore pliable in the crash. Their bodies flex and bend rather than tense and resist. The oak breaks under the force of the storm winds but the bamboo bends and survives.

So how does this apply to you, you ask? Once you are able to release judgment of the obstacles, you can begin to allow it to be simply as it is and you accept the facts of what it is; not the Truth, because that is related to the Higher divine energy back of all seeming obstacles. It may be a fact that you have no money to pay rent but the Truth is that you have access to a divine and limitless source of abundance that you can tap into. So on one level we accept the fact for face value as it is and we do not resist that. The doctor tells you that you are overweight. You hear the words; you do not judge them as being mean, wrong, or bad. You accept the words and allow them to be heard and felt, meaning you do not shut down and go to the land of denial. It is when you deny that you fortify your walls to resist, while arming for war! Want the weight gone, the rent paid for? Make peace with it by not resisting it; bend in the wind. Surfers don't fight the waves, they ride the waves feeling the water shifting and they go with the flow; they let go. Non-resistance is about letting go!

Let go of your egoic need to control. By entering into a place of allowance you release your need to control the outcome. You release your need to control all of the steps in between and you allow yourself the lowercase "i" to get out of the way for the "I" that is God to guide. This allowing does not mean you give up or give into the situation. It is not surrendering, as in allowing yourself to succumb to the debt, the disease, or the fear; rather it is surrendering to the power and presence, the Isness and Allness of the Divine. It is the letting go and letting the Infinite Wisdom step in and to manage through you.

I'd like to also mention another thing that I notice people manifest as they resist what it—regret. Regret is basically feeling sorry that something did not happen as you wanted it to happen. Someone may say, "I regret going to college right after graduating from high school." On some level they wish or desire that they had made a different choice. They are living in the past feeling sorry for what has already taken place. Instead of finding power in the now, they are regretting the past. If you recall, I started off this book by saying, "Hindsight is 20/20 and 'If I could have known then what I know now' was a reoccurring statement I frequently made at various times in my life. Then I realized two very important things. First, had I known then or had the lessons been presented to me then, I would not have been in a place to truly hear or learn from them. The pupil was not ready so the teacher could not appear. Secondly, on a deeper spiritual level, I did already know. It was this knowing that led me to the choices I made and the experiences that I had so that I could grow and develop as my Higher Self knew was necessary. Therefore, I did know what I know now; I simply was not ready to acknowledge that I knew it and live from that knowing. Every experience, misfortune, failed relationship, accident, injury, illness, success, book, chance meeting, etc are all "divinely" ordered. Synchronicity is all around us all the time and what we call accidents are miracles of providence." I remind you of this because it took me a long time to release the idea of regret. And just to be clear I am not referring to the feelings of remorse that one may feel for having harmed someone. I believe that feeling a sense of regret or remorse for such a thing is normal and healthy; however I also believe that it must be let go after a period of time. It is not healthy for it to be held onto and constantly re-opened like a scab that is picked at and in time becomes infected.

Have I made what people would call mistakes? Yes. Have been irresponsible and selfish at times? Yes. Have I hurt people either physically or emotionally? Yes. And I have forgiven myself for it all and I have released it and moved forward realizing that it all happened for a reason, whether I know the reason or not and whether others know the reason or not. I have learned and believe that on a soul level we all agreed to be there and to play our roles accordingly and to feel guilt, regret, and undue remorse would keep me bound to the boulder just as Sisyphus was for eternity. So I do what Michael Beckwith & Rickie Byars wrote in one of their many song collaborations.

> I release and I let go,
> I let the Spirit run my life.
> And my heart is open wide,
> Yes, I'm only here for God.
> No more struggle, no more strife,
> With my faith I see the light.
> I am free in the Spirit,
> Yes, I'm only here for God.

<u>Exercise Two: Play the What If Game</u>

The "what if" game is a simple game that many of us play without even realizing we are playing it. Every time we speak, write, or think the phrase—what if . . . we are deeply immersed in the game and a key difference is that many add a powerful prefix to the phrase by saying—but what if? But what if I don't get the job, but what if she says no, but what if the world does end in 2012, but what if the doctor is right, . . . to all of these and all the remaining but what ifs, I ask the simple question—but what if you changed your point of view and asked, but what if I do get the job, but what if she says yes, but what if the world does not end in 2012, but what if the doctor is wrong? Now what?? And if you really want me to get technical and blunt with you, let's revisit those initial questions:

What if I don't get the job? OK, so what if you don't? What does that really change or mean? What if you don't get that job but you get another, a better one. What if you don't get that job so that you can be available for the job you truly desire or to open your own business?

What if she says no? OK, so what if she says no? What does that mean? What does it change? What if her saying no turns out to be the best thing for you? What if her no is God's yes?

What if the world ends in 2012? OK, so what if it does? Can you do anything about it to prevent it? What if you simply enjoyed each day, each present moment instead of worrying about the possibility of what if? What if the world ends tomorrow? Wouldn't you rather enjoy today to the fullest rather than living in fear as people did about the Y2K fears in 1999? And what if the world doesn't end in 2012, then what do you do, jump on to the next fear-filled what if? What will you do to live a joy-filled and happy life instead of one run by fear?

What if the doctor is right? OK, what if the doctor is right, does that mean you give up? What can you do to live your life in the most health and whole manner possible? What can you do to heal yourself? What if the doctor telling you that is precisely the blessing you need in order to find the power within to heal yourself, cure yourself, and thus to help you heal others? What if the doctor is wrong? Will you change anything about your lifestyle or your beliefs?

As you can see, I could go on and on with the "what if game." It is quite easy to play and I encourage you to take each of your seeming negatives and ask the appropriate what if that allows you to shift your perspective to simply *entertain the possibility* of there being hope within despair and positive within the negative. This is the beginning of your ability to see with the eyes of love as you begin to playfully shift your perspectives to see everything as a potential positive no matter how "bad" something might seem. Oprah Winfrey tells a story where she says, "I remember a specific moment, watching my grandmother hang the clothes on the line, and her saying to me, 'you are going to have to learn to do this,' and me being in that space of awareness and knowing that my life would not be the same as my grandmother's life." What if Oprah had not had that epiphany and had agreed with her grandmother? What if it is like an Oleg Shuplyak illusory painting that looks like one thing but is, upon closer observation, something quite different? What if you took the time right now to shift your belief in bad to a belief in only good? What would that change in your life? For one day or even one hour, call it all good and speak only of the good. Just think about that before you move on to exercise three.

And by the way there is a great book to help you further along with this exercise is, What If It All Goes RIGHT? Creating a New World of Peace, Prosperity & Possibility by Mindy Audlin.

Exercise Three: Practicing Mindfulness

Mindfulness in the simple, but challenging form of meditation or exercise of being present in all of your activities and thoughts; it is being in the now not the later or the former. Many of us in this highly technological world with the internet and communication at the tips of our fingers have developed many tendencies to engage in what is called multitasking. Quick sidebar on multi-tasking, many researchers have determined that multi-tasking is a misnomer in that we are not doing several tasks at one time but are in reality switching between one task and another at a rapid rate of speed so that it may appear that you are doing multiple things. Research has also shown that those who engage in "multi-tasking" not only tend to suffer by being less productive, but they also tend to suffer in the areas of efficiency, creativity and long term memory.

If multi-tasking were the Joker then Mindfulness would be Batman. Mindfulness restores peace to our daily lives and increasing effectiveness, productivity, creativity, and overall sense of wholeness. What is mindfulness? A quote by Jon Kabat-Zinn defines it by saying, "Mindfulness means paying attention in a particular way; on purpose, in the present moment, and nonjudgmentally." So we see that mindfulness requires that our attention be consciously directed. We may be aware that we are driving but not consciously or actively engaged in doing so. I mean think about how often you get in the car and drive and before you know it you are at your destination. You were not particularly focused and so you drove by default. Or you missed an exit because your mind was elsewhere as you drove. Mindfulness asks us to be 100% present while driving or even something as simple as lacing your shoes.

Awareness is simply a knowing that it is being done, where as mindfulness is the quality of how it is being done. When you are cooking for example, are you cutting vegetables and adding ingredients while your mind is still crunching numbers that are due in a work report tomorrow? Or are you consciously aware and mindfully directing your actions and thoughts to the preparation of the meal? Do you sense the colors, textures, and aroma of the vegetables as you prepare them? A meal that is prepared mindfully is by far the more lovingly prepared meal. It is also said to be a healthier meal and more delicious due to the care that went into its preparation and presentation. And hopefully it was eaten with a similar sense of mindfulness rather than the typical mindless eating while watching TV, doing homework or talking on the phone when we barely take the time to taste and truly enjoy the food.

Therefore, mindfulness asks that when you cook, cook and when you drive, drive and when you walk, walk aware and consciously directing the steps along the way ever present in the now. There is a time and place for daydreaming or to engage in creative visualization and even then you are present in that activity not in the illusion of past or future. Can you even daydream while daydreaming that you are daydreaming? Sounds too confusing and I guess the point is, if you can, do it mindfully! ☺

What does mindfulness have to do with your obstacles? I'm glad you asked. By being in the now with each action and thought we open ourselves to the whispering still small voice of the Divine. By being mindful, we reduce fear, anxiety and worry. You cannot worry about the rent being due tomorrow if you are present in the now. Worry is a fear of something possible yet to come. Worry fears a future that is unwritten. No one worries about what happened last year. You may worry that something you did last year will be found out and change something once people know; and that is future based. If you truly focus on the right here right now, you cannot fear or worry about anything that has happened in the past or anything that could happen in the future because you are totally living in the now and in this expansive space all perceived limitations are cast off and there is greater freedom and it is in that state that answers become evident and the miracles that were there all along become visible!

"Unease, anxiety, tension, stress, worry—all forms of fear—are cause by too much future, and not enough presence. Guilt, regret, resentment, grievances, sadness, bitterness, and all forms of nonforgiveness are caused by too much past, and not enough presence" ** Eckhart Tolle

A great way to start being mindful is by selecting an activity you do daily, like brushing your teeth, taking a shower, or getting dressed. As you begin the activity, shift your awareness consciously so that you are aware and feel every element of the process. Feel the toothbrush in your hand, feel which fingers you use to hold it, and which part of those fingers are in contact. Notice how much pressure you use to hold the brush in place and how much pressure you use to squeeze the toothpaste from the tube. Notice the smell of the toothpaste. Feel the bristles running across your gums and your teeth and feel all the places you touch as you continue to brush. Becoming present you will notice many things that previously you were not present for. Your mind was elsewhere as you acted on autopilot. Simply notice, be aware and conscious of all you are doing and how you are doing it, do not judge it as too fast, too slow, not thorough enough or compulsive, simply be with it in the now. Do this at various points through your day. Be mindful of how you are sitting on the bus or standing in line at the store. As you become more mindful of these events you will increase your mindfulness in your communication as well. When the other person is speaking, listen with the same mindfulness you used to brush your teeth. Hear each word, each syllable, notice their pauses, their breathing, and listen to them with all of yourself. Many of us listen, but are already thinking about what we will say next. That is not truly listening and most definitely is not listening mindfully.

As you increase the amount of mindfulness to your daily activities the more you will find your obstacles will either fade into the ether or you will notice that they become manageable. I find this idea to be what is meant by the phrase, "God does not give you more than you can handle." When we see the obstacle or burden mindfully through the eyes of love, the obstacle becomes a challenge, a stepping stone, a goal in and of itself to move you to higher and greater states of being. The obstacle is then seen to have a purpose and reason for showing up before you.

Exercise Four: Shifting Paradigms

When we can see the barrier, obstacle, issues as stepping stones to lift us up, as a ladder to aid us in climbing higher, as the very catalyst to give us more strength to achieve our goals, we are entering the phase of paradigm shifting. Our paradigm, beliefs, and thoughts we hold in consciousness, are either enslaving us or liberating us. What you are being asked to do here with exercise four is to take each of the six areas to be discussed and shift your paradigm concerning them from what dis-empowers to what empowers you and places you in alignment with the Divine. We begin with that simple act of identifying. I want you to identify what each of these areas looks like in your life presently.

For example, what does your life look like physically? What is your body showing you? Is it overweight or underweight? Is it healthy and able to do what you want it to do? Is the body temple in disrepair or does it reflect the splendor that is its true essence? Do this with each of the six areas and simply identify what they are showing you. Do not judge, simply identify. The six areas are: Physically / Mentally / Emotionally / Relationally / Spiritually / and Financially.

Ok now that you have done that; let's look at each element closer so that you can shift your paradigms as needed in order to access the full potential you deserve. True abundance and prosperity is achieved when all six areas are aligned and in balance. Seek out the assistance of a life coach, therapist, or spiritual advisor to assist and support you in making the changes in any of the six areas.

Physically

All things physical relate to your actual body as well as to the conditions of your physical environment. Do you tend to your body as a holy temple for the Divine? Do you eat well? Do you exercise? Do you criticize your body for not looking how you want it to look? Do you vilify the body or do you bless it? What about your environment, is it clutter filled? Both how you tend to your body and your physical environments reflect what paradigms you hold in consciousness. A cluttered office indicates a cluttered mind. Disrespecting of your body begins with thoughts that disrespect and betray and can you truly respect another if you do not respect yourself? Begin here now to shift those thoughts and beliefs by making the necessary adjustments to your area of the physical.

Mentally

All things mental relate to your intellectual, analytical processes as well as all things thought related including core beliefs and to a certain degree your faith, as it is influenced by what you think and believe. Do you tend to over-think, over analyze things? Are you known for employing common sense or lacking it? Do you think of things in black and white with no shades of grey or do you take various ideas and assess them all? How would you describe the manner in which you process your mental capacities? How do you acquire information and knowledge? There are many ways of classifying the learning styles; here is one way that identifies seven areas:

1. **<u>Visual</u> (spatial):** You prefer using pictures, images, and spatial understanding.
2. **<u>Aural</u> (auditory-musical):** You prefer using sound and music.
3. **<u>Verbal</u> (linguistic):** You prefer using words, both in speech and writing.

4. **<u>Physical</u> (kinesthetic):** You prefer using your body, hands and sense of touch.
5. **<u>Logical</u> (mathematical):** You prefer using logic, reasoning and systems.
6. **<u>Social</u> (interpersonal):** You prefer to learn in groups or with other people.
7. **<u>Solitary</u> (intrapersonal):** You prefer to work alone and use self-study.

Do you know your learning style? Knowing how you formulate ideas and develop your beliefs is a very valuable skill as you shift from ideas and beliefs that no longer serve you as they once may have, this is the reason for shifting paradigms. Begin to pay more attention to how you learn, how you process information, and how you communicate, as it can give insight into the manner in which your mind and brain work.

Emotionally

All things emotional relate to your feeling nature, the manner in which you process and express emotions. Are you a sensitive, caring, compassionate person? Do you think crying shows weakness? Do you find your feelings are easily hurt or you offend easily? Do you prefer to be stoic and cold? Are you a romantic or do you believe romance is for fools? When you are complimented, what do you feel? What about when you are insulted? Do you tend to react impulsively only later to think about how you reacted? How would you describe your emotional constitution? Which do you feel more often, fear or confidence, love or anger, joy or worry? Do you ever ask why you feel the way you do? Now would be a great time to begin to apply awareness to your feelings. An ancient Samurai proverb states that, “The person who knows others is wise while the person who knows themselves is enlightened.” How well do you know you?

Relationally

All things relational relate to your relationships with others and the world in general. Do you have close friends or are they more acquaintances? Do you have any close or best friends? Are you close with any family members? Do you have a significant love interest in your life? What about children or even pets? How do you relate to any of them? Are you open or closed off? Do you openly communicate or do you withhold information from them? Do you keep secrets? Do you consciously or unconsciously manipulate the relationships so you are in control? Are your relationships liberating or co-dependent? Do you have fun when you are with your friends and family or are you stressed and anxious when around them? Do certain relationships bring you joy while others bring you pain? Your relationships are like a mirror, what do your relationships show you about yourself? How happy are you with how you relate to the people in your life? Do you see people as inherently evil or bad or are they good? Do you trust others? Are you yourself trustworthy? Take the time now to learn about yourself by the relationships you are engaged in. Every person comes to you bearing a gift of self discovery, are you willing to receive the gift?

Spiritually

All things spiritual relate to your connection with the Divine Source of all that is; call it whatever you desire, God, Universe, Christ, Oneness, Love, Yahweh, or the No-Thing from which All Things come. The name is irrelevant as words can at times limit the experience. Spirituality is the experience of the divine while religion is the system of dogma set up about a particular aspect of the Divine, so the question now is do you have any kind of spiritual connection to the Divine? Do you feel the divine in your life? Do you commune with the Source? Do you take regular time to engage in spiritual practices that in essence bring you into the presence of God? Do you pray, meditate, practice yoga, Tantra, Tai Chi, paint, play an instrument, walk in nature, engage in sacred service, or any of the thousands upon thousands of ways to enter into the presence of the Beloved? Do you feel that God is uninterested in you and your petty life? Do you feel unworthy of God's attention or love? Do you believe yourself to be a sinner born in sin or do you believe you are born in the image and likeness of God and blessed? How you feel connected or disconnected to something greater or something beyond simply the physical material world will affect how you live move and have your being in the world. Even the "atheist" can experience the Divine as he looks at a beautiful sunset and feels the awe of its amazing beauty! Take the time now to make that call and reconnect to the Divine in a new holy way where you consciously connect rather than wait for life's circumstances to knock you to your knees where you then feel it is time to pray. Prayer begins before you feel the need to pray. Prayer and meditation and spiritual practices are meant to be a daily part of your living, like eating, drinking, and breathing.

Financially

All things financial relate to your connection with money and all the things money can buy or provide. What is your current relationship to the all mighty dollar? Do you feel a lack of its presence in your life? Do you feel wealthy and living in abundance or are you struggling to get by, living paycheck to paycheck? Do you believe the old adage that money is the root of all evil? Do you believe that the rich get richer and the poor get poorer? Do you believe that you deserve to be rich? What does being rich mean to you? What does abundance mean to you? Can you be rich without having lots of money? If you had a million dollars, what would you do with it, would you waste it to load up on the hottest material items that offer a false sense of comfort or would you spend wisely? What does wise spending mean? Are you currently in credit card or other debt? Do you live beyond your means to satisfy your ego? Do you tithe to a church or organization or individual where you receive spiritual nourishment and support? Do you donate to an organization that you believe is doing great work in the community or the world? What does being wealthy look like to you? Money is energy and it needs to be circulated in order to continue to flow of abundance; however, it must be balanced wisely with proper intent if it is to circulate more abundance back to you. Do you squander money, disrespect money, hoard money, and feel a sense of scarcity? If so, you are stifling the flow of energy and cannot reap because you have not sown. Take the time to assess how you think and feel about money so that you can begin to understand your relationship with it on a deeper level. Once you are clearer on this level, you can open the floodgates allowing abundance to flow into your life. It is already present if we take the time to access it more consciously. It's like going to the ocean to get water from a never ending supply. Do you go with a cup, a bucket, a sieve, a thimble or a pipeline?

Exercise Five: Seek And Ye Shall Find

When we have taken the time to put into practice the things I have outlined thus far, we will begin to notice things shifting. For some the shift may be subtle and for others, it may be huge; that does not matter, what matters is that the shift occurs. Part of the process included in the shift is the setting of our intentions. The setting of an intention is likened to the archer who pulls back the drawstring, takes careful aim, and releases the arrow into the air. Once the arrow is sent from the bow, the archer has no control over it and so he must trust the power of his skill and part of that power is his ability to aim (setting the intention) and then trusting that aim and letting go! In order to shoot an arrow, the archer must "let go" of it. The arrow cannot be sent anywhere if the archer holds onto it. Your intentions cannot go anywhere if you hold onto them.

The setting of our intentions is therefore no different from shooting that arrow. We set a goal, take careful aim at the goal as we send the intention forward. The intention, backed by our will flies forward into the universe and through non-attachment we trust the universe to take hold of our intention as the laws of physics takes hold of the archer's arrow moving it forward through the air. Many people have weak intentions and weak will power and therefore their results in life are hit or miss at best; more misses than hits most likely. And honestly they are all hits! The question is, are they hitting the desired target or are they hitting the tree to the left of the target or are they hitting the ground five feet before the target? Again this takes a level of awareness and honest observation as we look at the areas in our lives where we are missing the intended target. Those previous six areas of divine prosperity or abundance are the targets each of us are aiming for. Each of us wants true prosperity and yet due to poor intentions and will, we stumble through life haphazardly as if using a faulty compass or virus infected GPS.

What goals do you currently possess in each of the areas? Physically what are you aiming for? A more nutritious diet, a healthier body, exercise three times a week, park further from the door and walk, get more sun, clean my office and keep it neater, take more time in the morning to iron my clothes and floss my teeth? Mentally what are your goals? Read one book a month about a topic of great interest to me, take a class at the community college or online to further my education, engage in stimulating conversations about thought provoking ideas and topics, play games like Scrabble, word searchers, Chess, or Sudoku to keep the mind active, and re-evaluate if any old beliefs need updating, rebooting, or removal? Emotionally, what goals do you have? Do you want to feel more joy and peace in your life, feel more compassionate, and feel both forgiving and forgiven, to express more love, or do you want to feel safe and secure? Do you want Relational goal such as more close bonds with friends and or family, to feel a sense of community and connection with others, to have strong lines of communication open with your children or significant other, to have dependable people in your life that are there to support and assist you when in need, or do you want to be able to see the face of God in all people you encounter? Spiritually, do you want to pray or meditate daily, go on a spiritual retreat where you are given tools and space to worship in your own way, to delve into the lives of spiritual masters who have lived before, or do you want to find deeper meaning in your religious beliefs so that you can have a true experience of the divine? Financially, do you want more money to go on vacation, pay bills, have enough money to live in comfort and with security, or do you want to have enough money to buy the clothes or car you want, or do you want money to help others in some philanthropic way?

If you are not sure what you desire in these areas of your life, I suggest you take a moment now and go back to pen and paper and write down at least three goals for each area. You cannot buy a plane ticket to go on vacation if you have no destination in mind. One should be a short range goal that you want to accomplish in a month or two, the second within six months to a year, and the third one to two years. Keep the list updated and in mind referring to is as you would a map guiding you across the countryside. Keep it in mind just as you would if you were the archer taking aim at the target before you. Intend it and put enough will into seeing it happen but then let go of it and allow the universe to carry it in flight. Remember what I discussed about how Oprah says she got the part in the Color Purple, remember this simple song, I surrender all, all to thee my blessed savior, I surrender all!

<u>Exercise Six: Life As If</u>

When you hear the phrase to "Act As If", what comes to your mind as the meaning of that phrase? You may well have heard the phrase previously as many teachers and coaches reference to the Law of Attraction or manifesting in general. I find that many people are so unsure of, or vague, and uncertain as to how they are to "act as if," that they rebel against the concept. This is a relatively simply concept if you think about what you desire and with a clear image in your mind's eye you live your life as if that image is already a part of your life. For example, suppose your goal is to earn one million dollars a year as the CEO of your own company. Where many get confused is to think that acting as if means spending money now AS IF you have those millions. That is the wrong place to begin. Acting as if begins with your thinking and feeling. Acting as if starts with asking the questions, If I were earning one million dolars a year as the CEO of my own company what kinds of thoughts whould I be thinking? What would I be feeling? How would I carry myself? How would I speak to people? You begin with these areas because they do not require you to do anything other than shift your belief system to one of a millionaire! If you begin to think like a millionaire and feel like a millionaire and speak like a millionaire then you will begin to behave like a millionaire and as I have said the Universe will conspire to give you what you are sowing into the soil of Divine Mind; it is the Father's good pleasure to give you the kingdom!

Before we go any further, I want to examine this a little further by asking you, how does a millionaire think? It is important to clarify what kind of millionaire we are refering to; one that is still caught up in victim and scarcity consciousness or one that is empowered and liberated? A liberated and empowered millionaire is thinking about ideas, improving him/herself, evolving, growing, and serving the community through their particular reason for being, their purpose and passion. They are feeling empowered, feeling free, feeling joyful at the opportunity to live on purpose, happy to share their passion, they feel love and loving. Can you feel any of this now, today, even without having the millions in your bank account? YES, you can and that is precisely where you begin! Begin where you are to think and feel as if that which you want is already manifested. All things begin in the unseen realm of existence in pure energy and then as we align, the energy of thought begins to slow down and it manifests into the physical realm. It exists already in mind so start there and get a clear vision of what you want.

As you think and feel as if, you will begin to speak as if and behave as if. Your actions and reactions will be as if. You will have relationships with people as if. And before you know it you will be living your life as if and then it will simply be!

Exercise Seven: Release Into Non-Attachment

As we enter into the seventh exercise, I want to clarify from the beginning that detatchment and nonattachment are not and I repeat are not the same thing. Detatchment is a form of denial where you refuse to fully engage or commit; you are absent. The archer who is detatched will not even bother to raise his bow, let alone take an arrow from his quiver and take aim. Think of detatchment as a form of apathy where your lack of caring is so extreme that you don't bother to set the intention or do the work. Non-attachment on the other hand is being fully committed to the action body mind and soul, but not being obsessed with the results or outcome. It is the willingness to risk "failure" to be creative and live your passion. Have you ever heard the phrase, "Dance like no one is watching?" That is non-attachment. You dance because you want to dance, you feel the inner music calling you to dance and you dance not for the applause or approval of another; you dance because in that moment you are a dancer! Think of how many fathers are detatched from their daughters because they were so connected to the outcome of having a son in comparison to those who are non-attached and love their child equally no matter if it is a boy or girl.

We aim to be non-attached to the final result; to let go and let God handle the details which are ultimately beyond our control. Non-attached we are able to fully commit to the present moment because we are not anxiously looking to the end results. You live according to your passion as a singer regardless if you get that million dollar album deal you want. You continue to write whether you get that contract from a well known publisher or not and self publish if necessary. You do what you desire because it is who and what you are. It reminds me of a recent movie I watched called "Something the Lord Has Made" starring Alan Rickman and Mos Def. The film which is set during the Jim Crow south era is based on a true story that recounts the emotional bond between two men who defied both the cultural and medical rules of their time to launch a medical revolution. The two men, Dr. Alfred Blalock (Alan Rickman) and lab technician Vivien Thomas (Mos Def) form an impressive team in the 1940s as they carefully research and work in Baltimore at Johns Hopkins to create an unprecedented technique for performing heart surgery on "blue babies." As Blalock and Thomas enter into unchartered territory, they are constantly faced with the social pressures of class, race, and doing the impossible which threatened to undermine their collaboration and tear their friendship apart. I mention this film because in the life of Vivian Thomas we see a man so committed to his passion that he was willing to do the work no matter the final outcome; meaning he was not doing the work for fame and fortune, he was doing it because it was who he was, it was his passion. He was non-attached to the end as he remained ever present in the now.

As we go about our daily activities it is good to take a moment and return to the now and ask how attached to (insert a situation, person's name, or anything that one might be attached to) am I? Am I so attached to getting that new job that I am wasting energy that could be best used elsewhere? Am I so attached to the person I believe I love that I smother them and refuse to let them live their own lives? Am I so attached to getting that promotion at work that I will sabotage my co-workers? Take some time each day to release those attachments and live from a state of non-attachment where you can let go and be happy no matter the outcome. In that space of true happiness, no obstacle can hold you back from living your purpose and passion right here and right now.

I pray continued success and joy to you as you live your sacred life!

It is so and so it is . . . Amen!

BIBLIOGRAPHY:

Bowen, Will. Acomplaintfreeworld.org 28 Dec. 2010 <http://www.acomplaintfreeworld.org/>

Cherry, Kendra. "Self-Actualization and the Hierarchy of Needs." About.com Psychology. 28 Dec. 2010 <http://psychology.about.com/od/theoriesofpersonality/a/hierarchyneeds_2.htm>

George. "Teachings of Bob Klein: Show Me Your Original Face." 11 Sept. 2006. Movements of Magic. 28 Dec. 2010 <http://movementsofmagic.org/blogs/bobklein/archive/2006/09/11/SHOW-ME-YOUR-ORIGINAL-FACE.aspx>

Goldman, Jonathan: <http://www.healingsounds.com/articles/overview-sound-healing.asp>

Hagelin, John S., Rainforth, Maxwell V., Cavanaugh, Kenneth L. C., Alexander, Charles N., Shatkin, Susan F., Davies, John L., Hughes, Anne O., Ross, Emanuel, and Orme-Johnson, David W. "Effects of Group Practice of the Transcendental Meditation Program on Preventing Violent Crime in Washington, DC: Results of the National Demonstration Project, June-July 1993." Institute of Science, Technology and Public Policy. 28 Dec. 2010 <http://istpp.org/crime_prevention/>

Hicks, Esther: <http://spiritlibrary.com/abraham-hicks/only-17-seconds-away-from-your-true-desires>

Hicks, Esther: <http://spiritlibrary.com/abraham-hicks/my-inner-being-communicates-through-emotion>

Kripalu Online. "Shamanic Wisdom and Healing: Cleaning Up Your River a conversation with Alberto Villoldo." Originally Published May 2007. Kripalu Center for Yoga and Health. 28 Dec. 2010 <http://www.kripalu.org/article/423>

Peske, Nancy. Villoldo, Alberto. "A Letter From Alberto." March 2009. The Four Winds Newsletter. 28 Dec. 2010 <http://thefourwinds.com/newsletter/march_09/AV_sub.html>

Nicholson, Ester. "12 Keys to Freedom." Esthernicholson.com 28 Dec 2010 <http://www.esternicholson.com/index.php?option=com_content&view=article&id=100:the-12-keys-to-freedom&catid=48:teachings&Itemid=65>

Ruiz, don Miguel and Ruiz, don Jose. "The Power of Doubt: When Being Skeptical Is a Good Thing." 23 March 2010. Oprah.com 28 Dec. 2010 <http://www.oprah.com/spirit/The-Power-of-Doubt>

Strand, Clark. "Green Koans Case 12: The Original Face" Tricycle. 28 Dec. 2010 http://www.tricycle.com/web-exclusive/green-koans-case-12-original-face

Van Warmerdam, Gary. "Living the Four Agreements: A life changing Journey."

Toltec Spirit | based on the four agreements™: Common Sense Wisdom for the Spiritual Warrior's Journey. 28 Dec. 2010 <http://www.toltecspirit.com/>

Vujicic, Nick. “About Nick Vujicic.” Attitude is Altitude. 28 Dec. 2010 <http://www.attitudeisaltitude.com/aboutus-nick.php>

Warner Bros. “The Matrix: Meaning & Interpretations.” The Matrix 101. 28 Dec. 2010 <http://www.thematrix101.com/matrix/meaning.php>

“Section 12 . . . The New Age/ Roots of Evil.” In Plain Site. 15 Jan. 2011 <http://www.inplainsite.org/html/roots_of_evil.html>

“The Titanic—Passenger and Crew Statistics.” History on the Net. 28 Dec. 2010 <http://www.historyonthenet.com/Titanic/passengers.htm>

“Transcendental Meditation Experiment Arrests Crime Study Shows Dramatic Drop in Violent Crime During D.C. Project.” 1 June 1999. All TM. 28 Dec. 2010 <http://www.alltm.org/pages/crime-arrested.html>

Wikipedia. “Maslow's hierarchy of needs.” 28 Dec. 2010 <http://en.wikipedia.org/wiki/Maslow's_hierarchy_of_needs#Self-actualization>

Wikipedia. “Samurai.” 28 Dec. 2010 http://en.wikipedia.org/wiki/Samurai>

Wikipedia. “Hagakure.” 28 Dec. 2010 <http://en.wikipedia.org/wiki/Hagakure>

Producer: Minsky, Alan. Host: Beckwith, Michael Bernard. Guest: Pearson, Carlson. Online Radio Archive Broadcast Friday, January 14, 2011 1:00 pm <http://www.kpfk.org/programs/187-michael-beckwith-sound-of-transformation.html>

FURTHER READING:

I Am By Howard Falco

Enlightenment for Everyone by Paul Ferrini

Real Magic by Wayne Dyer

Zen of Oz by Joey Green

The Secret by Rhonda Byrne

The Peaceful Warrior by Dan Millman

Illusions by Richard Bach

Jonathan Livingston Seagull by Richard Bach

Conversations with God by Neale Donald Walsch

The Five Principles by Ellen Debenport

Banishing Mind Span by Dr. Sheri Rosenthal

The Complete Idiot's Guide to Toltec Wisdom by Dr. Sheri Rosenthal

Spiritual Liberation by Rev. Michael Bernard Beckwith

Visioning by Rev. Michael Bernard Beckwith

Metaphysics by Rev. Paul Hasselbeck

Gay is a Gift by Salvatore Sapienza

The Science of Mind by Ernest Holmes

The Vortex by Ester and Jerry Hicks

The Map by Colette Baron-Reid

The Power of Now by Eckhart Tolle

A New Earth by Eckhart Tolle

Soul Mission Life Vision by Alan Seale

What If It All Goes RIGHT? Creating a New World of Peace, Prosperity & Possibility by Mindy Audlin